Advance Praise for *The Urba*

After decades of food delivered by industr
oil, we are learning the health costs to our
are too great. A revolution in food — where .... grown is
now sweeping urban centres. Read this book to see why it matters and
how we can do it.

—David Suzuki, co-founder, David Suzuki Foundation

As a farmer I'm amazed by the amount of discussion and debate there
currently is about food systems and farming. It's overwhelming, but Peter Ladner really separates the wheat from the chaff. If you want to get
your head around the important developments without ending up with
a headache, this is the book for you.

—Wally Satzewich, developer, SPIN-Farming

Peter Ladner has written a great book on food — food of, by and for the
people. He brings an insight and clarity to the issue that only a journalist,
turned politician, turned journalist, could achieve. His lucid and accessible book tells us how we have lost what used to be common, and how
we can make community agriculture common again. His book artfully
synthesizes the myriad strands of what is a large but still largely inco-
herent revolution — *The Urban Food Revolution*. This book should be
required reading for anyone in North America who has interest in food.
That would be all of us.

—Professor Patrick. M. Condon,
UBC James Taylor Chair in Landscape and Liveable Environments

Things are changing; our relationship with food, the land where it is
grown, the people whose hands harvest it, and how it is prepared and
eaten are coming back into focus and demanding our attention. *The
Urban Food Revolution* provides an overview of this movement, and
vignettes of some of it's key players; farmers, planners, activists, politicians, and all of us who eat. Here are the people and their ideas; a grand
experiment in re-imagining and re-creating one of the most fundamental aspects of our lives.

—Michael Ableman, farmer; founder, *Center For Urban Agriculture* and
Centre For Arts, Ecology, and Agriculture, co-director of *SOLEfood*;
author, *Fields of Plenty* and *On Good Land*

Government leaders, policy makers and teachers will want to read Peter Ladner's comprehensive view of what is driving today's urban agriculture phenomenon. With an academic background in urban planning, a successful career as a municipal politician and as a long time journalist, Ladner brings new insights to the subject in such chapters as 'Agriculture as the New Golf: Farming as a Development Amenity'. *The Urban Food Revolution* is a book by a passionate man who wants to change the way our food system works.

—Michael Levenston, executive director, City Farmer

This book is well-written, well-organized, and well-researched. It has lots of practical examples and a wonderfully balanced assessment of options. It was a treat to read. Peter Ladner's suggested policy interventions to promote urban agriculture are a great simile for parallel interventions required to promote sustainable enterprises. This book is a must-read for policymakers and CEOS with an interest in one of the most compelling issues of our time.

—Bob Willard, author, *The New Sustainability Advantage, The Next Sustainability Wave,* and *The Sustainability Champion's Guidebook*

THE
URBAN FOOD
REVOLUTION

Changing the Way We Feed Cities

PETER LADNER

NEW SOCIETY PUBLISHERS

To order directly from the publishers, please call toll-free (North America)
1-800-567-6772, or order online at www.newsociety.com

Any other inquiries can be directed by mail to:

New Society Publishers
P.O. Box 189, Gabriola Island, BC V0R 1X0, Canada
(250) 247-9737

New Society Publishers' mission is to publish books that contribute in fundamental
ways to building an ecologically sustainable and just society, and to do so with the least
possible impact on the environment, in a manner that models this vision. We are committed to doing this not just through education, but through action. The interior pages
of our bound books are printed on Forest Stewardship Council® acid-free paper that is
100% post-consumer recycled (100% old growth forest-free), processed chlorine free,
and printed with vegetable-based, low-VOC inks, with covers produced using FSC®
stock. New Society also works to reduce its carbon footprint, and purchases carbon
offsets based on an annual audit to ensure a carbon neutral footprint. For further information, or to browse our full list of books and purchase securely, visit our website
at: www.newsociety.com

LIBRARY AND ARCHIVES CANADA CATALOGUING IN PUBLICATION

Ladner, Peter
The urban food revolution : changing the way we feed cities / Peter Ladner.

Includes bibliographical references and index.
ISBN 978-0-86571-683-4

1. Urban agriculture.   2. Sustainable agriculture.   3. Local foods.   4. Food supply.
5. Urban health.   I. Title.

S494.5.U72L32 2011   630.9173'2   C2011-905558-9

NEW SOCIETY PUBLISHERS
www.newsociety.com

MIX
Paper from
responsible sources
FSC® C016245

Contents

Preface vii

1. What's the Matter with Food? 1

2. Past Forward to Local? Let's Be Real 11

3. Preserving Rural Agriculture Land for Food Production . . . 25

4. Converting Urban and Suburban Lands for Growing Food . . 35

5. Agriculture as the New Golf:
   Farming as a Development Amenity 49

6. In Praise of Technology 61

7. Economic Sustainability: Making the Economics
   of Agricultural Urbanism Pay 81

8. Economic Development through Urban Agriculture:
   Chasing the Local Job Dream 101

9. Rebuilding the Lost Food-Producing Infrastructure 119

10. Less "Waste," More Soil 133

11. Starting Young: Healthier Local Food in Schools,
    Colleges and Universities 151

12. Farmers markets and CSAs: Making the Most
    of Direct Sales 167

13. Growing Community with Community Gardens 181

14. Getting Food to Hungry People 197

15. Ending Food Deserts 217

16. Is Local Food Safe? 231

17. What We Can Do: Systemic Changes, Personal Choices . . . 239

References/Sources Consulted 259

Notes 275

Index 281

About the Author 291

Preface

People care most about what is closest to them. *Nothing* is closer to people than the food they put into their mouths every day. *Nowhere* is closer to people than their own backyard or schoolyard or front boulevard. The growing gap between our immediate world and the distant worlds that feed us is starting to gnaw at people. They see pieces of their lives fraying, and they see how much of that disintegration is related to the food they eat — or don't eat. They see the most primal element of personal survival put into the hands of underpaid foreign workers, a few large corporations, and distant mega-farms and processors dependent on diminishing supplies of cheap oil and water.

North Americans' health care costs, their children's obesity, their own health, their insecurities about the future of oil, water and soil, their uncertainties about climate change, and their anxieties over the loss of agricultural land are all related to accessing quality, affordable, nutritious food from reliable sources. The low-nutrient, low-quality "junk" food so many of us depend on is, literally, killing us. While the threats to our food supply in North America are trivial compared to the billion people elsewhere who go to sleep hungry every night, they're our issues and we must care about them.

The full story on urban food systems can't be told without looking at the corporate farmers and big global flows of food from one continent to the other that are laced with subsidies, floating in oil, and driving smaller farmers into bankruptcy. International treaties, national policies, commodity traders, and the price of tractors will always determine a lot of what we eat and how much we pay for it. This book will touch on that, but it will look more at what can be done at the local level, ramping up urban and near-urban local food production and distributing it more effectively. That's where the passion is. That's where we feel the wonder and simplicity of growing: *"I just planted this seed in a pot on my balcony and in three months I grew all these tomatoes!"*

What many are calling the "food revolution" is a groundswell of different actions that aims to take more control over the food that we eat. Bringing food production back into our cities and near-urban areas is part of a larger, more widespread urge — sometimes unspoken — to take back more control of our lives. It's a craving identified more than 50 years ago by the architect Frank Lloyd Wright:

> "Of all the underlying forces working toward emancipation of the city dweller, the most important is the gradual reawakening of the primitive instincts of the agrarian."[1]

And, as Matthew Crawford put it in his recent book, *Shop Class as Soulcraft:* "[The] struggle for individual agency...I find to be at the very center of modern life.... Both as workers and as consumers, we feel we move in channels that have been projected from afar by vast impersonal forces. We worry that we are becoming stupider, and begin to wonder if getting an adequate grasp on the world, intellectually, depends on getting a handle on it in some literal and active sense. Some people respond by learning to grow their own vegetables."[2] Writ large, this is the backbone of the worldwide "food sovereignty" movement, an international campaign to ensure people can exercise their democratic right to control their own food.

As Polyface Farm owner/author Joel Salatin says: "I can't wrap my head around global warming, but I can wrap my head around what I'm going to eat tomorrow."[3]

This book will look at people like Joel Salatin who are going "past forward" "back to the future" and celebrating messy organic things again. It will show how to pick up what we dropped beside the road to globalization, and how to take it down another road that combines the best of ancient farming wisdom with modern technology and the benefits of international trade.

I am not a farmer or even someone who grew up on a farm, although, like so many other people, some of my forebears were farmers. In my case, it was my great grandfather on my father's side, one of the first European settlers in Ladner, B.C., just south of Vancouver. The town was named after him and his brother. They farmed, and they also started a salmon cannery. I remember my maternal grandmother proudly showing me around her greenhouse in one of the tonier residential areas of Vancouver many years ago — and my mother's story of milking the family cow in that same backyard.

My interest in food systems comes out of a wider interest in changing the ways we live to ensure our children and grandchildren can live healthy and prosperous lives. It's what got me into municipal and regional politics after a career in publishing and journalism.

I've been a gardener all my life, having most recently converted the front lawn of a small lot I bought in Vancouver's Kitsilano neighborhood into a mix of berry bushes, fruit trees, and vegetable plots.

As a city councilor, I was the liaison to the Vancouver Food Policy Council as it struggled to get food issues onto the city's agenda — and into the budget. The city now has a food charter and succeeded in adding 2,010 food-producing community garden plots as a legacy to the 2010 Winter Olympic and Paralympic Games hosted in Vancouver.

As a member of the Metro Vancouver regional board of all the municipalities in our region, I couldn't help thinking that Metro Vancouver had all the ingredients for local food security — protected fertile farmland close to the city, great soils, a mild (for Canada) climate, plenty of water, and a large number of small family farms. It is said to be the most productive intensive agriculture area in Canada. Metro Vancouver now has a food strategy, for the first time. This book came out of my desire to push that agenda, as well as to promote what we and other jurisdictions in North America are doing to deal with the impending world food crisis.

For politicians, there are few decisions that don't have a downside — some group always seems to lose out. Food policy is one of those rarities. Bringing more fresh food production closer to home is an unparalleled win-win-win move. When urban agriculture flourishes, our children are healthier and smarter about what they eat, fewer people are hungry, more local jobs are created, local economies are stronger, our neighborhoods are greener and safer, and our communities are more inclusive. Everyone ends up smiling.

There are a lot of books written by people who know a lot more than I do about the world food situation, the health impacts of eating the wrong foods, water and fossil fuel shortages, and other mega-trends. There are also a lot of books being written about how to grow your own vegetables, fruit, chickens or bees in myriad small spaces. And there are even more celebrating local cuisine and recipes. What this book hopes to provide is advice to legislators, policy-makers, school officials, community organizers, developers, planners and health advocates about *what they can do to improve access to healthy food for all the people they represent.* What land use policies enable local food production? How do we zone cities to avoid food deserts? How can we make agri-culture part of mainstream culture? Who's getting it right? Eating more locally sourced food definitely feels good, but how do we ground public policy in economic, social and political sense, not just in emotion?

In the locavore spirit, I'll be talking a lot about my own city (Vancouver), my own region (Metro Vancouver), and my own country (Canada). But I'll also draw on my travels and research in other parts of North America and Europe.

Although a lot of the book is about planning cities, planning isn't just for professional planners. We all contribute to city planning by the choices we make every day: how we get to work, where we live, what we are willing to pay for water, and of course, what food we choose to eat or grow. Politicians, citizens, community groups, businesses and developers also shape the cities where most of us now live. If we can all get this right, we will transform our cities and our lives and give new hope to our children and grandchildren.

And when the talk is done, we have to do the dirty work. Let the farmers remind us:

"No amount of policy initiatives and foundation reports will successfully encourage food production in Canada until more people are willing to do the grunt work of farming. Farming these days is variously dirty, hot, sweaty, boring, menial, messy, wet, cold, frustrating and dirtier still. And that's when things are going well. Policy-makers would be more helpful to farmers if they got out from behind their desks, rolled up their sleeves, and helped with the work. The notion of delegating the workload, be it with chemicals, fancy machinery or migrant workers, is a tired initiative of the 20th century. A new generation of farmers, whether they're 18 or 80, knows that the future of successful food-growing is in the soil."[4]

1

What's the Matter with Food?

A NYONE WALKING into my neighborhood Marketplace IGA food store would be hard pressed to know why people are angry, anxious, or even concerned about the food that's available to most middle class North Americans.

Everything I could want is there: year-round organic bananas from Ecuador, fresh bread from local bakeries, so many dairy confections you need a nutrition degree to tell them apart, grains and nuts (in bulk *or* in packages), olives from Greece, local blueberries in season, spices from India, fair trade coffee from Nicaragua — there's more food and more choice than the richest people in the world could have dreamt of only 200 years ago. The average supermarket in the United States has 47,000 products. My grocery store has no shortages, no empty shelves. It does have massive waste, however. I witness it when I'm there at closing time and see them dumping everything from the deli section.

When I load up my bag in Canada or the United States, I'm paying the lowest percentage of my income for food than citizens in any other country in the world do. And I could be paying even less if I walked two blocks to the No Frills store, where the lighting is more austere and the "best before" dates are sooner.

In the United States, a food shopper gets to choose from an average of 50,000 different food products on a typical supermarket outing. The

American food system makes an average of 3,800 calories a day available to every person, more than one and a half times their average daily need. The invisible hand of the free market appears to be doing its job: nothing is rationed, and everything I see around me is being delivered efficiently and abundantly because of intense market competition for my food dollar. So why exactly are so many people engaged in a "food revolution"? Do we really need to intervene in the efficient, cheap flow of food provided by the free market?

Fewer Suppliers, Greater Risks

The answers are hidden in that store, mostly out of sight — and deliberately out of mind. The flaws in our food system start with the relatively few companies that control what's being sold. The invisible hand of the market is not concerned with how many suppliers there are, but it does demand that they focus on their own prosperity, not our dietary well-being, or farmers' incomes, or environmental pollution. Yet our lives, literally, depend on these few companies' industrial supply chains. "Never in the field of human consumption has so much been fed to so many by so few," notes British architect and historian Carolyn Steel.[1]

For example, five companies control 90% of the global grain market. In the United States, almost all the meat supply is controlled by four companies: Tyson, Cargill, Smithfield and JBS in Brazil. Cargill and two other companies process more than 70% of US soybeans, which are used to feed livestock and make much of the processed food we find in the grocery store.

Corn is a staple in livestock feed and is present in virtually all processed food and in an estimated 25% of all foods in a typical supermarket. Monsanto's genetically engineered corn covers 85% of total US corn acreage.

While corporate concentration doesn't necessarily mean that supplies are threatened, it guarantees that what food is supplied — and how those foods are grown and prepared — is in the hands of a few people completely outside our control, and mostly outside our regions. And the difference between food and those other two essential elements of survival — clothing and shelter — is that if someone stopped making our shelter and clothing for us, we would have time to regroup and adapt. With food, supply breakdowns have immediate and devastating impacts.

The same concentration and lack of diversity can be seen in the types of food we eat. The limited varieties of flora and fauna that meet the needs of a globalized food system are wiping more diversified products off the supermarket shelves and destroying the resilience that comes with biodiversity. This too adds vulnerability. Ninety percent of North American milk comes from the same breed of cattle; 90% of our eggs come from the same breed of hen.

The 'Gros Michel' banana is the type of banana our grandparents enjoyed. It was wiped out by Fusarium wilt (a.k.a., Panama disease). Because all commercial bananas are seedless, every banana is a clone, and thus equally susceptible to the same disease. "Billions of identical twins means that what makes one banana sick makes every banana sick," notes Dan Koeppel, author of *Banana: The Fate of the Fruit That Changed the World*.[2] The banana industry was rescued by the introduction of the now-ubiquitous 'Cavendish' banana, but it is susceptible to the same fate as its predecessor.

When the same species is planted in vast plantations, they become an all-you-can-eat restaurant for pests. Once a pest figures out how to attack that one kind of plant, it's open-season feasting on every plant in the field. As a response, we apply pesticides that contaminate the water, break down soil structure, deplete the soil's fertility, and decimate the soil's natural population of organisms.

To keep things growing, soil is replenished with loads of nitrogen, only a fraction of which is used by plants. The rest flows into rivers and waterways, feeding deadly algal blooms that suffocate aquatic life (most famously in the 6,000-square mile "dead zone" that flares each spring at the mouth of the Mississippi River). Much of the excess nitrogen is converted into nitrous oxide gas, which is accelerating climate change.

The vulnerability of any monoculture to disease and the concentration of production in fewer places compromises our food *safety*. In 2008, a *Listeria* outbreak at one meat plant in Toronto caused 22 deaths and hundreds of hospitalizations across Canada before all the tainted products could be identified and recalled. Typical carriers of food patho-gens are no longer just the usual suspects — meat, poultry and eggs — now, leafy greens can be the culprit. In the summer of 2010, a new strain of *E. coli* bacteria was found in ready-to-eat salad mixes packaged at one big center, triggering a new wave of recalls. Prepared salads are vulner-able both to contamination from handling and from bacteria taken into the leaves when irrigation systems are contaminated, or when improp-erly treated manure compost is used as fertilizer. Unlike meats and eggs, there's no cooking to kill pathogens.

Also invisible in my neighborhood grocery store are the antibiotics used to accelerate growth in cattle, poultry and hogs. These drugs are directly related to the spread of antibiotic-resistant bacteria in humans.

Less Soil, More Meat, More Competition for Water

The way our food is grown also undermines the likelihood that it will remain healthy, cheap and plentiful. Soil is eroding off North Ameri-can farmland at an alarming rate. The vast prairies — the famed North American breadbasket — have lost half their original topsoil. And ero-sion from agriculture continues to sweep away soils 30 times faster than new soil is being produced.

Around 2 million acres of cropland go out of production every year because of erosion, soil depletion or waterlogging. Another million acres a year are lost to development. Because food crops drain more nutrients than natural grasses, the soil that remains is increasingly dependent on fossil fuel-based fertilizers for nutrients.

Growing water shortages cannot help but hit agriculture hard. In Asia, 70% of all fresh water is used for growing rice. In a world where 2–5 million people already die every year from lack of potable water, the demand for fresh water will exceed supply by over 60% within a gen-eration. Half of the world's people live in countries where water tables in aquifers are falling because of overpumping. Saudi Arabia used to be self-sufficient in wheat, which was irrigated by a now-depleted fos-sil aquifer. From 2007–2011, Saudi wheat production dropped by two thirds. By 2012, it's expected that Saudi Arabia will have to import *all* its wheat.

The Ogallala Aquifer, which sits in the middle of the United States, is the source of irrigation for 20% of America's farmland. It is being overdrawn by 3.1 trillion gallons a year. As available water supplies shrink, the cost of foods requiring large amounts of water is bound to go up, as does the chance that those foods will become less available.

Table 1.1 Gallons of water required to produce one pound of food.

Beef	1,857	Sausage	1,382
Pork	756	Processed cheese	589
Chicken	469	Eggs	400
Fresh cheese	371	Figs	379
Plums	193	Avocados	154
Yogurt	138	Corn	109
Bananas	103	Apples	84
Oranges	55	Strawberries	33
Potatoes	31		

Source: *National Geographic supplement*, April 2010

Food shortages are already commonplace in many parts of the world. Globally, an estimated 963 million people — or about 15% of the world's population — were undernourished in 2008. In March of that year, riots broke out from Haiti to Bangladesh to Egypt as people were hit with annual price increases of 130% for wheat, 87% for soy, 74% for rice, and 31% for corn.

Food shortages and price increases in 2009 sent another 75 million people into the ranks of the hungry. A drought in Russia in 2010 triggered a ban on wheat exports — part of a disturbing trend of food-producing nations protecting supplies for domestic needs. As the world's population keeps growing and consuming resources faster than they can be replaced, future food shortages and price hikes are inevitable.

In 2010, the food price index hit record highs, and the United Nations' Food and Agriculture Organization estimates that food production will have to increase 70% by 2050 to feed a world population that's headed to 9.1 billion people (from 6.8 billion in 2010).

Of the food that is produced, distribution is skewed to the point that there are as many obese people as there are starving people. Ironically, in Western societies obesity is closely related to low income, where people aren't getting enough healthy food, resorting instead to sugar- and fat-laden fast foods — when they can find food at all.

Food shortages are exacerbated by the growing appetite for meat in countries like China and India. Grains that could go a lot further feeding people directly are being diverted to feeding animals for meat.

Although the United States rightfully prides itself as the breadbasket of the world, in 2006 — for the first time — the value of food imported into the United States exceeded the value of food exported from the United States. In 2009–2010, Australia had its first year as a net importer of food — and that was *before* the Queensland floods of 2010 that ruined thousands of acres of agricultural land.

The changes in imports and exports could be a reflection of the shrinking land base for agriculture, as agricultural lands around city edges get turned into housing lots and pavement. According the American Farmland Trust, more than 6 million acres of agricultural land in the United States were lost to development between 1992 and 1997 alone.

No Oil, No Food

Our food is "swimming in oil." The food industry is dependent on oil for all its materials and at every stage of production: fertilizers, farm equipment, distribution to markets, refrigeration, getting it home from the store, etc. To be complacent about peak oil is to be complacent about ensuring our future supplies of food. A July 2010 report from the UK is one of the direst warnings to date. The Lloyd's insurance market and the Royal Institute of International Affairs say Britain has to be ready for "peak oil" and disrupted energy supplies at a time of soaring fuel demand in China and India, constraints on production, and political moves to cut CO_2 to halt global warming. They might also have mentioned competition with biofuel producers. Their report says companies and industries (they could have added "cities") that fail to take advantage of the new energy reality could face "expensive and potentially cata-strophic consequences."[3]

Richard Ward, Lloyd's CEO, says we're in a period akin to a phony war. "We keep hearing of difficulties to come, but with oil, gas and coal still broadly accessible — and largely capable of being distributed where they are needed — the bad times have not yet hit."[4]

One strategy for combating dependence on oil is to grow biofuels, but that collides with our need for those crops for food — another pressure point on our food supplies. In the United States in 2009, almost 30% of the grain harvested went to ethanol distilleries to produce fuel for cars. That's enough food to feed 350 million people for a year.

Sadly, the oil that grows our food is also contributing to climate change. Floods such as those that devastated Pakistan and Australia in 2010, the Russian drought in the same year that decimated harvests, and rising sea levels are all reducing agricultural production. So are record high temperatures: crop ecologists estimate that for every 1 degree Celsius rise in temperature above optimum levels during the growing season, grain yields will decline by 10%. As of 2011, rising sea levels are threatening 20 major rice-growing river deltas in Asia.

Policies created to lessen the impact of climate change by reducing CO_2 emissions are more bad news for affordable food. Twenty-five percent of greenhouse gas emissions in the world are from agriculture. One study found that 83% of total household emissions stemmed from the production of food. By one calculation, the production of meat is responsible for more greenhouse gas emissions than the entire transportation sector.

One way to reduce oil dependency is to eat more local food. A Canadian study on "food miles" estimated that sourcing 58 food items locally or regionally rather than globally could reduce greenhouse gas emissions by about 50,000 tons annually. That's the equivalent of removing almost 17,000 vehicles from the road.

And what about all the fish on display at my local grocery store? That supply is shrinking too. According to the UN Millennium Ecosystem Assessment, "the demand for both freshwater and marine fish will expand because of increasing human population and changing food preferences, and the result will be an increasing risk of a major and long-lasting decline of regional marine fisheries."[5]

All fish stocks are currently in decline, with some researchers predicting the collapse of all our seafood sources by the middle of this century. That doesn't necessarily mean they'll disappear or that we won't do something to reverse those catastrophic trends. It almost certainly means fish will get more expensive and out of reach to a growing number of people. Fish farming, which still depends on feedstock from the oceans, won't be able to fill the void.

No Farmers, No Food

Back on the farm, the financial squeeze on farmers is driving the next generation of farmers off the land, leaving aging farmers to provide us with our food. The average age of farmers in North America is around 60 years old. In Canada, it's 52.

A quarter of US farmers and half of farm landlords are at least 65 years old (compared to only 3% of the US labor force). With the consolidation of farms, there are now more prisoners in the United States than there are full-time farmers.

While US farmers have doubled their productivity over the past 40 years, they now earn $40 billion less from farming than they did in 1969 (in inflation-adjusted dollars). It's a similar story in Canada, where the average Canadian net farming income is $8,000 a year, a number that has decreased steadily since the 1950s. (To keep things in perspective, that number includes all the hobby/tax farms, and comes after deducting every imaginable expense in running a farm, home and property.)

A lot of young people would like to go into farming, but the money just isn't there. As one son of a farmer told me, "The prospect of taking over my family farm is both lovely and awful." It's the money that's most awful: farm debt in Canada is soaring, as are operating costs and total farm cash receipts, resulting in net farm incomes declining for decades — and now hovering around zero. Since 1985, the average net income for farmers in Ontario has been below that of 1930's levels. More than half (52%) of Ontario farmers are losing money on their farms; most earn the majority of their income from off-farm jobs.

The picture in India is shockingly horrible: farmers there are saddled by impossible debts incurred to pay for seeds, tractors, fertilizers and pesticides that didn't used to be necessary. They are committing suicide by the thousands — as many as 200,000 by one count.

These trends are compounded by rising energy prices, increasingly onerous regulatory regimes, and the steadily falling percentage of income that consumers in northern countries spend (and expect to spend) on food. In Canada, we spent 24% of our incomes on food in 1960. Today we spend 11%. The people growing our food will soon be too old to grow it anymore. Then what?

Our Choice of Foods Is Killing Us

As if that's not enough to set off alarms about our future food security, we're also going to have to make some huge changes in *what* we eat. Diet-related obesity and diabetes are epidemics. A third of American children born after 2000 will get diabetes. Among minorities, the rate will be 1 in 2.

The Canadian Diabetes Association warns that the economic burden of diabetes in Canada could escalate to nearly $17 billion by 2020, an increase of more than $10 billion from 2000. Nearly 10% of all Canadians risk getting or having diabetes by 2020.

A lot of that onslaught is due to obesity. USDA Deputy Secretary Kathleen Merrigan told the May 2010 Farm to Cafeteria conference in Detroit that the cost of obesity-related medical spending in the United States in 2008 ($147 billion) was more than three times what it was in 1998 ($40 billion). Statistics Canada found that 26% of children aged 6 to 11 are overweight or obese. The percentage rises to 28% for Canadian teenagers and a staggering 61% for Canadian adults.

It's not too much to say that the food we're now eating is, literally, killing us. The US Centers for Disease Control and Prevention and other health organizations estimate that three out of four deaths in the United States can be linked to diet and other behavioral habits.

The largest grocery retailer in Canada is Loblaw. They are also the biggest private-sector employer in Canada. When their CEO, Galen Weston, spoke at the 2009 Global Politics of Food conference in Couchiching, he cited soaring health care costs as a reason his stores are planning to be on the good side of the food revolution: "We're looking at unsustainable health care costs, 70% of them driven by behaviors, with diet a driving force in 75% of diseases."

Americans spent almost $300 billion at supermarkets in the past year, with the #1 item being carbonated beverages, which clocked in at about $12 billion.

Pick your problem: soil erosion, biological and corporate monoculture vulnerabilities, water shortages, population pressures, peak oil, carbon pricing, wild fish population collapse, farmer shortages, biofuel competition, sickening diets, or antibiotic contamination. Any one of these by itself loads a big problem onto our plates. Put them all together and all that bountiful food in my corner IGA store is certain to become more costly, less safe, less nutritious, and less available. No wonder so many people are kicking into action to do something about this. For many, the first step is to go back to growing their own food, not just on farms in the countryside, but all over our cities.

2

Past Forward
to Local?
Let's Be Real

I STILL REMEMBER PULLING my chair up to a table in the third-floor lobby of Vancouver City Hall as a member of city council to join James MacKinnon and Alisa Smith for a "100-Mile Breakfast." It was 2005, and they were well into their year of living by eating only food from within 100 miles. She looked very thin. The tomatoes and eggs were good, but mint tea just didn't cut it compared to coffee. We walked away satisfied, buoyed by the excitement of the idea of a 100-Mile Diet — but were secretly looking forward to a conventional, globally sourced lunch.

MacKinnon and Smith were the people who coined the phrase and the project that encapsulated the essence of local eating. The idea of a 100-Mile Diet planted a seed that blossomed around the world. Groups trying the 100-Mile Diet have sprung up in France, Norway, Australia, California and all over Canada. MacKinnon and Smith's 100-Mile Diet experiment was covered by every major news media in North America, followed by a best-selling book, a reality TV show, and the formation of the 100-Mile Diet Society. In Manitoba in 2007, 100 people ate food grown within 100 miles for 100 days. The "100-Mile Challenge" TV show has spawned a *100-Mile Meal Planner*.

Locavorism is really a conceit, even if "locavore" was the New Oxford American Dictionary's word of the year in 2007. (The word was

introduced on World Environment Day 2005 to describe the practice
of eating a diet consisting of food harvested within a 100-mile radius.)
Seriously, how many of us really want to restrict what we eat to what is
grown around us? Few, I'm sure, but locavores are here to stay. The new
word was just one small manifestation of the craze for local food that
is sweeping the Western world. It's like a giant, self-organizing community barn-raising that is rebuilding the foundations of healthy food
self-sufficiency in our cities and surrounding farms. Restaurants are featuring local food and recipes: in 2010, the top five Canadian menu trends
were locally sourced food, sustainability, organic produce, artisanal
cheeses and simplicity/back-to-basics.

Community gardens are popping up everywhere (some of them un-
authorized "guerilla gardens"), and newbie gardeners are lining up for
plots. On rooftops in cities all over North America, people are tending
beehives, growing herbs, supplying leafy greens to restaurants, and dem-
onstrating that rooftop greenery can also be edible. I've stood in a long
line just to get into a "Feast of Fields" afternoon at a local farm showcas-
ing local food producers in a carnival of gustatory delights. Schools are

James MacKinnon and Alisa Smith's 100-Mile Diet experiment spawned a book,
a TV show, and a new international standard for eating locally sourced foods.
They never meant to imply that only 100-mile diets are acceptable.

connecting with nearby farmers to get salad greens onto their menus next to the microwave-heated fries. Grocery stores are beginning to brand local foods separately. Planners, food policy councils, legislators and urban conferences are diving into the local food pool. Businesses are team-building by pulling weeds at community gardens. Community kitchens are teaching people how to cook with the food that comes from their neighborhoods. Community Supported Agriculture — pre-paying a farmer for a season's worth of food — is exploding. Boxes of good food that is locally produced are replacing food bank handouts of imported industrial leftovers.

Why Canadians Like Locally Grown Food

The majority of Canadians polled in 2006 say buying locally grown fruits and vegetables:

- helps their local economy (71%)
- supports family farmers (70%)
- tastes better (53%)
- is cheaper (50%).

Slightly less than half of Canadians believe in the following benefits of locally grown fruit and vegetables:

- not genetically modified (48%)
- healthier (46%)
- no chemical or synthetic pesticides (45%)
- safer (44%)
- environmentally friendly (43%)
- preserves green belts (41%).

Similar proportions said each of these is also a benefit of locally grown meat compared to "regular" fresh meat. In addition, 46% of Canadians believe a benefit of locally raised meat is that it has no added hormones or steroids.

While these Canadians' trust in the safety, nutrition and low price of local foods can't always be backed up by evidence, it's a positive sign for the local food market.

Source: Canadians See Many Benefits of Locally Grown Food, Ipsos Reid poll, Dec. 2006

Feast of Fields Day in Delta, B.C.: Curious city-dwellers line up to meet local farmers at events like this festival of local foods, chefs and suppliers.

Given all the crises facing the trade-dependent globalization of our industrial food supply, the craving for local can be explained very simply: The surest way to control the supply and quality of the food we eat is to grow it ourselves. The next best way is to buy it from someone we know.

In 2009, author Thomas Homer-Dixon told Vancouver's Fraser Basin Council: "The number one lesson in resiliency is to make sure you can grow your own food." In a world that is increasingly out of our control, eating local food is something we can all do for ourselves. Not only do we get fresher, more nutritious food if it's grown close by, but we also get to support local farmers and keep our food dollars in the community. We can turn back toward more self-sufficiency. It's a "past forward" move that would do our grandparents proud.

Local food is imbued with the same underlying wisdom as local lending: the bad loans that undermined the United States and other banking systems wouldn't have been made if the lenders lived in the same place where the loans were being approved. The more we control where our food and money are coming from, the more resilient we are.

Reducing Food Miles Isn't Everything

The simplest and best-understood case for buying and growing local is that it reduces the fossil fuel transportation costs locked into food that travels thousands of miles from field to fork. (Most of our food travels between 1,000 and 1,500 miles.) In his book, *Why Your World Is About to Get a Whole Lot Smaller,* former CIBC World Markets chief economist Jeff Rubin argues that in a world that will soon see triple-digit oil prices due to increasing scarcity, "distance suddenly costs money, and lots of it.... Your neighbors and your neighborhood are about to get a lot more important in the smaller world of the none-too-distant future." Without cheap oil, globalization doesn't work.

Building a case for local food based on savings on high transportation costs may get a lot of horns honking in favor, but it's a weak argument. In fact, it's a unfortunate distraction that gives naysayers a legitimate platform for dissing the local food movement. Although food miles will always have the enduring value of intuitive simplistic importance, they are far outweighed by other unsustainable aspects of our food system. Shipping so much food huge distances by trains, trucks, freighters and airplanes to our plates (5,000 miles on average, in one UK study) is indisputably offside and ridiculous in a post-carbon era. Still, citing the reduction of food miles as the main justification for local food steers us away from much more serious problems. James McWilliams makes this point with a vengeance in his article, "Just Food: Where Locavores Get It Wrong and How We Can Truly Eat Responsibly": "In focusing on food miles at the expense of so many other detrimental factors of production and consumption, we're wasting time, energy, and a heap of good intentions that could very well save future generations from the mess that previous generations have dumped upon us."[1]

Most greenhouse gas emissions and fossil fuel uses occur *before* any food leaves the farm gate. One US study found that food miles account for only about 4% of the total GHG emissions from food production and distribution. Another said it was 20%. Whatever the percentage actually is, latching onto food miles alone lets people like writer James McWilliams blame the food miles argument for what he calls a "cultish attraction to the fetish of localism."

Most arguments for local food assume the advantage of proximity. There's no denying some advantages: local and regional transportation costs tend to be lower than trans-continent or trans-ocean transportation. A study in Iowa found that food coming from conventional (global) sources used 4 to 17 times more fuel than food from Iowa-based regional and local systems. Sourcing food globally also released from 5 to 17 times more CO_2 than food sourced from the local region. Unfortunately, specific regional studies like this don't always lead to conclusive generalizations applicable elsewhere.

A National Resources Defense Council study in California had a wider range of data to prove that transporting local goods is far less harmful to the environment than importing food. They looked at six top food and beverage imports into California (table grapes, navel oranges, wine, garlic, rice and fresh tomatoes). These were all foods that are both grown and exported from California. The study tracked greenhouse gas emissions, pollution, air quality and health impacts based on the number of miles traveled and the means of transportation from the originating country. The study found harmful air pollution from these food imports was 45 times the pollution caused by local or regional transportation. What they called "global warming pollution" (presumably, greenhouse gas emissions) was 500 times higher for imports than for locally grown food when the imports came in by plane.[2]

After pointing out the hypocrisy of ignoring long drives to the farmers market and the energy costs of home fridges, freezers and dishwashers, science writer and journalist Stephen Budiansky figures that home preparation and storage account for 32% of all energy use in our food system, the largest component by far. His conclusion: "The best way to make the most of these truly precious resources of land, favorable climates and human labor is to grow lettuce, oranges, wheat, peppers, bananas, whatever, in the places where they grow best and with the most efficient technologies — and then pay the relatively tiny energy cost to get them to market, as we do with every other commodity in the economy. Sometimes that means growing vegetables in your backyard. Sometimes that means buying vegetables grown in California or Costa Rica."[3]

Agriculture is far too complex to boil local food's virtues down to a simple matter of fewer miles traveled to get it to the market. When local food is only available at a farmers market 15 miles down the road and accessed in a single-occupancy SUV on a single-purpose trip, or when it comes from a fossil-fuel-warmed greenhouse, its economic and environmental benefits wither.

Many of us are indeed wasting gas on the road to the supermarket. Food miles for consumer trips to food stores in the UK are rising dramatically: Between 1985–1998, the distance of car shopping trips in the UK increased by 57%, and the average number of shopping trips increased by 47%.

Local Isn't Always Environmentally Friendlier

It's easy to get up in arms over fruits and vegetables that are grown in New Zealand to be sold in the UK. But dig deeper into food energy costs and the picture gets muddier: New Zealand has a much milder climate than northern Europe, so farmers get much higher yields. In addition, two thirds of New Zealand's energy comes from renewable resources. So an apple can be produced in New Zealand for half the fossil fuel energy that would be used on equivalent farms in the "local" market of northern Europe. If you add in the relatively low energy costs of shipping by sea, the GHG emissions for apples produced and consumed in the UK (in winter) are about two thirds higher than they are for New Zealand apples imported into the UK.

Arizona conservation activist Gary Nabham looks at local food from Arizona and wonders: "If a farm near Tucson, Arizona is irrigated from a canal that transports Colorado River water hundreds of miles (and at high ecological cost to wild riverine species), or if it uses fossil groundwater set down during the Pleistocene pumped by fossil fuel set down in Iran during the Pennsylvanian era, what is to be gained by promoting its food?"[4]

Similarly, if sources of hay, compost, nitrogen and feed grain are traveling thousands of miles to get to a "local" producer, simply measuring the miles from that producer to the consumer misses a lot of points. How "local" is that producer after all that? "Why call lamb locally produced in Idaho when its flock has wintered part of the year in California and its hay comes in from southern Colorado?" asks Nabham.

Professor Peter Tyedmers, an ecological economist at Dalhousie University's School of Resource and Environmental Studies did some revealing studies comparing the greenhouse gas emissions from farmed salmon in Norway vs. Scotland: "Let's say you're a British consumer. You say, 'I'm going to eat local because it'll have less environmental impact.' Why import salmon from Norway? Because it has much less greenhouse gas emissions and getting it to you would be trifling if you can move it by containerized ship." [5] Especially after looking at the feeds used on the salmon farms and the global commodities that go into them, he calculated that greenhouse gas emissions per tonne of salmon harvested in Norway were almost half those of salmon harvested in Scotland.

It is not really that hard to see that James McWilliams is right to ask us to look at life-cycle assessments of food products and recognize the virtues of large-scale production for some crops.

Energy Reduction: Putting Local Food in Context

Looking at the bigger energy picture, food production and consumption amount to only about *10% of first-world energy consumption.* This means that even the most fastidious eaters can only reduce their total energy footprint marginally through diet alone — and that's by changing *what* they eat, not where it comes from. That isn't to say that we shouldn't be doing everything possible to lighten our ecological footprint, but obsessing on local food just isn't enough.

Cutting meat out of our diets would have far more impact on saving water, reducing fossil fuel dependency and mitigating global warming and pollution than buying only local food. Roughly 25 times more energy is required to produce one calorie of beef than to produce one calorie of corn. Vegans, whether they eat local or imported food, can boast that their diets use 90% less energy than the average American's, and even those who include eggs and dairy in their diets can claim credit for significant energy efficiency. One pound of beef requires 1,857 gallons of water — if you include the water needed for irrigation, cleaning, growing feed, etc. — compared to 31 gallons for a pound of potatoes. Going without meat and dairy products for one day a week is more environmentally beneficial than eating locally every single day.

"I don't believe local trumps organic," adds Arran Stephens, the CEO of Nature's Path, the largest organic cereal producer in North America. Stephens is a passionate advocate for sustainable agriculture, sponsoring school gardens, community gardens and educational outreach to promote organics. While his company processes cereal in plants in the United States and Canada (some using grains from Nature Path's own organic farm in Saskatchewan), he also finances a community garden and organic teaching center in his own backyard in Richmond, B.C. "Local is great, but it's not the full answer," he says. "It can only supply supermarkets with fresh food in season. Local *and* organic is best."

An unfortunate legacy of the 100-Mile Diet is that it makes some people think eating local has to be all or nothing: "If I can't eat everything from within 100 miles, eating local is never going to work." Or, as the son of a farmer described to me: "I remember going down to that root cellar on the farm in the winter when I was a kid and bringing up yet another cabbage for dinner. Why would I want to go back to that? No thanks." For most of us, for now, local food has to be seen as *a part* of our diet, not a complete replacement diet. But even if it only means eating more local fruit and vegetables in season, that's a step toward a more sustainable food system.

The environmental benefits of eating local are decidedly mixed. Energy costs are usually lower for local than imported food, but not always. It depends where the imported food is coming from, how it's being transported, whether local food is in season, whether we're talking carrots or CO_2-heavy tomatoes, how long local food has been stored, how local food is grown (organic or petroleum-based fertilizers? indoors or outdoors?), what kind of fuels are used at every step, and how far your SUV has to drive to the farmers market. Organic growing, reducing meat consumption, eating what's in season and eating vegan are all at least as important as eating local in reducing the energy embedded in what we eat and becoming more energy self-sufficient. But eating local is about a lot more than saving energy.

Local Food Isn't Always Cheap or Easy

A big barrier to eating more local food is that it doesn't always save money. Lori Stahlbrand, who is campaigning out of Toronto for a "Certified Local Sustainable" labeling system in grocery stores, says consumers should expect to pay about 10% more for local produce than they do for imported industrial food (see localfoodplus.ca for more information). This is actually less than the typical markup for organic produce, and, for consumers who value the better flavor, nutrition and freshness usually found in local food, a higher price can be worth it. (Chapter 11 discusses prices at farmers markets in more detail.)

Growing our own food, while increasingly popular, isn't easy. Here's what it was like for James MacKinnon and Alisa Smith during their year of living entirely on a 100-Mile Diet:

> "Autumn, it turns out, is exhausting. Every corner of the apartment is at work. On a recent weekend we had hot peppers and sunflower heads drying on the balcony, herbs drying in a closet, 45 pounds of tomatoes waiting to be canned, onions curing in my clothes cabinet, two enormous salmon to be cut into steaks, and spinach, cauliflower, carrots, collards, brussels sprouts, basil and edamame waiting to be blanched and frozen. Preparing for a 100-Mile winter is like adding a part-time job to our full-time lives."[6]

Eating local doesn't have to be a career. It can just as easily be a marginal change in what we buy and eat. While you don't have to grow your own food to be a locavore, a whole lot of people are giving it a try. Canning courses offered by the Vancouver Food Bank's Fresh Choice Project have become so popular that they're now giving special two-day courses to train trainers to lead workshops in the 50-plus community kitchens around Vancouver. Sales of canning supplies in Canada were up 11% in 2009. Mason jar sales were up even more — by 20%.

Almost half the people who checked in at AllRecipes.com and who can their own food are under 40. Some of them were prodded into rediscovering the survival art of their grandparents by concerns about the security of their food sources. A pantry of canned food is protection against power outages, freezes, hurricanes and floods. In a new age where weather patterns aren't what they used to be, that's a smart strategy.

Being a locavore has quite a different meaning in regions where climate, soils and water limit local growing. I remember going to a 100-Mile banquet for the Federation of Canadian Municipalities in Calgary and discovering to my surprise that the only fruit we could eat was Saskatoon berries. (But the steaks were huge.) The uneven distribution of available food — especially fruit — can be a problem for a locavore. Many of us northerners are envious of people who can grow avocados, lemons, oranges and bananas in their backyard.

Through most of history, though, most people have eaten mostly what was grown or hunted around them. They didn't expect to have croissants, oranges and coffee every morning. North Americans looking at urban agriculture for the first time are usually skeptical about how much can be grown locally, especially within city boundaries. The question is usually "How much of what I now eat can be grown here?" The truth is, cities all over the world are actually huge sources of food. Urban farmers supply food to about 12% of the world's population.

Urban and near-urban agriculture provide 45% of all vegetables consumed in Hong Kong, 80% of poultry in Singapore, 70% of the poultry and eggs in Dakar and Kampala, and in Shanghai, 60% of vegetables, all the milk, 90% of eggs and 50% of pork and poultry. Hanoi sources 80% of its daily fresh vegetables from within urban and near-urban areas, and cities like Beijing have built urban agriculture into their city plans. The town of Rodas, Cuba, population 33,600, was entirely self-sufficient in fruit and vegetable production in 2001.

A study in Toronto concluded that the city of Toronto has enough available land and rooftop space within its own boundaries to produce 10% of the fresh vegetables currently consumed. A "Forbes 2020" team of experts and authors predicts that by the year 2018, 20% of all food consumed in US cities will come from rooftop and parking lot farms.

The biggest lessons about urban agriculture's potential in Western cities can be learned from the use of Victory Gardens during World War II. By 1945 in the UK, 1.5 million allotment plots were producing 10% of all the country's food, including half of all fruits and vegetables.

In the United States, by the end of the war, over 20 million home gardens were supplying 40% of US domestically consumed produce.

A more current example is Village Homes, a 70-acre upscale residential development in Davis, California that boasts community gardens, orchards and edible landscaping. It provides 24% of its residents' food needs.

Knowing what's possible, some cities are aiming for getting targeted percentages of their food needs from within their own boundaries. Toronto, for example, hopes to supply 25% of its fruit and vegetable production from within the city limits by 2025. A study by Michigan State University estimated that with the use of hoop houses, trained farmers, proper storage and bio-intensive techniques, just 570 of Detroit's vacant 5,000 acres of city land could produce 70% of the city's vegetables and 40% of its fruit.

Think how much the food industry has changed in the last 50 years in North America, from when the interstate highway system, supermarkets and franchise restaurants were just starting to catch on. Why could it not change equally as profoundly in the next 50 years, this time driven by ecological, social and economic sustainability, and concerns about food security?

Consumers Want Safety, Reliability

What ultimately matters is not what report writers say is possible. It's what people actually want and will pay for. More and more people at least say they are prepared to pay a fair price to farmers they can trust to produce good, clean food. In a recent poll, 91% of B.C. residents agreed that "it is important that B.C. produce enough food so we don't have to depend on imports from other places."[7] Local foods have replaced organic foods as the fastest-growing sector of the retail food market. For many people, *local* has become more important than *organic*.

In July 2010, Ontario grocer Dale Kropf switched five of his family-owned grocery stores from their Sobeys affiliation to team up with four other stores to form the Hometown Grocers Co-op. He did this because he wanted to stock more local food, but Sobeys's corporate policies wouldn't allow the sale of local meat that had been only provincially approved, not federally inspected. "We feel that local food, local presence is huge in our market and we wanted to take advantage of that," Kropf told CBC news.[8] He said his customers were concerned about the safety of food from overseas and from large corporations.

Vancouver-based studies indicate that nearly three quarters of the population would pay a premium for Canadian-grown products — if they knew the premium would go to Canadian farmers.

In a Toronto survey, 79% of respondents in a telephone poll agreed with the statement: "I prefer to buy locally grown fruits, vegetables and meats." Only 18% agreed that "It makes no difference to me whether the fruits, vegetables or meats are locally grown or imported," and only 1% agreed that "I prefer to buy imported fruits, vegetables and meats." The same survey found that 90% of respondents agreed that the distance a food product travels is a concern. And almost everyone — 97% — agreed that supermarkets should create dedicated and visible sections to make it more convenient to buy locally grown food.

Grocer Dale Kropf admits that local food appeals to the minority of buyers who put quality first, price second. For all the desire and noble intentions to buy local, the majority of consumers still look at price first, and local food is generally more expensive. But that isn't stopping its appeal from growing. Many who can afford it are willing to pay more for higher quality food — and reap the satisfaction of all the other benefits of buying local.

Conclusion

The new "lunge to local" is easy to criticize as a simplistic response to a single issue like global warming or peak oil vulnerability. It's actually a lot more than that. It helps local economies and local farmers, and it puts fresher, tastier food on the table. It satisfies a widespread urge to make our lives more resilient and self-sufficient.

For whatever reasons, no matter how misinformed locavores may appear in the eyes of economists and free traders, people want local food. Our own history, and examples from around the world, show that urban agriculture can be a big contributor to a nation's food supply. People get this, and they are growing and canning with an enthusiasm reminiscent of previous generations. In 2009, the number of Americans growing fruits and vegetables (41 million) grew by 13% over the year before. Even in Japan, more and more metropolitan families are becoming weekend agriculturists in the fields outside Japan's major cities, joining a movement based on *jisan jisho*, which roughly translates as "local food for local consumption."

The local food movement educates kids, restaurant patrons, farmers market customers and community gardeners about the food they're eating, where it comes from, and how it affects their health. Food from closer in is typically — though not always — fresher, which means more nutritious. Although not necessarily safer from contamination, local food can be far more easily traced than food from abroad. The only verifiably dependable source of healthy food is local food. Backyard and community garden food-growing eases poverty and adds income for people who can find even a small lot — and it provides a feast of spinoff health, community-building, exercise, green space, community safety, recreational and educational benefits.

The North American urban food revolution feeds on all these benefits, which is why it's growing so fast.

3

Preserving Rural Agriculture Land for Food Production

W E CAN'T HAVE LOCAL FOOD if we don't have local farms. It doesn't get much simpler than that. But anyone watching cities grow knows that growing cities pave over farmland. It's so easy. The land is already flat and is usually close to roads and water sources. What's worse for the farmland (and better for the city) is that farms are often at the city's edge, which is the obvious location for more homes, stores, factories, schools, temples, community centers and senior housing. In Canada in the last 40 years more than 5,000 square miles of fertile soil have been lost to urban development. In the United States, *each year* an area two thirds of a mile wide that would stretch from San Francisco to New York is converted by urban sprawl. Farmland acreage in the United States peaked in 1954 and has been decreasing ever since.

Between 2002 and 2007, the United States lost 3.2 million acres of farmland each year, mostly to development. The overall loss of farmland coincides with professional planners' absence of interest in food, even though it's an enduring necessity, as important as air, water and shelter, all of which get a lot of planning attention.

Most urban dwellers concerned about local food security are passionate about protecting high-quality farmland close to cities, which is where most of it is being lost. But do we really need all that agricultural land close to cities? What if we could do more with less? Shouldn't improving agricultural technologies continue to increase yields, making the supply of land less important? Shouldn't we be able to just grow more on less land?

As it turns out, adding pesticides, fertilizers and genetically modified varieties on open-field crops is producing smaller increases in yields, sometimes even lower yields, as soil breaks down and erosion increases. So a growing population is dependent on growing, not shrinking, cropland acreage. In B.C., for example, the Ministry of Agriculture estimates we would need another 225,000 acres of irrigated farmland to produce a healthy diet for people in B.C. in 2025.

Driving this relentless onslaught on borderline farms is the irresistible lure of big money. The closer to the city, the higher the price of land. A farm that's worth $2,000 an acre for growing food or raising cattle can be worth 20 times that (it goes up with each zoning upgrade) when it's subdivided. A developer can make more money from turning an acre of farmland into housing than a farmer could make from a lifetime of selling produce off that acre. Combine this financial bonanza with dwindling incomes for aging farmers, and the pressure to get rid of near-urban farmlands is firmly in place.

"It's all about land costs," says UBC food economist Jim Vercammen. "That's the thing. Even if someone inherits a farm that's worth a lot, the opportunity cost of keeping it in farming is too high."

Ironically, the new taxes reaped by a city from a greenfield suburban development are illusory gains. The American Farmland Trust (AFT) studied scores of US counties and found that for every dollar of taxes raised by residential development, public costs were $1.16. By comparison, private working agricultural land and open space cost only 35 cents to service for every dollar of tax they generated. What the trust calls "working and other open lands" may generate less revenue than residential, commercial or industrial properties, but such lands require little public infrastructure and few services. In nearly every one of more than 150 communities studied, farmland generated a fiscal surplus that helped offset the shortfall created by residential demand for public services. The only exceptions were where a community decided to pay for agricultural conservation easements. "Converting agricultural land to residential use

Vanishing farmland in Quebec: Farmland keeps disappearing as farmers cash in their pension assets and cities continue their assault on arable land.

should not be seen as a way to balance local budgets," the AFT study concluded.[1]

In Canada, a similar study in Red Deer County, Alberta, came up with similar numbers: Residential development cost the county $1.81 for every $1.00 in tax revenue, compared to only 70 cents in costs for agricultural land.

Not to be overlooked are the important "urban backyard" land uses that are also competing for agriculture land: sand and gravel pits, garbage disposal sites, equestrian centers, golf courses, driving ranges, car-racing circuits and the like.

Stopping Conversion of Agricultural Lands Isn't Easy

Stopping this long trend and bucking these market forces can only be done three ways: prevent farmers from selling to developers; prevent land from being developed; or have someone else (usually a public agency) buy and preserve the land.

Everybody knows that we need enough land to feed ourselves, although not everyone thinks it has to be close by. Outside of owners and developers with financial interests in converting farmland to other uses, most people like the idea of preserving local farmland. Although many people realize that this land needs to be part of our food system, some people like the idea of preserving farmland simply because they just like driving by it on the weekends and enjoying its green pastoral splendor. They might be neighbors who like the views and tranquility, especially if it's a non-working farm, as so many urban-edge "farms" are. By contrast, people living right on the edge of farmland are understandably eager to see the end of farming that is noisy, smelly and messy, even if it's all an essential part of a farmer's livelihood — and even if the farm was there long before their subdivisions were.

But deep in the public gut is a feeling that farmland is a community resource, not just a commodity, and one day we all might have to depend on our own local farms to supply a lot more of our food. Fields used for export crops and animals today are our insurance against food insecurity tomorrow. It's a primal, practical instinct to protect ourselves against food shortages, however disconnected that might be from the reality of what's being produced on farms on the edges of our cities. That might be horses, Christmas trees, ornamental shrubs, flowers, or produce and livestock for export — all completely unrelated to what we are eating today, but grown on land that could feed us tomorrow if we really needed it.

Lands around North American cities are home to a hodge-podge of initiatives to protect agricultural land for food production, all riding on a deep, widespread belief that agricultural land is a scarce and valuable community resource, but all under attack by economic forces pushing for non-agricultural uses.

For example, only about five percent of the massive province of B.C. is agricultural land, and only part of that has good soil. During the 1960s, we were losing between 4,000 and 6,000 hectares of arable land every year to development in the prime valley bottoms and river deltas. Urban intrusion onto agriculture land was particularly rampant in the lower

Fraser River Valley, on the outskirts of fast-growing Metro Vancouver. The hemmed-in geography of this fertile delta helped trigger action. With wilderness mountains to the north, the US border to the south, the ocean to the west, and a constricted valley to the east, there was no Plan B. Either the province's best agriculture lands were preserved, or there wouldn't be any agricultural land left.

In 1973, the provincial government created the Agricultural Land Reserve (ALR), which stopped the building of subdivisions on land designated as agricultural. The government identified lands for agriculture based on the capability of the land, its current use, local zoning, and input from public hearings. Five percent of the province (4.7 million hectares) ended up in the reserve — lands deemed most critical for the province's food production, where non-agricultural uses would no longer be allowed.

The ALR set off a frenzy of opposition. Two thousand people rallied on the lawn of the legislature, and farm leaders urged farmers to protest by not planting crops. A Provincial Agricultural Land Commission was set up to deal with exclusions, starting a tug-of-war that continues to this day as municipalities, individuals and developers make the case for taking certain parcels out of the reserve. For a few years, until that government was defeated in 1975, the Commission bought farmlands that were rented out to farmers for a "career-long" term. That was in line with the objective of the original Land Commission Act that created the ALR: to not just preserve agricultural land but to encourage the establishment and maintenance of farms. Today the Commission does little or nothing to encourage the establishment and maintenance of farms; it struggles with a reduced staff barely able to assess requests to have lands removed from the reserve. (The city of Surrey, just outside Vancouver, has a tough but easy answer to requests for excluding land: they will recommend removal of land from the ALR if the proponent can provide double that amount to add to the reserve.)

In spite of some highly contentious debates over removal of lands from the reserve (one lasted through 25 nights of public hearings), public commitment to the ALR has stayed strong. In the early 1990s, the B.C. Fruit Growers Association and the B.C. Federation of Agriculture both passed resolutions demanding the abolition of the ALR, but by the end of the decade, more than 80% of British Columbians thought it was unacceptable to remove land from the ALR for urban purposes.

Surprisingly, even within five years of its establishment, a survey of property owners with land inside the reserve found that 80% of them were in support of it. Supporters came from groups who might have been expected to be strong opponents of the ALR: people who used their property for non-farm purposes; people who had tried to change their land use designation; people who had protested against the legislation in 1973; holders of small-sized properties; owners of properties with poor soil; very old farmers; childless owners; and owners in rapidly growing and urbanizing regions. The case for preserving farmland had become firmly rooted, even among those who lost out on personal opportunities to rezone and sell at a higher price.

That support has stayed strong: a survey in 1997 found that 90% of British Columbians felt government should limit urban development to protect farmers and farmland. Seventy-two percent believed it should be difficult or very difficult to remove land from the ALR.

The sometimes stormy success of the B.C. Agricultural Land Reserve served as a guide to Quebec's establishment of a similar commission in the late 1970s. It also informed the Ontario government's 2005 Greenbelt Plan to protect farmland and undeveloped land from urban expansion in the Golden Horseshoe (from the Niagara region in the south, to cities such as Toronto, Hamilton and Peterborough). Ontario's Greenbelt Plan prevents non-agricultural uses on lands designated as "prime agricultural areas" or "specialty crop areas." Encompassing 1.8 million acres, it's the largest and most diverse greenbelt in the world.

Cities around the world with similar protected greenbelts include Melbourne (Green Wedges), Sao Paulo (Green Belt Biosphere Reserve), Frankfurt (Grün Gurtel), and other cities in Germany in the "Iron Curtain" Greenbelt.

Limiting Sales of Farmland

Many countries in Europe have preserved their farmland by limiting sales of land to speculators or to passive owners. In Denmark, Norway, France, and to a lesser extent, Germany, it's almost impossible for an individual or company to buy farmland as a passive investment. (The simplest way to define "passive investment" is an owner who's not a farmer.) The only way for a company, co-op or institution to buy farmland in Denmark is by getting permission for uses such as agricultural research. Otherwise, a purchaser has to have farming as a main occupation and move onto the land within six months of buying it. This has reduced inflationary pressure on farmland prices.

In Norway, County Agricultural Committees have a duty to intervene in sales and potentially do their own valuations where agricultural property seems to be offered for sale at a disproportionately high price.

France's Société d'Aménagement Foncier et d'Etablissement Rural (SAFER) can similarly intervene in high-priced farmland sales, exercising a right to purchase and resell at a lower adjudicated price.

In Sweden, Germany, France and Ireland, the "hobby" farmer and the "weekend" or "second residence" buyers are targeted as uneconomic users of rural land. Irish land policy encourages farmland coming onto the market to be made available to enlarge existing uneconomic farms.

All these zoning and selling restrictions do the job, but they require strong state or regional land use control, something that is often politically challenging. Politicians have to take heat from landowners who feel they've been robbed, and also, indirectly, from new homebuyers who figure out that restricting the land base available for housing raises the cost of the land that's left for housing. A University of B.C. real estate expert calculated that by tying up one out of five acres in the ALR in the geographically constrained Greater Vancouver region, housing prices are squeezed up by 22% because land prices get pushed up.[2]

Paying Farmers to Stay Put

Instead of banning farmland sales, a common practice in the United States is to reward farmers for staying on their land or restricting urban development on their property. This is done by harnessing private market forces to transfer density rights from the farmland to somewhere else. (These don't work in Canada because there are no constitutionally protected property rights; local governments can change zoning at will in the public interest.) Under a Transfer of Development Rights (TDR) scheme, a farm landowner sells or donates the right to develop land for non-agricultural purposes on some other location to a government or non-profit land trust. The receiving property, where high-density development has to be desirable, can sometimes get five times the density that would have been allowed on the farmland giving up its development rights. That provides compensation to the farmer and saves farmland — at no apparent cost to anyone.

The downside of TDR schemes is that they require a sophisticated administrative system to line up development sites in disparate locations and negotiate individual deals. That capacity is beyond the reach of many communities, which limits the effectiveness of TDR. As well, many farmers are reluctant to embrace that restriction on behalf of their offspring, and many communities don't support added density.

In spite of those challenges, TDR zoning can work. For example, in Montgomery County, adjacent to Washington D.C., TDR zoning has protected 40,000 acres in 20 years, achieving half the area's farmland preservation goal without any public spending.

Serenbe, Georgia, a master-planned farm community in the newly created city of Chattahoochee Hills, Georgia, on the edge of Atlanta, is a model for the successful integration of farming and development. It used TDRs to protect existing farms and the farming way of life by letting a conservancy organization oversee the purchase of development rights.

Unfortunately, "preserved" farmland even with no development rights can be almost as costly as farmland with development potential, according to new farmers struggling to find land in New Jersey.

Another option is for motivated farmers to voluntarily put a restriction on their land title, limiting the land's development potential, essentially providing a personal subsidy to future farmers. Even that doesn't always work. In B.C., the Agricultural Land Commission protecting the ALR has to approve any restrictive covenant registered on ALR land, and it is increasingly reluctant to do that.

In Marin County, about 40 miles north of San Francisco, proposed developments in the early 1970s spurred Marin ranchers and environmentalists to come together to oppose the developments and give family farms and ranching a second chance. In combination with restrictive zoning, land use regulations, and active support for ranching by the county government, the Marin Agricultural Land Trust's (MALT) agricultural conservation easement program was set up in 1980. It was the first program in the United States to focus on farmland preservation by persuading landowners to sell agricultural conservation easements on their land. These legal agreements prohibit non-agricultural residential or commercial development or any use of the land that would destroy its agricultural value. The land remains privately owned.

"Typically we get approached when there has been a death in the family, or siblings can't agree on the future of the ranch," says Jeff Stump, Easement Program Director for MALT. "We capitalize a portion of their assets and they use that to build a new creamery or something else that needs to be funded." MALT has protected more than 41,800 acres of land on 66 family farms and ranches — and the program's administrators have an eye on another 60,000 acres still unprotected from development.

"In Marin County we lose very little farmland; we have been able to fend off most conversions," says Stump. Still, he recognizes that his county's 100,000 acres of farmland could be lost in a day in another part of the country. As recently as the 1990s, California was losing more than twice that amount of agricultural land every year.

A 2005 study of 46 conservation easement programs in 15 US states found that most are successful in protecting farms for farming. But the easements couldn't keep vital agricultural service industries intact, and many didn't adequately monitor compliance with easement restrictions.

MALT gets some of its money from private funders passionate about farmland preservation, open space, and local food. It also gets state funds (some of them protected by ballot-endorsed specific-purpose bonds) and money from federal programs like the US Department of Agriculture's Natural Resources Conservation Service.

Land trusts have sprung up all over. The Southern Alberta Land Trust Society is another example; it was started by a group of ranchers in 1997 to buy conservation easements on ranch land.

Planners on the fringe of the rapidly growing city of Calgary, Alberta, are looking at agricultural lands not as greenfields for paving, but as economic assets to be enhanced while residential, commercial and business uses are constrained to designated corridors. Giving farmers a tax break is another way to make farmland available for those who will really farm it. Many jurisdictions have preferential taxes for farms, but they could be a lot stricter in the definition of non-agricultural uses, or in the level of agricultural production required to get the tax benefit. The USDA considers a farm as any place from which $1,000 or more of agricultural products were produced and sold, or normally would have been sold, during the census year. Such low thresholds encourage what has become known as "rural sprawl."

B.C. Ministry of Agriculture and Lands Senior Agrologist Mark Robbins would like to see people who tie up rural agriculture lands for exclusively residential uses pay a premium tax rate. "If someone is living on protected agricultural land but using it as a big backyard with no farming, we should classify that the same as a city residential use for tax purposes." Some jurisdictions go at this problem with "home plate" restrictions, which limit the percentage of an agriculturally zoned property that can be taken up by housing.

Conclusion

Growing more local food means having access to products from local farmland, but farmland near cities is under intense pressure for redevelopment. Farmers near cities struggle to make ends meet. Some want more protective tariffs. Many dream of the day they can cash in their land and retire. Expanding cities need new land for housing and are eager to convert farmland, even though residential developments cost cities more than they gain in new tax revenues. But urban residents like the idea of protecting nearby farmland, and politicians around the world have responded with a mix of farmland conversion restrictions and financial incentives to keep farmers on the land.

In spite of all these efforts, the combination of struggling farmers, eager developers, and space-hungry cities continues to conspire to pave over arable lands. Sprawl continues its relentless march over much of North America's most valuable farmland, especially lands at the edge of spreading cities.

4

Converting Urban and Suburban Lands for Growing Food

I FELT JUST A LITTLE CONSPICUOUS walking through the South Side of Chicago; I was the only white person in view since I got off the bus many blocks away. I was headed to Growing Home's Wood Street Urban Farm in the Englewood neighborhood. "You must be going to the garden," a man said to me as I walked past a cluster of friends chilling on a porch a few blocks away from the garden. The garden and I are both relative newcomers to the neighborhood. Its parent organization, Growing Home, was started in 1992 by Les Brown, Director of Policy for the Chicago Coalition for the Homeless, but this farm has only been around since 2007. It's a beacon of hope and fresh food in a depressed neighborhood with few real food stores. A restaurant I passed on the way, Pappy's Restaurant, featured shrimp, fish, chicken wings, tacos and burritos. A "Fresh Meat" store had nothing but liquor ads in the window.

Hidden at the end of a cul-de-sac in a resolutely residential neighborhood, Wood Street Urban Farm's trim, neat rows of vegetables under hoop-house frames bespeak a new standard of eating and growing local. Through the back of one hoop house, I could see the homes right across the street. This two-third-acre site is a farm, but it is far away from typical farmland.

Fresh meat, maybe. Liquor, definitely: Food sellers add to food deserts as they struggle for economic survival in neighborhoods like this one in Chicago.

Three collegiate-looking young people are bunching turnip greens, mint and radishes for an upcoming farmers market on the north side of town. Selling produce at the various farmers markets is just one way the farm makes money to support itself.

The Wood Street Urban Farm provides job training through its nonprofit organic agriculture business. Upstairs, in the brand new office building (finished July 2009), the day's training class breaks for an afternoon smoke. These trainees are people with employment barriers who are learning the basics of finding work. They look more like hip young people than farmers, but they're being trained for any job they can get that's food-related. This year has been better than last: one member of the class already has a job. Today's class is trying to figure out how to attract neighbors to the Wednesday veggie stall set up on the premises.

Before the spartan but classy new offices were built, vandalism was an issue with the farm's on-site trailer. Now things are better. In 2008 the farm produced approximately 5,000 pounds of produce; a year later it was double that. Spinach, lettuce, arugula, swiss chard, tomatoes, zucchini, beets, turnips, kale, mustard greens and collards all grow happily in the warm, moist hoop-house climate, oblivious to the traditional urban surroundings.

Wood Street Urban Farm is just one of many new intrusions of agriculture and food production into the urban food revolution landscape. To think of food production in cities as an intrusion is odd. Historically, food has been an integral part of city life; in fact, the first cities came into being to store and protect domesticated agricultural produce. In the developing world, live food is still everywhere in cities. Without that urban produce, many more people would be starving than already are.

Live food — cattle, chickens, orchards, pigs, vegetables — has been a major presence in cities through the ages. Only in very recent years has food production been pushed out beyond the city boundaries and processed food been brought in the back way — through suburban warehouses and hidden loading bays behind centralized supermarkets; now, food magically appears out of trucks, trains, planes and ships from places we know nothing about.

Vegetable stall, farm office, classroom: Wood Street Urban Farm's headquarters is a multi-purpose community development center.

Cheek by jowl: A commercial greenhouse at Wood Street Urban Farm in Chicago blends with residential homes across the street.

Today's challenge is to bring food back into our cities in a much more visible and tangible way, "past forward" to a 21st century model that feeds on the new technologies *and* the old reality that everything we eat has to grow somewhere — the closer, the fresher.

Friction at the Edge

There were some good reasons why farmers left cities for the comforts of the country. But even in the country, especially at the rural boundary, you can feel the friction between urban dwellers and their farming neighbors.

"Urban infrastructure and rural infrastructure are diametrically opposed," says Kim Sutherland, a regional agrologist at the B.C. Ministry of Agriculture and Lands. "Farmers need easy access to their fields, and roads with little traffic. They don't want a lot of neighbors who will complain about noise and odors."

There Goes the Neighborhood

May 28, 1998: Swine-farm neighbors say stink bugs them

HOOKER, Okla.—Julia Howell has stuffed feather pillows up her chimney. She said it was to help keep neighboring hog-farm odors from seeping into her home.

She even caulked the windows in her two-story, 17-room home and bought an air cleaner, she said.

Three years before, Seaboard Farms Inc. constructed a corporate hog farm about a mile from the Howell home, she said.

Nearly 10,000 hogs are housed at that facility, said Mark Campbell, vice-president of operations for Seaboard.

A hog-waste lagoon is less than a mile from her home, Howell said.

"We have...masks we wear outside, and sometimes I come in from working in my flower bed because of the toxic fumes," Howell said. "We have a golf driving range out here, and people used to come out here and use it and I used to give a few golf lessons, but that doesn't happen anymore."

"You can't breathe; it's that bad—regardless of what the hog people say," she said. "They say 'Well, you know this is agriculture, what do you expect?'"

"They tell us...if we're worried about it, we're radicals against agricultural growth and economical development. And this is as far from the truth as it can be," she said.

Howell and her husband, Bob, are long-time Hooker farmers. But they haven't invited dinner guests to their home for two years because of the smells from the hog farm, she said.

"It changes your life," she said.

Bob Duke, a long-time farmer and rancher in Darrouzett, Texas, said he does not want large corporate hog farms moving into Lipscomb County.

"It's almost impossible to drive a tractor and live next to them because of the smell," he said. "It's just almost unbearable."

A small enclosed hog farm rests about seven miles northeast of Duke's home. He said hog odors don't drift as far as his home, but the odors are prevalent while he works in his fields.

"I am just not for them. I feel they will be a detriment to our country, and I think down the road people are going to be sorry they let them in," he said.[1]

People with homes close to farms, especially farms with livestock, have to put up with noises, foul smells and bad air quality. One farm neighbor in Aldergrove, in the Fraser Valley east of Vancouver, filed a complaint with the Farm Industry Review Board about the dust made up of chicken manure, skin, feathers and feed that was settling on his house. He said the dust, which came from the fans on the side of his neighbor's chicken barn, gave his family breathing problems, irritated their eyes and throats, and caused flu-like symptoms. The review board, a quasi-judicial tribunal that balances "right to farm" legislation with excessive disturbances, ruled in favor of the farmer, but they couldn't remove the inherent conflict between these two land uses.

The common practice of manure spreading on dairy farms is another frequent cause of complaints. One resident in the Okanagan area of B.C. filed a complaint saying it was "like living in an outhouse" after manure had been freshly spread.

Noise—from blueberry and cherry cannons, chickens being caught and moved in the middle of the night, or boisterous guinea fowl—is another reason more urbanized residents get upset with their farm neighbors. The city of Surrey, B.C. forces some new developments to include information on land title documents that a particular lot may be subject to agricultural "noise, smells and dust." Many municipalities have buffer zones of hedges, ditches or linear parks to reduce disturbances from farms.

Ironically, people who own small farmland plots mainly as a backyard for sprawling "rural lifestyle" houses tend to be reluctant to let farmers come and work their land.

Farming at the Urban Edge Adds Value Both Ways

But let's not forget that farms can add value to the residential communities around them. One study in Abbotsford, B.C. tried to quantify the benefits of farmland. After taking away a dollar value for the "public nuisance cost" of farms, it added up the "amenity benefits" (most notably, access to local foods, greenspace and rural lifestyle) and concluded that "the present value of the stream of public amenity benefits and ecological services provided by each acre of farmland in Abbotsford in 2007 is estimated to be $29,490." Comparing this to the net tax benefit from industrial and residential land, the study concluded that industrial land provided a benefit of only $14,000 per acre, while residential lands cost taxpayers $13,960 per acre.

This community benefit provided "free" by farmers has led to proposals for compensating farmers for providing those public benefits. It's a nice idea, but how would you quantify the payments, and where would the money come from?

Having farms close to cities also has advantages for the farmer. Farmers like Delta, B.C.'s Terry Bremner take advantage of their proximity to the city to add new revenue streams. He bottles and processes his blueberries on-site, sells his products at his own retail store, hosts classes, classic car shows and musicals, and rents out the barn for festivals. He got permission to rezone some of his farmland for these multiple uses so he could make a living as a farmer. He thinks all farmers should be able to carve off a small slice of their land for light industrial agriculture-related uses like a welding shop or warehouse. This would help them make a decent living.

"Doing something like that could give the farmer either more productivity or another $150,000 from commercial rental — that would keep him on the farm."[2]

Being at the edge of the city makes Urban Edge Agricultural Parks work in California. Pioneered by Sustainable Agricultural Education (SAGE) in a partnership with landowner San Francisco Public Utilities Commission, the 18-acre Sunol Agriculture Park, 40 minutes from Berkeley and 30 minutes from Oakland, provides land and infrastructure for four small organic farms run by city folk. The farmer leases the land, and SAGE provides a farm manager, fences, roads, irrigation and a watchful eye on maintaining hedgerows and natural habitats for pollinators and beneficial insects.

The current wave of urban farming is very much alive in Europe. In the UK, the first modern urban farm was started in North London in 1971. By the mid-1990s, 60 similar farms had popped up around the country. Some market gardens thrive on the edge of cities by catering to the luxury urban markets. Others, like the Wood Street Urban Farm in Chicago, grow food in poorer areas of cities, providing environmental education and engaging the community in ways a larger rural farm wouldn't.

Is turning suburban lots into farms undermining the need to densify suburbs to reduce automobile dependence and create walkable neighborhoods? Not at all. First, there is still lots of opportunity to densify suburbs along transportation corridors and around commercial/industrial centers. That's where density belongs. For those who lament that outer-ring suburbs are doomed to become abandoned ruins of a cheap-oil lifestyle, what better way to revitalize the ruins than to bring them back to life as suburban farms? New approaches to farming inside city boundaries are changing the meaning of "city boundary."

Cities Without Edges

Many cities are blurring the boundary line that used to dictate that food is grown "out there" and eaten "in here," give or take a few backyard gardens. Architect/designers André Viljoen, Katrin Bohn and Joe Howe make the case for an "edgeless city" in their book *Continuous Productive Urban Landscapes.* "The emerging 21st century city can be identified as 'the Edgeless City'.… The concepts of city boundary, greenbelt and suburb are all obsolete. Cities are becoming formless, edgeless and seemingly endless."[3] These authors advocate for the creation of city-traversing open spaces providing a mix of leisure, recreational and green transportation uses. But their main focus is the introduction of agricultural fields into urban life — green strips farmed by local residents who rent the land and work it commercially for local food production.

When this happens, agricultural urbanism becomes a growth-containment mechanism. By integrating agriculture into suburban settlements, residents learn first-hand the value of preserving agricultural land. It's part of their lives, rather than the next land waiting for development at the city's edge. When we're all living with agricultural land in some form as part of our everyday lives, it is more valued and less in need of draconian protection measures. Still, it's hard for local governments under pressure to provide land for other community purposes, like low-income housing, to give the nod to urban agriculture uses.

Traditionally, many cities have had commercial suburban farms associated with prisons and mental institutions that provide food for the institution, with the added benefits of providing therapeutic healing and teaching responsibility, work ethics and self-sufficiency. The New Jersey Department of Corrections is the largest farmer in its state, supplying milk and processed foods to state departments at lower rates than commercial farms. The 800-acre Frontenac Farm in Kingston, Ontario is believed to be the largest urban farm in Canada. Bizarrely, it and five other prison farms across Canada are being shut down because the federal government believes they are too costly ($4 million a year) and that they compete with local farmers and don't provide relevant skills to inmates. How can they not provide relevant skills if they compete in the marketplace with other farmers?

Fed Up on the Roof

Some urban farmers and their farms are well disguised. Eli Zabar is a Manhattan baker, retailer and restaurateur. Up on the roof of a three-story brick complex on 91st St., under the eye of neighboring apartment buildings, his big commercial rooftop greenhouses cover raised beds pumping out herbs, salad greens, radishes and tomatoes. A compost grinder helps convert bakery and deli waste into compost. Exhaust pipes from the ovens downstairs keep the greenhouses at the precise temperatures that work for growing tomatoes in the winter.

Restaurants all over North America are doing the same thing — growing what they can on-site, either in a ground-level garden, or, like the restaurant at the Fairmont Waterfront Hotel in Vancouver, on an upper-level courtyard. At the Uncommon Ground restaurant in Chicago, volunteers hauled six tons of topsoil up to planter boxes on a 2,500-square foot rooftop garden.

Converting a roof to a garden isn't easy. The weight of the soil and the constant human traffic up to a rooftop requires extra support, which can be expensive. One of Uncommon Ground's owners estimates he spent $150,000 on construction. "We resupported the entire building. We dug down five feet and put in all new posts and beams. That was all to support what we wanted to do on the roof.... My structural engineer said we could probably land the presidential helicopter on the roof."[4] Uncommon Ground's roof also features a pair of beehives that produce 40–50 pounds of honey for the restaurant.

Brooklyn's Grange Farm has gone one better. Boasting the world's biggest rooftop farm — on the Standard Motor Products building in Long Island City — its one acre of garden required 600 tons of soil to be hauled up six stories in a 91-year-old building. The Long Island Business Development Association was so impressed, it presented Gwen Schantz and the Grange Farm with its 2010 Green Business Award.

Or would you like rice with that? Mori Building, developer of Roppongi Hills in Tokyo, is using rooftop gardens to create "vertical garden cities" to add green space to a depressed area and dampen its intense urban heat island. The company's Keyakizaka complex rooftop boasts a seventh-floor rice paddy — yes, rice paddy — and vegetable plot. The paddy is small (155 square feet) and largely symbolic, but still capable of producing 135 pounds of rice, with elementary school students doing the planting and harvesting under the instruction of rice farmers.

There's lots of rooftop space potentially available. By one estimate, the 4.8 million commercial buildings in the United States have about 1,400 square miles of roof, most of it nearly flat. That's an area larger than Rhode Island. Not all of it is useful for rooftop gardening. Aside from the obvious structural loading issues, acceptable access to the roof is critical. In many multi-family residential or commercial buildings, occupants may not want urban farmers with wheelbarrows of compost and muddy tools traipsing through a public lobby. But even leaving out the roofs that are shaded, inaccessible, or structurally unable to support rooftop activity, that's a lot of growing space.

Finding Farming Space in Cities

Back at ground level, the lands most often being converted for urban farming are those that are underused (lawns, parkland, abandoned backyards and schoolyards) or eyesores (brownfields). In Milwaukee, Growing Power's Will Allen bought the last remaining farm in the city and brought it back to life as a 1.7-acre complex of greenhouses, compost production and aquaculture ponds.

To make space for livestock, a British company makes portable (designer!) hen-houses that sit happily on the front lawn. Hens are being kept by half a million British families; 10,000 of them are using these "Eglus," high-tech chicken coops with fox-proof runs.

Single-family homeowners are taking a second look at their lawns and wondering why they're working so hard on a manicured look when they could be reaping tomatoes and lettuce. Dan Goosen, general manager of Intervale Compost Products, says the average American lawn uses 8,000 gallons of water a year, compared to 3,000 for a one-acre organic plot. According to the EPA, one lawnmower can emit as much carbon in one hour as a car does in a 200-mile ride.

"There's so much land in cities we're spending money mowing," says Ward Teulon, who has a backyard food harvesting business in Vancouver called City Farm Boy. He used to be in the lawn care franchising business, opening new franchises across North America. He says his average clients were spending over $300 a year keeping their lawns mowed, weeded, fertilized and aerated. He offers to take over the land and start growing food, saving the homeowner those costs and paying her in all the produce she can eat.

Some food sources don't even need cropland allotted to them. Some cities are replacing decorative boulevard trees with edible fruit and nut trees, and new developments pride themselves on edible landscapes. Developers with projects in Vancouver's Southeast False Creek downtown housing development are required to include edible landscaping and food-producing garden plots for rooftops and courtyards. Rooftops feature espaliered fruit trees and raised vegetable beds, and courtyards are framed with blueberry and raspberry bushes and trellises supporting fruit-bearing vines.

Legalizing Urban Farming

Cities all over North America are struggling to figure out how to allow farm uses in traditionally residential, commercial or industrial neighborhoods. Baltimore, for example, is revising its zoning to officially recognize community gardens and urban farms; the change is expected to become law in 2011.

Cleveland has already added a new "urban garden district" designation in its zoning code that allows for both community gardens and urban farms. The code includes details about allowable structures, including chain-link fencing up to six feet high, something not allowed elsewhere in the zoning code. Cleveland's director of planning says there was initial public resistance to having farms in the city, but since the zoning changes were made, not one person has complained. Cleveland is now considering allowing an "agricultural overlay" on lands zoned for other uses, allowing temporary agricultural uses until other development takes over.

Philadelphia has changed its zoning code to open up residential districts to "agriculture and horticulture, except the commercial keeping or handling of farm stock or poultry; and except commercial greenhouses or establishments for sale of farm or horticultural products." This effectively allows community gardens but not commercial farms.[5] Philadelphia's next step is to recognize urban agriculture as a primary land use in its new zoning code, including commercial farming. The goal is to bring local food within 10 minutes of 75% of residents.

Milwaukee has generous provisions for "raising crops or livestock" in residential districts, not just allowing community gardens but also a range of livestock unheard-of in most cities: cattle, horses, sheep, swine, goats, chickens, ducks, turkeys, geese or any other domesticated livestock permitted by the health department.

It's Hard to Lock Up Urban Farmland

The biggest issue surrounding converting urban lands for farm use is security of tenure. In Milwaukee, as in many cities, bringing in permissible zoning but only allowing short-term leases of city-owned plots for community gardens begs the question: how can a community gardener or urban farmer be assured they're not going to get kicked off the land just when they've got the soil built up and everything growing?

Cities are now recognizing that securing tenure for urban farmers is the key to opening the gates on urban agriculture. Serious urban farmers aiming at commercial food production look for underused lots that can be converted to growing food with some certainty that they'll remain as urban farms for many years.

That's where an organization in Chicago is showing the way. NeighborSpace has been working with community groups since 1996 to buy land on behalf of local partners and end the uncertainty about future possible redevelopment (neighbor-space.org). Their goals are a mix of conservation, recreation, preservation, community food production and beautification. Their sites, always public, also provide opportunities for socializing and educational activities. It helps that they get money and support from their founding partners, the city of Chicago, the Chicago Park District, and the Forest Preserve District of Cook County. Those public entities set up NeighborSpace when they discovered that Chicago ranked 18th out of 20 similar-sized cities for open green spaces. By 2010, NeighborSpace owned or leased 61 sites, with another 20 under acquisition.

Yes, guerilla gardeners are jumping in and starting farms and gardens on rooftops and in underused lands all over our cities, asking forgiveness while politicians craft bylaws of permission. But serious food

---

How to Tear Up a Lawn

Converting lawn to productive garden space is pretty simple: here's a good "weaken, kill and rot" recipe:

- Cut the lawn as short as possible
- Cover it with black plastic or old carpet—or any material that will completely block the light.
- Leave it a few weeks, then uncover and sprinkle the area with a complete organic fertilizer.
- Spade the sod upside-down, then re-cover it with plastic to bake for a few more weeks.
- Uncover and plant potatoes or, to bolster organic matter, plant a quick crop of green manure (clover or field peas) and give it five weeks.
- Till in the new plants and let them rot for a few more weeks, then plant your food crops.

Source: Randy Shore, Vancouversun.com.

production on urban sites isn't going to happen until urban farmers are sure enough that land will be theirs for long enough to reward their investments in time and soil-building.

It's conceivable that small agricultural reserves inside city limits could one day become a new civic amenity as important as parks and school grounds. In the meantime, farm spaces will more likely be carved out of underused properties in both cities and suburbs, protected by zoning permission, and swarmed by city farmers eager to ramp up local food production. Declining cities, where vacant land is widely available, will have the easiest time converting to agriculture. But every city, even if it has to squeeze farm sites onto rooftops, is going to be looking for ways to grow more food closer to home. The reason is simple: people really want it.

5

Agriculture as the New Golf: Farming as a Development Amenity

THERE ARE 16,000 golf course developments in the United States. "People want the view over the fairways, but it costs millions to build and maintain a golf course," says Ed McMahon, of the Urban Land Institute. "Developers are asking, 'How can we build open space at less cost?'" Enter the farm.

When Linda Weins met me at the Prairie Crossing train station (the one that connects with O'Hare airport, not the other one, that connects directly with downtown Chicago), it was immediately apparent that Prairie Crossing wasn't just another suburban development. The fact that she would eagerly volunteer to take a stranger around this prototype "agricultural subdivision" was the first clue. The fact that we could walk from the train station to the subdivision entrance (if we had wanted; she actually gave me a ride) was another clue. The sense of purposeful community was palpable. The development might be mistaken for the set of *The Truman Show*, a film about a tidy, ordered community inhabited by actors creating a fantasy existence for an unwitting protagonist.

Homes in Prairie Crossing are carefully laid out and designed under strict guidelines. There are well-kept boulevard lawns and identical white stands for identical rural-style mailboxes stationed at identical intervals along clean streets. Every home has a view over green space.

Linda can confidently point out which people are strangers.

Situated at the juncture of two railway lines about an hour's ride north of Chicago, Prairie Crossing is a 677-acre development in the 5,000-acre Liberty Prairie Reserve. In some ways it is like a thousand other bedroom suburbs — it is a bunch of detached homes on former farmlands a long way from jobs and commercial centers. But one big difference is that the farm hasn't gone away. The mostly low-density, detached housing occupies only 20% of the developed land; 145 acres are devoted to an organic farm, and the rest is reserved for wild habitat preservation. Ten miles of trails wind through a landscape of farm fields, pastures, newly created lakes and ponds, restored native prairies and wetlands, and acres of historic hedgerows — all set on top of formerly depleted corn and soybean fields.

The 20-year-old development is grounded in the vision of its founders, George and Vicky Ranney. In the words of Vicky Ranney: "On the assumption that the ground under our economy may be shifting…the future of development lies with community designs that take into account climate change, public health concerns and new forms of agriculture."[1]

What really makes Prairie Crossing different is its complete integration of residential housing and farming. Agriculture is an integral part of the community. A salaried manager looks after the on-site organic farm, and 15 acres are available for community farming. Most of the residents rent community garden plots and grow food for themselves. And some of the food comes from edible landscaping that residents have planted around their own properties. A quarter of residents have volunteered on the farm. It is just part of a sense of community engagement built around growing their own food.

"I've been checking out other lots in other subdivisions, and what a difference," says Linda Weins. "They're just a development, not a community." Prairie Crossing has its own school, community center, and a small, struggling commercial zone in a mixed-use town center that has 36 condominiums.

The Community Barn at Prairie Crossing is part of the agricultural amenities package at this farm-centered residential development.

Six different farmers work individual farm sites, five of them apprenticing through the Farmer Business Development Center incubator, modeled after Will Raap's Program at Intervale Center in Burlington, Vermont (see Chapter 7).

The Center sets farmers up with mentors, five-year low-cost leases, and low-cost access to shared equipment. The farmers all sell at the weekly farmers market, including Matt and Peg Sheaffer of Sandhill Organics, who work 30 acres, the biggest farming plot. A berm between the community and the farm separates the working agricultural land from the nearest homes, symbolic of the freedom the Sheaffers have been given to run the farm as a successful independent business without interference from the residents.

The farmers market is a popular social gathering place, as are the community gardens and the rebuilt timber-frame barn that serves as a community center and meeting place for the residents' association. People also meet less formally on the tidy man-made white sand beach on the shore of Lake Aldo Leopold. The farmers sell weekly boxes of produce through a Community Supported Agriculture (CSA) network in the community.

Prairie Crossing also supports a small educational farm on the site that works with students from local schools. The stewardship costs for all the non-profit endeavors are covered by grants, a 0.5% levy on all house sales, and fee-for-service charges. The Prairie Crossing Homeowners' Association chips in $10,000 a year to help out the farm, in recognition of its services to the community.

Prairie Crossing has been visited by hundreds of planners, developers and agriculture advocates, and spawned a rash of similar developments across the United States. They are all part of the movement variously known as *New Urbanism, agroburbia, agricultural urbanism, conservation developments* or, more glibly, *"farming as the new golf."*

How to Make Community Gardens Work in Planned Communities

Residents in conservation communities enjoy having access to community gardens, especially in neighborhoods built to New Urbanism standards of small lots and higher densities. These community gardens work best when they're near residences. Each one needs:

- water
- a composting system
- trash collection
- occasional access for trucks or tractors
- enough plots (20–25) to create a sense of "garden community."

Source: *Building Communities with Farms, Insights from Developers, Architects and Farmers on Integrating Agriculture and Development* by Vicky Ranney, Keith Kirley and Michael Sands, Sept. 2010, Liberty Prairie Foundation.

You Design Your Own Utopia

One of New Urbanism's most prominent proponents is evangelist Andrés Duany, of Duany Plater-Zyberk & Company (DPZ), architects and town planners. Speaking at the 18th Annual Congress for New Urbanists in Atlanta in May 2010, Duany danced into the branding circle with the moniker "Agrarian Urbanism." Bigger than both "urban agriculture" (cities that are retrofitted to grow food) and "agricultural urbanism" (intentional communities built in association with a farm), "Agrarian Urbanism is a society involved with the growing of food." Duany points out that America already abounds with intentional communities; there are golf course communities, equestrian communities, even "fly-in" communities. So why not build communities for locavores? Residents could have as much land as they like — but they would plant gardens instead of yards. Apartment-dwellers could tend community gardens and window boxes. A commitment to "hand-tended agriculture" could be part of a legally binding agreement with a homeowners' association. Instead of a strip mall in the town square, there would be a "market square" comprised of green markets, restaurants, cooking schools, an agricultural university, and so on.

"This thing pushes buttons like mad," says Duany. "The excitement this triggers — [people] get as excited about this as they did in the old days about the porch and the walkable community."[2]

Duany was awakened to these concepts by a group of planners, academics and developers from the suburb of Tsawwassen, B.C., just south of Vancouver. In May 2008, they invited Duany to lead a charette for an agricultural urbanism design proposal for Southlands, a piece of prime farmland. The plan they came up with would put housing on a third of the land, preserve another third, and create a mix of working farms on the remaining third, completely integrating agriculture into the lifeblood of the community. The project is still awaiting approval — local politicians are caught between passionate opponents who insist on preserving farmland for future farming uses only, and supporters willing to compromise to compensate for today's abysmally low returns for conventional farming.

Food is rapidly becoming part of more and more planners' agendas. Galina Tachieva of DPZ has stated: "Almost every project we've done is looking at ways to incorporate food production, in both urban and suburban settings."[3]

In developments like Farmview in Makefield, Pennsylvania; Serenbe in Chattahoochee Hills, Georgia; South Village in Vermont; and Qroe Farm Preservation Development projects in Massachusetts and Virginia, as much as 80% of the farmland and natural habitat is preserved as part of a housing development. In some cases, an existing farmer can stay on the land, compensated by new owners who cover taxes, lost development potential, and farm costs. Homeowners pre-purchase crops through a CSA food box program.

Other projects have been retrofitted to include agricultural urbanism, including the New Town at St. Charles in Missouri, and Sky in Florida, where land is preserved and sustainable building is encouraged in a predominantly rural (and formerly agricultural) community.

Troy Gardens in Madison, Wisconsin, is a community-owned 31-acre urban agro-ecology project. It has 30 co-housing units integrated with a large community garden, an urban CSA farm, a prairie restoration, and edible landscaping that includes fruit and nut trees and herbs.

When they work, these "conservation developments" free a new generation of farmers from the cost-price squeeze that's driving so many aging farmers out of business. Although politically volatile (and easily subverted into a token sweetener for urban sprawl onto farmland), this model has a powerful potential to marry homeowners' willingness to pay a premium for being part of an agricultural community with an urban-edge farmer's need for new sources of funding.

In Serenbe, about 30 minutes from Atlanta's airport, a working farm backed by a CSA is at the heart of a new community of 1,000 planned homes where 80% of the farmland is permanently preserved. The surrounding 35,000 acres are almost totally undeveloped, and they were recently incorporated, predominantly to support a zoning code that requires that same sort of dense nodal village development, with 70–80% preservation over the whole area.

In the Netherlands, a new town development proposes to take this to the next level. In cooperation with a network of stakeholders, the

Table 5.1 Benefits and Challenges of Incorporating Agriculture into New Communities

Potential Benefits	Potential Challenges
For Developers, Design Consultants & Landowners	
Creates identity for project and community	Loses land for competing profitable uses such as more houses
Enhances marketing potential for the community	Adds complexity to design, financing, permitting, management
Creates civic space for community interaction	Requires nontraditional development team capacity
Enhances potential for entitlements	Requires a suitable farm entrepreneur
Provides fresh and healthy food locally	May increase commercial traffic through community
Provides opportunity for education programs	
For Farmers	
Creates affordable access to farmland and favorable lease terms	Involves close proximity of nonfarm neighbors
Provides high-value customer base at farm gate	Increases potential neighbor complaints—farm nuisances
Makes farmers members of a community	May increase distance to farm colleagues
Gives access to urban or suburban amenities	Reduces privacy
Developer may subsidize infrastructure	
For Public Officials	
Adds jobs and commercial activity	Doesn't fit conventional zoning regulations
Adds taxable economic activity on open space	Adds complexity to permitting
Protects open land without use of public funds	Invites potential future complaints of farm nuisances
Requires relatively few municipal services	May require health department inspections
Provides an alternative development model	
Enhances status and property values outside the development	

Source: Ranney, Vicky et al. *Building Community with Farms: Insights from Developers, Architects and Farmers on Integrating Agriculture and Development.* Liberty Prairie Foundation, Sept. 2010.

Dutch University in Wageningen designed a virtual rural-urban city district called "Agromere" that has agriculture and urban living tightly enmeshed. In 2009, the city council of Almere (30 kilometers east of Amsterdam) committed to urban agriculture as the main element of green infrastructure in the development of 15,000 homes. As the city nearly doubles in size (from 190,000 to 350,000 inhabitants) over the next 20 years, sustainable food production will be tied in with green energy production, water purification, waste management, recreation and tourism — all aimed at reducing greenhouse gas emissions and fossil fuel dependence.

According to Ed McMahon, Senior Fellow with the Urban Land Institute, these projects in North America are still mostly "boutique" developments, but many developers are waking up to the attraction of providing an open space amenity that generates a cashflow even before any lots are sold. "The only way these are going to go mainstream is if the developers can pencil out the numbers," McMahon says. "Already we're

Farm Views Compared to Fairways

Conservation developers have subdivided different farm uses based on how much friction they cause with nearby neighbors:

- Commodity crops (corn, soybeans, wheat, rice; non-organic): large vistas, soothing monoculture. **Downside:** often require herbicide and pesticide spraying from industrial-sized equipment, sometimes nighttime harvesting from lighted combines.
- Vegetables: diverse views, labor-intensive, lots of activity. **Downside:** need buildings and field storage of equipment.
- Orchards: Attractive three-dimensional vistas. **Downside:** usually require spraying of significant amounts of pesticides.
- Grazing animals: Well-maintained pastures can provide views comparable to golf courses, with animal activity. (Prairie Crossing residents paid a premium for views of horse pastures.)

Source: *Building Communities with Farms: Insights from Developers, Architects and Farmers on Integrating Agriculture and Development*, by Vicky Ranney, Keith Kirley and Michael Sands, Sept. 2010, Liberty Prairie Foundation.

seeing farmland going from being an amenity to being central to the development." On most residential developments around golf courses, the majority of residents don't play golf, but they love the green pastoral vistas of the manicured fairways. While farms are messier neighbors, they have a green funky pastoral appeal, as well as providing agriculture's community-building ability and weekly supplies of reliable fresh food right in the neighborhood.

South Village (South Burlington, Vermont) developer David Scheuer says his only regret in building his farm-linked development was not getting the farm working earlier. He underestimated the power that the farm would have in establishing and promoting the community, which includes the wider community that gets brought in through the CSA program.

Marketing Bonus: Journalists Eat Up the Story

The growing public interest in local food and agriculture delivers a financially juicy side benefit to developments built around agriculture: free marketing. The link to the local food movement is irresistible to journalists. Developer Steve Nygren, a former restaurateur, built the story of Serenbe in Chattahoochee Hills, Georgia, around his high-quality restaurants. Serenbe has three restaurants, and there are plans to add four more. They all use produce from Serenbe's farm, and focus on farm-to-table dining. Because they attracted so much positive attention, Nygren reduced his advertising budget to zero. He still kept selling homes thanks to the stream of press covering the community and the farm. "People come for a cupcake and end up buying a house," Nygren says.[4]

Prairie Crossing got a similar boost: "At Prairie Crossing, we started the project by hiring a couple as farm managers. They did a great job developing a successful working farm and hosting a large number of events that were critical in marketing the Prairie Crossing community and house sales," says Vicky Ranney. "Feature articles about the new local food farm helped to drive sales more effectively than ads in the real estate section of the *Chicago Tribune*."

Having a community with a trusted, on-site fresh food source turns out to be a powerful market differentiator.

Political Pitfalls on the Way

Marketing agro-developments once they're approved is a lot easier than getting them approved if they are on protected agricultural lands. In 1970, George Spetifore gave up on his 42-year-old farm in Tsawwassen, a mixed rural-residential suburb abutting the US border in Metro Vancouver. He just couldn't compete with imported food. He proposed a development of 2,000 homes and a golf course on the land, which would have to be taken out of the Agricultural Land Reserve (ALR). After the longest public hearing in Canadian history, that application was turned down, as were seven others in the following years. In 1981, Spetifore used his political connections to finally get the land removed from the ALR — in a highly contentious decision.

The latest owner of this land, developer Sean Hodgins, leaned on the wisdom of academics Patrick Condon, Kent Mullinix (a former commercial orchardist) and grad student Edward Porter to put together a farm-based plan for the land. It focuses on the premise that simply protecting our agricultural lands is not enabling us to feed ourselves. Food prices are still too low for farmers to make a decent living growing for the local market, especially with agricultural land prices in the area as high as $100,000 an acre. A sustainable farm needs other sources of income.

In return for being allowed to build 1,900 homes, some of them multi-family, on a third of the fertile land, Sean Hodgins offered to dedicate the other two thirds of what he now calls "Southlands" to a mix of parkland, a training center for young farmers, a farmers market, and food-growing plots ranging from backyard gardens to commercial farms. All the amenities would be subsidized by the revenues gained from the rezoning. The 40% of the land dedicated to agriculture would be protected under a Community Trust to guarantee that it remain farmland in perpetuity. "We can talk about preserving farmland all day long, but if we don't preserve the farmer we've got nothing," says Hodgins.

Hodgins's project is stalled in the face of fierce political opposition. Some are saying that every acre of scarce farmland in the geographically hemmed-in Fraser Valley in Metro Vancouver needs to be preserved: "Grow food, not houses," goes the cry at standing-room-only public meetings. Some are NIMBY neighbors who don't want the traffic or changes in their neighborhood. As long as the fields stay green, they don't care that agriculture will never be financially viable. Some have memories of previous attempts to develop the land for purely commercial gain, and they distrust any developer purporting to have a higher purpose. Local politicians deciding on the proposal have a bigger downside to saying yes than to saying no. The constituency of supporters (agricultural urbanism advocates, future residents) is a lot smaller and less organized than opponents (long-standing residents, those who blocked previous developments on the site).

Few opponents understand or trust the new conservation development/agricultural urbanism model. They distrust the unknowns: Will the covenants on the land be strong enough to secure the farmland forever? Will the business model keep the farm financially stable in tough times? Who will keep this all going after buildout — the developer, a new land trust organization, the homeowner association, a non-profit, a farmer?

If you look at the Southlands development as a way for a devious developer to dress up the rape of agricultural land in fancy concepts, it's easy to agree with Sean Hodgins's opponents that agricultural urbanism is "one of the greatest threats to farmland and food security that B.C. has ever seen."[5]

Southlands's proponents insist it's about putting agriculture first, and tolerating development as a way to support it. "We can't wait for the price of food to go up to make food production economically viable," says Mark Holland, one of the key planners on the Southlands project. "This is a model for artisan agriculture — high value, high labor, high productivity, with processing adding value." Local residents and their municipal representatives who have the final say on this development will have to be convinced of that — as will all approving bodies of agricultural urbanism in any location.

Conclusion

Developers all over North America are jumping on the local food bandwagon with "conservation developments" that have agriculture built into the physical, social and economic life of the community. Working farms become part of suburban life as residents of these communities participate in community gardens, CSAs and farming education. Restaurants featuring food grown in the neighborhood add to the marketing allure and bring nearby residents into the development's local food orbit. Farmers feed off new sources of income not possible on traditional rural lands. Politicians and the public need to truly understand that it is impossible for conventional agriculture to make its way financially on expensive suburban land without some innovative sources of revenue. Getting these developments approved depends on selling the integrity of the plan as an authentic agricultural shift, not just a gimmick.

6

In Praise of
Technology

A WEEK AFTER THE WETTEST September on record, farmer Bill Zylmans called into a local radio show from his tractor on his farm in Richmond, B.C. You could hear the resignation and despondency in his voice:

> "I'm sitting here on the tractor, looking out over the fields. Unbelievably I'm in the first of 18 fields I'll be able to finish harvesting today and this 12-acre field is the only one I'll actually be able to get the whole crop off. At this time of the year, we just don't have the sun to dissipate the water into the air, and the soil is so saturated from all the rains we've had in September. Remember we had the 50 mm [2 inches] of rain on the 31st of August. We just have never been able to recover from that. The only thing that has happened is that as we moved into October, the crops are deteriorating every day.
>
> "It's not just potatoes. It's cabbages. It's broccoli. It's brussels sprouts. It's cauliflower. It's corn. It's beans. It's carrots. It's beets. Right through the whole library of fresh vegetables that everyone will want to enjoy on this Thanksgiving.
>
> "Farmers have been trying. They've been going to the high spot of their fields, taking risks, taking chances, trying to rescue a

few potatoes here and there. It's all but over. Even the high places on the fields, you just don't have enough room to harvest and get turned around in the slop and the mud to go back and make another pass.

"On this farm alone, our loss is hundreds of thousands of dollars. It could be close to three quarters of a million dollars before the dust settles. The analysis right now in the potato and vegetable industry is that the loss is up to $38 million. This is serious — unprecedented. We have no knowledge of where we're going to end up. This is the worst this farm has ever experienced, and we've been in existence since 1948.

"Young farmers who started this year, will they be around next year? Family farms that have been around since the early 1900s — will they be able to go through and carry on? The repercussion of this is not just for one season. It's going to last for a while to come. We have a crop insurance program, but it's in 1997 dollars. That's a big hit for agriculture. Those dollars are not going to take a tip off the iceberg for us. They'll barely cover the cost of land rental and partial fertilizer and maybe a little bit of seed. It's just not going to be enough to help farmers get around the corner and have another season."[1]

Being at the mercy of the weather is the fate of farmers throughout history. Actually, not all farmers.

A few miles away, hundreds of acres of greenhouses sitting on agricultural land keep humming away, raising peppers, tomatoes and leafy greens year-round regardless of the weather.

The difference between Bill Zylmans's fate and the greenhouse harvests is the control over weather conditions offered by technology. Ever since the invention of the plow, technology has been helping farmers.

The earliest known use of technology to protect plants dates back to the Roman Emperor Tiberius Caesar (14–37 AD), whose doctor told him he needed a cucumber a day to preserve his health. So he had moveable garden beds built that could be brought inside during bad weather and put outside on winter sunny days under a frame glazed with transparent mica.

The development of cheap artificial light — especially the LED lighting that's taking over from sodium growlights — has made the use of indoor lighting for growing a lot more affordable and easier than hauling around mica frames and waiting for sunny days. "Early adopters" include British Columbia marijuana growers. The renowned "B.C. bud" marijuana, estimated to be worth billions of dollars annually in the underground economy, is grown almost entirely indoors, sometimes in huge underground chambers that never see any natural light.

The widespread adoption of GMO seeds, pesticides, herbicides, fertilizers and antibiotics has revolutionized agriculture. The harm from the collateral damage to natural ecosystems and rural societies from these technological advances is still being tallied, a measure of the mixed blessings that come from technology in agriculture. While genetically modified seeds may end up costing the planet more than the benefits they deliver, that legitimate fear shouldn't let us forget that without technological advances, most of us wouldn't be alive today. As the writer P. J. O'Rourke once famously pointed out: Anyone who doubts the benefits of technological progress should think about one word: "dentistry." He could equally have said "computers" or "refrigeration" or "electricity."

Tech advances on large-scale farms are beyond the scope of this book. Such advances include the sophisticated GPS field maps that allow computer-controlled application of fertilizers that can be customized to subtle changes in soil type across a farmer's fields. But there are many ways technology is going to increase food production for smaller-scale growers in and around cities.

Self-proclaimed "lunatic organic farmer-entrepreneur" Joel Salatin is very clear about the advantages technology can bring to even the most down-to-earth farming practices. "I'm not afraid of using technology," he says. One example is the moveable electric fence system he uses to contain chickens and cattle on different parts of his property. The fences let the animals feed themselves and, at the same time, fertilize the pastures with manure — so Joel no longer has to buy and transport feed and fertilizer. For him, it's about efficiency: "The weak link is not making better use of the resources we already have."[2]

Greenhouses offer one of the most effective technological boosts for producing more food on less space with fewer resources. One acre of hydroponic greenhouse can produce 600,000 pounds of food per year; that's ten times what a one-acre field could produce — and there's no wasted fertilizer.

Hydroponic and aeroponic technology has increased yield potential 20-fold while using 30 times less water than outdoor growing. Those impressive efficiencies have led to booming greenhouse industries around the world — without the genetically modified seeds, pesticides and herbicides that have played such a big part in the Green Revolution.

The pressure to produce more food in smaller and unconventional spaces has led to vertical farming — adding height to the traditional one-story greenhouse. Will Allen at Growing Power in Milwaukee is using part of his 2008 $500,000 "genius grant" from the John D. and Catherine T. MacArthur Foundation to build "a five-story vertical building totally off the grid with renewable energy, where people can come and learn, so they can go back to their communities around the world and grow healthy food."[3]

Arctic Greenhouse Feeds on Round-the-Clock Sun

One hundred and twenty-five miles north of the Arctic Circle, behind Igloo Church, at the corner of Gwich'in Road and Breynat Street, is the Inuvik Community Greenhouse. It is the northernmost commercial hothouse on the continent, and it may be the only community greenhouse of its kind in the world. Since November 1998, the former hockey arena has been home to a variety of crops and flowers. There are two growing areas: a 12,000-square foot community garden, where residents and local groups can rent 40 square foot plots for $100/year; and a 4,000-square foot commercial greenhouse that pays for itself. Despite a relatively short season — mid-May to late September — eight weeks of non-stop sun intensifies the growth. Now, residents of Inuvik (which has a mean temperature of 15 degrees Fahrenheit) have access to fresh local produce for as many months of the year as most of the rest of Canada.

Vertical farms are a natural extension of the evolution of human living spaces into denser, higher, more efficient buildings.

One back-to-the-land prototype for self-contained, homespun vertical farming is the legendary Solviva greenhouse pioneered by the indomitable Anna Edey at Martha's Vineyard in Massachusetts. She designed and built the 3,000-square foot Solviva Solar Greenhouse in 1983, with the goal of producing high yields of high-quality organic food year-round, with no backup heat, no cooling fans and no toxic pesticides. The heating was to be primarily solar, with additional heat provided by living resident heaters: chickens and rabbits. It worked.

To fill orders for what she claims was North America's first fresh, cleaned organic greens packaged mix, Edey stacked four tiers of "grow-tubes" in her solar-and-chicken-heated complex, which allowed her to harvest 90 pounds (1,500 servings) of "Solviva Salad" each week at peak production. Unfortunately, the pressure of keeping her multifaceted operation operating and solvent became too much for her, and she was forced to sell the property. The greenhouse was later demolished. But she did prove her point.

No Soil, No Sun, No Problem:
Hydroponics and Vertical Growing

A big advance in vertical growing in a greenhouse or a closed building like a vacant warehouse is coming from Valcent Products Inc., developers of Europe's first vertical farm at the Paignton Zoo in Devon, UK. It's a hydroponic greenhouse that has 11,000 lettuce, spinach, chicory, chard and herb plants growing in stacked trays that move slowly around a suspended track. On each computer-controlled loop, the plants pass a feeding station that provides water and nutrients and a "shower of lighting" that supplements the natural light. Water and nutrient runoff from the feeding station is captured and recycled. On 1,075 square feet, the zoo is growing $160,000 worth of crops, using only 5% of the water that would be required to grow them outdoors — and even that 5% can be recycled. Valcent CEO Stephen Fane says some animals actually know the difference between vegetables from the greenhouse and commercially grown ones, and they prefer the greenhouse products, if given a choice.

Credit: valcent.net

Valcent VertiCrop carousel: At the Devon Zoo, animals prefer these greens grown on-site to lettuce purchased from stores.

The zoo calculates that it is saving $25,000 a year on its lettuce bill alone. And the advantages of fresh lettuce go beyond the monetary savings: Lettuce kept at room temperature for four days loses 82% of its water-soluble protein, 61% of its vitamin C, and 54% of its chlorophylls.

A similar greenhouse has been developed by TerraSphere Systems in Surrey, B.C. It has 11 levels that hold 400 plants each; this allows 20,000 plants to be grown in just 120 square feet of space. That's five times more spinach, for example, than can be grown on a comparable space outdoors (terraspheresystems.com).

"Without the use of pesticides, herbicides or fungicides, and zero water waste, we can mass-produce food all over the planet," says TerraSphere inventor Nick Brusatore. "We have the ability to mass-produce spinach, strawberries, all the lettuces, all the herbs. We have the ability to grow food in remote locations and urban centers."

A TerraSphere-technology 8,000-square foot lettuce operation opened in September 2010 in Vancouver. It supplies "Eco Spirit" brand lettuce to eight Choices Market stores in Metro Vancouver. Consumers have been, as they say, eating it up. They pay $5.00 for a 5.3-ounce container of the locally grown lettuce. "The quality is excellent, the nutrient levels are high, the shelf life is long," says Choices CEO Mark Vickars. "We're always trying to go local, and this gives us local 365 days a year."[4]

It's hard to believe these high-tech indoor growing systems will not become a vital contributor to food production in the near future. I look

Higher Productivity Indoors

The advantages of these advanced greenhouses are compelling:
- year-round production
- more efficient use of a limited land base (one indoor acre is generally equivalent to 4–6 outdoor acres, with some crops like strawberries generating as much in one indoor acre as 30 outdoor acres)
- no weather-related crop failures
- dramatic reduction in fossil fuel costs due to tractors, plowing, transportation, chemical fertilizers, etc.
- organic premium due to easier pest control
- recycling water means extremely low water use (5% of outdoor crop water demand)
- potential energy sales from methane produced by compost
- ability to include on-site processing, so there is no agricultural runoff
- proximity to employees and markets
- high nutritive value compared to field-grown crops (according to NASA tests at its Martian Base prototype indoor growing center).

Source: cornellcea.com/about_CEA.htm.

forward to seeing them in urban industrial settings, on rooftops, and alongside grocery stores. Because they use little water and don't make a lot of noise or produce unpleasant odors, there's no reason they can't fit into almost any urban space without disturbing the neighbors.

Lighter-weight *nutrient film technique* (NFT) hydroponics is another technology we should be seeing more of soon. It has an advantage on rooftops because most of the water weight is in a reservoir that can be put on a stronger part of the roof.

One expert has calculated that most of a family's fresh vegetable needs could be met by a 50-square foot indoor hydroponic garden. One 600-watt light could cover the tomatoes and peppers, and two 400-watt lamps could cover the lettuce and herbs.[5]

The big unknown for these new technologies (and one that can spook investors) is the cost of energy for the lights and climate controls. The big greenhouses on the outskirts of Vancouver struggled when natural gas prices rose, then had difficulty with air quality regulations when they tried to switch to wood pellets or hog fuel (leftover bark chips and wood fiber from mills). One Vancouver greenhouse grower, CanAgro Greenhouses, teamed up with Maxim Power Corp. to demonstrate an eco-industrial approach by capturing methane that would otherwise be released to the atmosphere by an adjacent landfill. The methane is piped under a highway to a co-generating plant that makes power for the grid and uses heat from the manifold for the adjoining 63-acre greenhouse.

Some urban growers have found a similar solution by heating rooftop-grown plants using waste heat from the building below. Eli Zabar, for example, heats his Manhattan rooftop greenhouse with exhaust heat from the bakery below.

Investors Are Discovering Hydroponics

Companies that manufacture indoor growing technology are scrambling to get the technology, energy savings, financing and management aligned to meet the huge demand that's coming as outdoor-grown food prices keep rising and people are demanding local fresh food. An executive with Valcent said he is following up on 150 requests for orders from 20 countries.

Investors from the green tech world are just waking up to the financial opportunities. "Sustainable agriculture is a space [for investment] that looks as big or bigger than clean tech," says Paul Matteucci, a venture capitalist with US Venture Partners in Menlo Park, Calif. "Historically, we have not seen a ton of entrepreneurial activity in agriculture, but we are beginning to see it now, and the opportunities are huge."[6] Investors are waking up to conventional agriculture's contribution to climate change, and they are increasingly aware of its dependence on huge amounts of water and fossil fuels that are becoming more expensive and less available.

Investors already into clean tech and life sciences are realizing they can make money out of the coming transformation of industrial agriculture. One Silicon Valley green tech firm is backing a company that's making tools to measure the nutrient content of soils in real time, allowing more precise applications of fertilizer, which saves money and avoids nitrogen runoff and pollution of waterways. A New York firm, NewSeed Advisors, has started "Agriculture 2.0" conferences to showcase new ag tech opportunities.

Once a critical mass of financiers, lawyers and investors understand the entrepreneurial sweet spots in meeting new demand for indoor urban food production, a lot of new companies offering tech solutions will be jumping in.

One dream project that continues to be held out as a beacon of what's possible is Columbia University Public Health Professor Dickson Despommier's 30-story futuristic vertical farm. The size of a city block, it would cost hundreds of millions of dollars — but it could feed 50,000 people. Build 160 of them, and you could feed all of New York, he says. He came up with the idea after his students went looking for rooftop garden spaces in Manhattan that would be suitable for growing food. They identified only 13 acres (and concluded that rice would be the best crop to grow). That amount of space could satisfy only about 2% of Manhattan's food needs. So, his students then turned to NASA, and they learned that numerous small-scale projects have demonstrated that anything can be grown indoors. But nobody was seriously considering growing food in tall buildings. The main reason — aside from uncertainty about whether it would work — is the cost of construction and energy. "Scores of companies have tried to do this, even the big guys like General Mills 15 years ago," says Bruce Bugbee, a professor of crop physiology at Utah State University. "It's too expensive. People don't realize how much light it takes to grow plants."[7]

Despommier set out to design a completely closed-loop system:

"All the water is recycled, all the nutrients are recycled. The only thing that actually leaves the building is the produce.

"The big question is who's going to be doing this? Who wants to do it? Who needs to do it? And who can do it? The answer is: countries that don't have agriculture — Iceland, all the Emirates.

You've got a lot of people and you've got almost no land. Here's a wonderful way of conserving water and providing food for everybody.

"What about those places that want them? China and India have been wanting these for years. The technology has finally caught up to the desire, and now, I think they're going to start building them.

"What if you had a vertical farm that specialized in one crop, like we have outdoors — corn, rice, wheat. Imagine the ancillary industries that would spring up around these farms in an urban setting, to employ even more people. From wheat you can make flour, from flour you can make bread or cupcakes, and it comes from that building. The biggest social benefit is that everybody gets fed healthy, clean food, and you can remediate it to clean water. So you can have safe water and safe food wherever you live.

"I've had no negative reaction to this idea. I think the idea is about to develop into reality."[8]

Energy Costs Undermine Growing Indoors

Before getting too excited about indoor growing, keep in mind that these are costly man-made systems that recreate what's available free in nature. A greenhouse has to use man-made energy to regulate temperature, irrigation, fertilization, light, CO_2 content, and air circulation. Eliminating nature's unpredictability and rough edges comes at a cost. Current state-of-the-art closed greenhouses can cost more than $1 million/acre. However, these greenhouses have yields 40% higher than open or vented greenhouses because of better pest management, lower energy costs, and better use of captive CO_2.

A Netherlands study found that vegetables grown in greenhouses require 57 times as much non-renewable energy than the same vegetables grown in an open field. That number is disputed by those who say energy productivity has to take into account food miles for distribution (what if the greenhouse is on the roof of a grocery store?) and food waste in the field (nothing is wasted in greenhouses).

"The only viable food we can ever produce is that which is a by-product of our relationship with the soil," Vandana Shiva reminds us in *Dirt! The Movie*. Taking into account fertilizers needed to feed soil and distances to market, the viability of soil-grown food in an oil-challenged world is changing. Finding soil for growing is one of the biggest challenges for the future of food. With the human population expected to top 9 billion within 50 years, feeding all the new people will require an additional 270 million acres of farmland that doesn't exist today. Carving it out of dwindling forests comes at a huge cost to the planet's biodiversity — assuming that the required amount of forested land is even available.

A big threat from indoor agriculture is that it provides an excuse to stop preserving agricultural lands and soils. If we can grow all we need indoors, what's the problem with paving over farmland even faster than we are now? But billions of the world's farmers depend on the free ecological services provided by nature. The vast majority of these farmers will never be able to afford to build greenhouses. They will be challenged enough by the trend to price "free" natural assets (such as potable water) in an effort to protect them and ration their use.

We will always need farmland. Indoor growing has to be seen as a supplement to outdoor growing, not a replacement for it. Fields will always be more suitable for growing crops like grains, rice and corn. Hydroponics and urban and near-urban plots will increasingly supply other crops.

Less Land, More Technology: More Revenue

What makes controlled-environment agriculture especially appealing in cities is the relatively large payoff from a small area of land. One acre of crop agriculture produces a typical annual wholesale cash value for grains of $300–$500; for field-produced fruits and vegetables, it's $3,000–$5,000; for ornamental nursery stock, it's $30,000–$50,000. But for greenhouse agriculture, one acre can generate $300,000–$500,000. Those returns can cover a lot of input and operating costs.

Benjamin Linsley, managing director of Bright Farm, showed off his hydroponic systems on a floating "Science Barge" operating along the Manhattan waterfront in the summers of 2007 and 2008. He claims one of his one-acre Better Food Solutions greenhouses on a supermarket roof could produce between 750,000–900,000 pounds of produce a year. That's about $1.3–$1.6 million worth of produce at wholesale prices — all the greens and many of the vine vegetables a supermarket would need in a year (brightfarms.com).

Using technology for growing doesn't have to be limited to high-production commercial greenhouses. Simpler technologies can equally benefit the small, hands-on home gardener. Blake Whisenant, a fourth generation family farmer and inventor of the EarthBox, credits "more than a decade of dedicated scientific work" for the development of his raised-bed box of soil on wheels that features fertilizer that stays on top of the soil and water that comes from the bottom (earthbox.com).

"Our scientific research proves that the EarthBox system provides higher yields and minimum maintenance, healthful homegrown vegetables without guesswork or toil," he says.

Google uses EarthBoxes in their employee garden in Mountain View, California. A reporter visiting the company noted that the sub-irrigated EarthBox requires very little maintenance, which makes sense for workers who really don't want to be hoeing on their lunch break. "For some employees, beanpoles quickly become just another part of the office scenery. On a visit last fall, the special self-watering EarthBox container garden was filled with fewer actual gardeners than with workers hurrying through on their way back to their desks, cafeteria trays filled with free food balanced on their laptops."[9]

The Windowfarms Project is another example of small-scale technology opening new urban agricultural possibilities, this one suitable for apartment-dwellers. Windowfarms sell modular hydroponic "farms" made from recycled plastic bottles that hang in a window frame (windowfarms.org).

Aquaponics: Bring on the Fish

One new technology that has the potential to produce vast amounts of food with low inputs and high outputs is *aquaponics* — a combination of aquaculture (farming fish) and hydroponics (growing plants in water). Aquaponics mimics the natural system of a lake or pond, except it's in-

Aquaponics: Growing Power CEO Will Allen harvests tilapia from tanks that feed plants that process fish waste that comes back as clean water.

doors. The beauty of aquaponics is that it offers a balanced nutrient cycle without added fertilizers. It also solves one of the big problems associated with aquaculture: what to do with fish waste.

In these systems, fish are grown in tanks using water filtered by plants. The plants in turn filter the fish waste, using the ammonia-rich nutrients as fertilizer, producing crops and clean water that is pumped back into the fish tank. The vegetables require 80–90% less water than they do with conventional growing. In one system, the plants grow on floating rafts sitting on 14 to 16 inches of water. The rafts are moved down the line in stages from seedling to fully grown, then harvested at the other end. The whole cycle of a plant's life can be seen in one row. Cuttings from the plants are usually sold, but the plants can also be composted to grow worms that are fed back to the fish, which closes the loop. Aquaponics UK, a non-profit that promotes aquaponics, estimates that 5 pounds of fish food (worms, pellets) produces 110 pounds of vegetables and almost 2 pounds of fish.

Since the only inputs to this system are fish food, a little water, and sunlight, it's not hard to set up a small aquaponics operation in a greenhouse, with fish tanks on the ground level and growbeds on top. The weight of the water in the fish tanks would make rooftop aquaponics a challenge, although the tanks could be at ground level with the hydroponic operations on the roof.

AquaRanch Industries in Flanagan, Illinois started commercial operations in 1992. They grow tilapia and organic lettuce, kale, chard, herbs, tomatoes and hot peppers in a 12,500-square foot warehouse. Owner Myles Harston says he's having trouble keeping up with demand for his products.

Sweet Water Organics, a company spawned by Will Allen's success with aquaponics at Growing Power, raises perch and leafy green vegetables in a converted mining warehouse in Milwaukee. Started by James Godsil and Josh Fraundorf in January 2009, Sweet Water is now producing 154 pounds of vegetables a week (sweetwater-organic.com). "The fish it produces are a 21st century form of protein that won't harm planet earth," says Godsil.[10]

Nelson and Pade, Inc., the leading North American firm involved with aquaponics (and publisher of *Aquaponics Journal*), sells packaged aquaponic farming systems that include tanks and raft hydroponic trays. Its small commercial system that sells for $4,000 can fit into a greenhouse as small as 16 feet by 20 feet and produce 180 pounds of fish and 1,500 heads of lettuce a year.

On the Big Island of Hawaii, Friendly Aquaponics is claiming "first in America" status for its aquaponics business, having incorporated in 2007. It sells organic lettuce to Costco (friendlyaquaponics.com).

Aquaponics is still in its infancy, with only five operations bigger than an acre as of September 2010, but its appeal is catching on quickly.

In Australia, where farming has been devastated by drought and floods over the past decade and low water use is a huge focus, Backyard

Aquaponics in Perth is selling 300 systems a year in what the owner claims to be the first aquaponics retail store (backyardaquaponics.com).

San Francisco-based Cityscape Farms CEO Mike Yohay claims that by eliminating transportation and fertilizer costs, a 10,000-square foot aquaponic greenhouse could produce $500,000 in profit from 20–30 tons of food a year. But Silicon Valley entrepreneur Paul Matteucci isn't so sure: "For the most part the quality of the product is excellent, but the costs are still too high."[11]

Urban Farming 2.0 Is Here

Not to be overlooked is the relentless expansion of online communications. These technologies are making networking, ordering, buying and selling local produce a whole lot easier and cheaper.

Cities are bursting with new networks linking people with people: homeowners with empty backyards to farmers looking for land; people with spare fruit to food banks in search of produce; people who want to raise chickens to people who know how to raise chickens; and city food buyers to nearby local food sellers.

James MacKinnon, co-author of *The 100-Mile Diet*, shows how simple it is to tap new technology: "A friend of mine and I went on to Craigslist and asked if anybody had fruit trees they just weren't using. We were contacted by somebody who had a plum tree. We went out and we harvested all the plums we could take. We didn't have to pay anything. Then we canned those plums and turned them into jam. And that was all the jam we needed for two households for more than a year. That, to me, was indicative of the kind of power this has."[12]

"Crop mobs" are even starting up, mimicking "flash mobs" that use social media to bring people together in a public place for some brief (often bizarre) act. Crop mobs, originally started in the Triangle area of North Carolina, use Google Groups to get wannabe volunteer farmers together with small-scale farms in need of short-term labor. According to the project's website, "Any crop mobber can call a crop mob to… work together, share a meal, play, talk, and make music. No money is exchanged. This is the stuff that communities are made of" (cropmob .org).

One online educational leader is Vancouver-based City Farmer, launched in 1994, which claims to have the first website to publish information about urban farming (cityfarmer.info). Today it has hundreds of pages and links to teach people how to grow food in the city, compost their waste, and take care of their home landscape in an environmentally responsible way.

Information online is just a start. How about an online marketplace linking scattered buyers and sellers? Greenbeltfresh.ca connects producers, consumers and institutional and commercial buyers in the Greater Golden Horseshoe in southern Ontario. Go online to the free Fresh Food Finder and pick a category (e.g., wholesale or CSA), a postal code area, and the kind of food you're looking for, and up will pop a list of farms in that area that have what you want, with e-mail contacts and web links to them. More than 400 farms are listed (as of September 2010).

In the Pacific Northwest, Portland-based EcoTrust has gone one step further, setting up an interactive marketplace — like a Craigslist for regional food — at food-hub.org. It's a business-to-business tool open to food buyers and sellers of all types in Alaska, California, Idaho, Montana, Oregon and Washington. It's a live feed of products, either available for sale or wanted for purchase, that's constantly changing. "On the buyer side, it's everybody from restaurants to caterers to hospitals to schools to resorts," says Deborah Kane, EcoTrust's vice-president of food and farms. "On the seller side, it's anyone large or small producing or processing food in the Northwest, from fruits and vegetables to dairy, meat and fish. It's big packers and processors, little companies making jams or pickles, wineries and distilleries. And it's not just for the certified organic operator; it's for Northwest agriculture of all kinds."[13]

Distribution methods vary "from Alaskan fishermen who freeze and ship their product via UPS, ranchers who run their own trucks into town, and farmers who ready wholesale orders for pickup at farmers markets, to all those who gladly rely on the services provided by mainline distributors" (food-hub.org).

Participants (625 as of October 2010) each pay $100 to join this one-stop shopping network, which is designed to accommodate everyone from a farmer with one case to sell, to buyers looking for semi-truckload quantities. Buyers post what they need, and sellers offer their bids on filling the order.

Several food-buying clubs have joined FoodHub. These clubs allow a group of individuals to act as a wholesale buyer, sometimes taking on the complexities of individual deliveries themselves. These groups often accept non-uniform but perfectly good produce that grocery stores don't want — a huge opportunity for small-scale producers.

"Some people call it the Facebook of local food, or the Match.com for food buyers and food sellers," says Kane. "If you're a buyer looking for corn, you type in the word corn, add a specific variety if you want, and FoodHub will return a list of all the people in the system with corn in their profile, both buyers and sellers."

Grand Central Bakery in Portland posted this message: "We are in search of local rhubarb for pie season. We prefer once a week deliveries to our North Portland Bakery. We need 250–350 pounds per week while in season (April–July)." Another member, Big B Farms, responded. The two struck a deal to deliver the rhubarb. "It was like magic," said Grand Central Bakery's cuisine manager Laura Ohm.

Portland Green Parenting, a network of over 200 families who make bulk purchases from local farmers and food producers, made a post to the FoodHub Marketplace asking whether any ranches would be interested in starting a meat CSA for Green Parenting members. Dustin and Lisalyn Taylor of Taylor Made Farms in Lebanon, Oregon responded, and a few months later they began delivering monthly meat CSA boxes to 12 families through the network's pickup location. The families get pasture-raised, hormone- and antibiotic-free pork, chicken, lamb and beef.

Melissa Williams at Adam's Sustainable Table in Eugene wanted to buy organic Oregon cranberries to sprinkle on salads. She knew they were grown in bogs around Coos Bay. "Somebody must be drying them," she remembers thinking. She posted her desire for cranberries on Food-Hub and learned that Hummingbird Wholesale — only ten blocks from her restaurant — not only stocked the cranberries, but also dried them locally and finished them with a touch of Oregon blackberry honey.

The FoodHub community uses its Marketplace function for whatever comes along. Deborah Kane says, "An ice cream maker in Puget Sound was running refrigerated trucks into Seattle for deliveries, then coming home empty. They were looking for someone to use that refrigerated space on the return trips. A Willamette Valley seed grower had lost all his beet stock in the freeze, and did a shout-out to all the farmers in the valley, looking for storage beets." Kane thinks FoodHub could do more to help make transportation more efficient: "I'd like FoodHub to look at distribution amounts and transportation efficiency. You'll have five farmers that are running the same route into Portland. We feel like we have an opportunity to really maximize efficiencies. So that maybe instead of five trucks, we can get it down to two. Those five farmers may not even realize they're running the same route, but we can see it in our system."

Kane says she's getting calls from all over the country from people who want to use her technology in their region. "We decided to build FoodHub with open-source technology so it could be easily transferred and adapted by local experts once they got the baseline platform from us. But we're very committed to making sure FoodHub hums in the Pacific Northwest. It'll be at least a year before we focus on sharing the information," she said (in August 2010). FoodHub has three employees and a $500,000 budget; it was initially funded with government and corporate grants, but intended to be self-supporting through membership fees in two years.

Catching Fishing Customers Online

Otto Strobel is a retired Kelowna, B.C. high school chemistry teacher and long-time fisherman. "Skipper Otto," as he is known online, has teamed up with his family to set up Canada's first Community Supported Fishery (CSF). Because of its tech-enabled efficiencies of direct sales, Strobel's take-home revenue from a bin of fish has gone from $1,200 to $4,000. It is hard to imagine this being possible without online communications. Members sign up online, and are alerted by e-mail, blog or RSS feed to show up — typically on a Saturday morning — at the False Creek dock by Granville Island in Vancouver to pick up their orders.

"They pick what they want," explains Strobel's daughter-in-law Sonia, who runs the online communications end of the operation. "We throw it on a scale and subtract the total from $250 [the CSA seasonal advance payment] on the spreadsheet. We can tell members at any time how much is left in their share. In the fall, we let them know when the last date is to collect the remainder of their share."

How Food-hub.org Connects Buyers and Sellers Online

Samples from the "WANTED" Category:

Does anyone want my excess duck fat? Will sell cheap, or work out a trade.

Looking to buy 40–60 dozen farm raised eggs in the Seattle area.

Blueberries from Skagit, Whatcom, Snohomish county in WA. Will buy fresh and field packed blueberries 100–200 lb/week during the season for resale at our farmstand.

Need 17.5 pounds of chicken livers.

Seeking local octopus.

Looking to contract with local farmer(s) to purchase entire season's crop. We use approx 80+ bushels of habaneros per year. You can process/store or we can. Let's Talk! We also need suppliers for market season—tomatoes, tomatillos, onions, jalapenos and cilantro.

In the "AVAILABLE" Category:

Sun-cured candy sweet onions for sale.

New crop walnuts. Excellent freshness and flavor. In shell or hand cracked.

Hard red and soft white wheat.

Red potatoes and red beets.

Wagyu beef: Restaurant cuts of Tenderloin, New York, Top Sirloin & Prime Rib, Grade A-5. We also have hamburger in patties, in 15 lb boxes.

Source: food-hub.org

She does this — and most everything else enabling this model to work — through the miracle of free social media. Customers and media have been attracted through online connections to the website (wildbc salmon.org). With the help of Farm Folk/City Folk, a non-profit organization promoting local food (ffcf.bc.ca), she set up the website through Google, then traded maintenance and updates to a webmaster for fish. The webmaster set her up on Twitter ("Sept. 1: El Dorado [Otto's 35-foot gillnetter] is on her way down the coast with a tonne of fish on board!"). She sends weekly emails to her members to let them know about the week's delivery, then she books their pickup appointments using event brite.com. Meanwhile, her husband, Shaun, engages customers with blogs from the boat: "Aug. 18: Otto had a great first 24 hours of fishing and pulled in over 300 sockeye. Unfortunately, he also caught the net in the prop…He had to sell off some of his fish to a local buyer because the holds were full and he was out on the fishing grounds with no way to get the fish to Vancouver!"

It's a strange mix: hunting and gathering and social media.

Conclusion

Technology has always been part of agriculture. Its advantages are ever more in demand as climate changes upset old growing patterns and rising oil prices further distort traditional farm economics. Hydroponic growing offers huge advantages: water conservation, pest control, freedom from vagaries of weather, and dizzying levels of production in confined spaces, especially rooftops. Aquaponic developments are creating new businesses growing fish and vegetables out of the marriage of aquaculture and hydroponics. Even simple systems for mobile growing and "window farming" in apartments are adding new food-producing possibilities in cities. Social marketing through online food hubs is making food distribution and marketing vastly more efficient and flexible, especially at the urban scale. Investors, tantalized by the profit-making possibilities, are piling on, with new companies geared to on-site vegetable production for grocery stores. Expect rooftop greenhouses to become a standard feature of grocery stores over the next decade.

7

Economic Sustainability: Making the Economics of Agricultural Urbanism Pay

W ARD TEULON HAS TO TIME his compost deliveries carefully. He needs an empty elevator so he has room for his bins as he rides up in the Fresia condominium in the heart of downtown Vancouver. "Don't be there at 4:30 or 5 PM when everyone's getting off work," he warns. Teulon, the self-dubbed "City Farm Boy," uses the elevator to haul compost and soil up to one of his less-accessible gardens, 65 raised beds on a fifth-floor rooftop terrace designed for the building's residents, but now part of his urban farm network of gardens. An agrologist who grew up on a farm in Saskatchewan, Teulon is one of a growing number of entrepreneurs across North America ramping up community food production from a backyard hobby to a serious business — except that he's building his serious business in backyards — and on the Fresia rooftop.

When he first got the call to come to the Fresia and take over the abandoned beds, they were overgrown with weeds and moss. They had become a litter repository for residents who ventured out on the roof but didn't really have the time or the urge to do their own gardening. It sounded like a good idea when the building went up — add a gardening option to enrich the residents' lives, help build community, let them grow a few veggies.

Rooftop farm: Self-titled City Farm Boy Ward Teulon and helper tend to his commercial crop five stories up on a condominium balcony in downtown Vancouver. If residents don't want these sites, urban farmers do.

"They got the demographic wrong," says Teulon. "The single people in these 500-square foot condos, many renters, aren't interested in gardening." So Teulon now uses those beds for growing carrots. "It works out well," he says. "The carrot flies don't get up that high, so I get natural pest control." The building owners appreciate Teulon's help in keeping the rooftop terrace in order. "People don't throw garbage in gardens." And the carrots don't seem to mind the elevator music on the ride down to Teulon's van.

Teulon loves farming, but he also wants to make it pay. Unlike many worthy urban agriculture endeavors, Teulon's stands out for its bottom line focus. He's trying to make a living doing this; he simply can't afford to be a social worker or food bank donor on the side.

Teulon is riding a wave of urban agriculture that could lift yard farmers and smaller-scale urban farm operators higher than their larger industrial counterparts. Commercial urban farms in the United States already get 13 times more revenue per acre than non-urban farms. How can urban and near-urban farms and food producers find new economic opportunities not available to their rural counterparts? The key, ironically, is to keep it small and very simple.

I am sitting with Mike Sands, executive director of the Liberty Prairie Foundation, in the dining room-turned-boardroom in the restored original farmhouse that's now the headquarters for the Prairie Crossing Corporation — the suburban development an hour train ride north of Chicago. Says Sands, "Some traditional farmers think we're crazy. That's partly because they don't know we can support a family on 30 acres, compared to a good conventional farmer who can expect to make $50–$90 an acre, of which at least a third is subsidies. We can net $5,000–$7,000 an acre because of the intensity of our cropping, our direct sales, and our proximity to customers. The most lucrative crops are tomatoes, which gross $55,000–$70,000 per acre. The next most valuable crop is mixed salad greens."

Cheap Land in the City?

I don't mean to imply that farming in and around cities is easy. For those not able to get free plots, or who need more space than their backyard provides, buying affordable, sizeable plots — when almost every other

---

Urban Growing Advantages

Farmers growing in and around cities are discovering they have a lot of advantages over their rural counterparts. Working under the radar of big agriculture, their strengths are:
- access to cheap land
- a variety of readily accessible niche markets
- friendlier growing conditions
- easy access to water and organic waste
- plentiful opportunities for supplementary income from second jobs
- eliminating the need for hired labor
- minimal capital costs.

use provides a higher financial return — is next to impossible. The closer to the city center, the higher the price of the land. Where farmland isn't protected, speculators typically drive up the price of suburban land, and then don't care a lot about whether it's in production or just waiting empty for a rezoning. The exception to this rule is the significant number of shrinking cities. There, finding productive green uses for vacant land can be the highest and best use of that land — for a while.

Ironically, this huge barrier to rural farm economic success — the cost of land (even the opportunity cost of inherited land) — vanishes for micro-scale urban farmers like Ward Teulon. His 15 small plots are all free: "I don't pay cash for plots — my currency is vegetables," he says.

His customers are also paid in reduced yard maintenance costs, stimulating garden views from their kitchen windows, and social interaction when he comes to work in their yard. One of his landowners is a single older man who gets few visitors. He enjoys coming out to talk while Teulon works in the garden.

Some "free" land in cities provides other benefits — sometimes bankable — that are unique to dense living areas and lie outside the metrics of conventional farmlands. Food gardens that replace abandoned brownfield sites make neighborhoods safer, cleaner and more beautiful. For example, Allen Street Community Garden in Somerville, Massachusetts is on a former contaminated residential property that was cleaned up and converted to a community garden at the city's expense in 2007. It is now seen as an oasis for the residents of New England's most densely developed city, with a lineup of gardeners waiting for plots.

Community food gardens in place of lawns in public parks save mowing costs; instead of paying city employees to mow, volunteer gardeners often *pay* to work their plots. A study in Philadelphia looked at the costs and benefits of farms within the city and estimated that turning ten half- to one-acre public lawns into farms would save the city treasury $50,000 per year in mowing costs.

Food gardens tied to feeding and engaging people in low-income neighborhoods provide so many "soft-revenue" benefits that many cities happily hand over land funded by city taxpayers. Alemany Farm in San Francisco is entirely funded by grants and volunteer labor (aside from some minimal funds from produce sales). The payback is jobs and better nutrition for the Alemany Housing Project's low-income residents. The Intervale Center in Burlington, Vermont depended on a formal partnership with city, county and state officials to get the financial leverage to secure its land and capital.

Urban Niche Markets Bring Higher Returns

Cities are hotbeds of niche markets and specialized marketplaces, in contrast to bulk export markets for industrial commodity crops. Every financially successful urban farmer depends on selling high-value niche products to some combination of restaurants, farmers markets or passionate, dedicated customers.

Selling direct is always more lucrative — and more feasible in a denser urban area with plenty of options for customers. Selling at farmers markets, for example, brings twice the return of selling to a wholesaler, notwithstanding the extra hours, spoilage, and opportunity costs involved in sitting under a tent at a farmers market on a sunny Saturday.

Successful urban farmers find the best direct sales route — whether it's roadside stands, farmers markets, direct home delivery, Community Supported Agriculture (CSA) programs or food-buying clubs. In Saanich, B.C., three young small-scale farmers teamed up in a cooperative venture that meets their particular needs by selling through a combination of large-volume sales to restaurants, a direct-to-customer box program inspired by CSA projects, and farmers market sales. Ward Teulon sells direct to his CSA group, saving money by making them do their own pickups. He sells only surpluses at the farmers market.

For urban agriculturalists, customers are much closer and more plentiful than they are out in the country. A big market of easy-access customers has a better chance of including wealthy people who will pay more for local food for ethical and political reasons. Shorter distances from the garden to the customer also allow just-in-time picking, which guarantees enhanced flavor and freshness, which is an important selling point that justifies the higher prices for many customers. Legendary urban farmer Michael Ableman, for example, says the key to the success of his Fairview urban farm in Goleta, near Santa Barbara, California (at one time grossing $1 million a year in revenues), was selling high-end, high-priced specialty items.

Credit: Peter Ladner

Go for the niche: Organic farmer and community organizer Michael Ableman says the key to the success of his Fairview urban farm in Goleta, California, was selling high-end, high-priced specialty items.

Friendly Urban Growing Conditions

Unlike rural areas, North American cities have established water systems and a wealth of backyard compost sources. Even where water shortages are an issue, cities are rife with opportunities for collecting and diverting rainwater. Gutters and downspouts are everywhere, ready to be directed into rain barrels and garden plots. Cities also have a lot of food scrap and yard waste, which is increasingly being diverted from conventional waste streams and turned into compost that finds its way into gardens.

Cities also have a wealth of fall-back income sources for the majority of farmers who have to supplement their incomes. (Same for their spouses and partners. Ward Teulon's wife is a lawyer.) They also are home to many credit and financing sources, including non-profit funders who tend to look more fondly on projects they can see on the way to work every day.

Financial sweet spots in urban farming are both direct and indirect. In many cases, especially where there is grant funding or volunteer labor, the shortage of financial returns can be shrugged off — or compensated for by outside funding — in return for the indirect financial payback of building neighborhood bonds, making streets safer, feeding people, supplying food banks, educating children about where food comes from, improving diets, creating civic green spaces, and keeping prisoners or senior citizens productive. All of these goals are highly desirable rewards in themselves and often provide a financial payback — but not directly to the farmer.

One tantalizing grant option is the proposed Community Gardens Act of 2009, working its way through committees in the US Congress. It proposes a program within the US Department of Agriculture to compensate community groups for up to 80% of the costs associated with starting and maintaining a community garden.

Small Is Better

Exactly what does it take to be financially successful in today's hybrid world of agricultural urbanism? Wally Satzewich has one of the clearest, most accessible, most systematic answers. He's the founder of SPIN farming, an abbreviated name for Small Plot Intensive Farming, specifically tailored to the high-end jewels of urban agriculture: the free-land, no-capital, labor-intensive, high-value plots.

Wally's Urban Market Garden in Saskatoon, Saskatchewan, is made up of 25 residential backyard sites rented from homeowners, with an aggregate size of about half an acre. (Rents are nominal, sometimes traded for produce.) They range in size from 500–3,000 square feet. Satzewich claims to be grossing over $50,000 a year, selling mostly at the Saskatoon Farmers Market.

You can tell he's focused on revenue just by visiting his website at spinfarming.com. Right at the top of the home page, he's selling instruction manuals. Minimal mechanization, maximum fiscal discipline, and planning are the hallmarks of the SPIN formula. It emphasizes precise revenue target formulas and intensive relay growing, which can produce as many as three crops a year in a northern climate like Saskatoon's. Satzewich would be the last to claim he's doing anything new, but he has managed to package and systematize his knowledge in a way reminiscent of a business franchise — except all he sells is knowledge. But the knowledge he sells is vitally important. According to one study, the most important factor in determining yields is the management skills of the farmer.

"We are producing 10–15 different crops and sell thousands of bunches of radishes and green onions and thousands of bags of salad greens and carrots each season," says Satzewich. "Our volumes are low compared to conventional farming, but we sell high-quality organic products at very high-end prices." SPIN's low-cost simplicity is stunning. "All we needed to buy was a van, a used rototiller, and an old Pepsi cooler we put in the garage," says Pauline Scobie, an Oak Bay, B.C. SPIN practitioner. "We have our market right next door."[1] She had to get around a municipal bylaw forbidding agriculture in the city, but that's changing everywhere.

There are two things all SPIN farmers have in common, says Satzewich — markets to support them and an entrepreneurial spirit. His own entrepreneurial spirit is in evidence in the range of books and learning guides he sells online. Similarly, Ward Teulon supplements his farming income with garden tours, building raised beds, and garden consultations.

SPIN's claims of revenues were proven in a carefully monitored experiment on the Somerton Tanks Farm property in Northeast Philadelphia. Backed by city and state funding to promote local economic agricultural development, the Institute for Innovations in Local Farming (IILF) and the Philadelphia Water Department, the half-acre SPIN farm on donated land grossed $26,000 in its first year of operation. After four years of refining the system, improving the soil and building the farm's reputation for quality produce, revenues were up to $68,000. A follow-up economic feasibility study projected that revenues could reach $120,000 on less than an acre of growing space using the SPIN methods.

Unfortunately, the plot had to be abandoned when the property was needed for other uses.

Will Allen's two-acre Growing Power, Inc. in Milwaukee has established some impressive markets and prices for its year-round produce coming out of six greenhouses and eight hoop houses. In 2010, Growing

Table 7.1 Income & Expense History: Somerton Tanks Farm, Philadelphia 2004–2006.

	2004	2005	2006
Revenue			
Community Supported Agriculture Shares	$15,700	$23,800	$24,900
Farmers Market Revenues	$12,700	$19,600	$36,900
Restaurant/Wholesaler Sales	$7,600	$6,500	$5,800
Farmstand Sales & Other	$2,800	$2,800	$400
Total Revenues	$38,800	$52,700	$68,000
Operating Expenses			
Growing Supplies & Irrigation	$2,900	$3,500	$5,100
Sales Supplies	$900	$1,700	$1,400
Vehicle Insurance	$5,400	$5,000	$4,300
Vehicle Operations & Repair	$1,600	$3,000	$3,000
Equipment Purchase & Repair	$1,800	$2,900	$1,900
Marketing	$900	$200	$400
Farmers Market Fees	$1,000	$1,500	$2,300
Employee Labor — Part-Time	$0	$10,200	$11,500
Business Liability Insurance	$200		
Other	$600	$0	$0
Total Non-Farmer Expenses	$15,100	$28,000	$30,100
Net Farmers Wages	$32,400	$37,500	$39,700
Total Expenses	$47,500	$65,500	$69,800

Source: "Farming in Philadelphia: Feasibility Analysis and Next Steps," prepared for the Institute for Innovations in Local Farming by Urban Partners, December 2007.

Power sold $500,000 worth of produce, meat and fish — boosted by 3,500 volunteers.

Sprouts, grown in trays year-round, can bring in from $5–$30 a square foot. Growing Power produces 2,000 trays a week. The watercress from Growing Power's aquaponics contraption, fed by tilapia waste pumped up to an overhead filtration garden from ground-level pools, sells for $16 a pound. The tilapia, ready for harvest in 6–12 months, sell for $6 each. They eat anything from food scraps to duckweed. Allen figures that three 55-gallon drums in a basement could produce 50 fish a month, enough to feed a family.

"A critical success factor is markets," points out Roxanne Christensen, president of IILF. "It is here that urbanization can be turned to the farmer's advantage — because cities provide a variety of sales channels — farmers markets, CSAs, restaurants, high-end specialty food stores — that are able to pay premium prices." Christensen says SPIN now has a network of more than 500 "sub-acre farmers" around the world using these methods.[2]

GROW BIOINTENSIVE® Sustainable Mini-Farming is another micro farming system (growbiointensive.org). Its promoters say it will produce all the calories and nutrients needed for a complete diet for one person — on a tenth of an acre of growing space. GROW BIOINTENSIVE methods have been spreading since they were researched and proven at the University of California-Santa Cruz in the late 1960s. By 2011, when it celebrated its 40th anniversary, more than 1,500 people from 46 states and 24 countries had been trained in the methods at "Ecology Action" workshops, taking the lessons to small gardens in 141 countries around the world.

According to Ecology Action's Executive Director John Jeavons, GROW BIOINTENSIVE farming techniques can feed one person on a vegan diet (1,100 lbs. of vegetables) on 4,000 square feet of land (0.09 acre), or 10–12 people (15,000 lbs.) on 43,560 square feet of land (1 acre).

Predicting economic returns from those yields is difficult because it would depend on the local market and the management skills and intent of the growers. Regardless of the financial outcomes, GROW BIOINTENSIVE confirms the SPIN farming claims that urban farming on small plots can be highly productive.

Renowned author, farmer and teacher Eliot Coleman has four prin-
ciples that enable him to gross $100,000 a year from 1.5 acres of farm-
land in Maine, which has a limited growing season. His mantra is:
- Simplify production techniques.
- Use efficient small machinery and tools.
- Reduce expenses on external inputs.
- Market produce to bring the greatest return.

Stepping up from sub-acre plots to more acreage can add new costs that
can't be covered by the smaller increase in revenues. Wally Satzewich
didn't start like Ward Teulon with small city plots. His first farm was a
one-acre plot just outside Saskatoon. Eyeing economies of scale, he then
moved onto 20 acres on the South Saskatchewan River where he and
his partner Gail Vandersteen grew vegetables. After three years of fighting natural pests and paying the capital costs of more machinery, they
realized they could do better growing multiple crops in the city. "People
don't believe you can grow three crops a year in Saskatoon," Vandersteen
says. "They think it's too much work, but the truth is, this is much less
work than mechanized, large-scale farming. We used to have a tractor
to hill potatoes and cultivate, but we find it's more efficient to do things
by hand. Other than a rototiller, all we need is a push-type seeder and a
few hand tools."

Finding the right scale of operation is an important factor in getting
favorable financial results. Wally Satzewich discovered on his own that
small-sized plots are financially beautiful. A 1997 economic analysis of
sustainable community food systems found that small-scale on-farm
processing can be more efficient because some of the work can be done
by farm family labor in on-farm kitchens. When quantities get too big
to use hand-processed, low-overhead production methods, but not big
enough to capture economies of scale, the profit margins disappear.[3]

Chicken production is similar: the profit per bird under homestead
production is higher, although the total net income at small volumes
can't match that of higher-volume industrial chicken producers.

The challenge is finding the right volume for maximum revenue
while keeping production costs at homestead levels. The path to profitability for community-scale processors is to achieve a high margin on

small production quantities instead of producing high quantities of low margin products.

Another path to profitability is to go indoors. Stephen Fane, a former accountant and hothouse vegetable grower, lays out these numbers for his backyard-sized Valcent high-tech greenhouse (proven in operation, but not available commercially):

TABLE 7.2 Estimated revenues from Valcent's automated growing system.

Capital cost of a 5,800-sq. ft. growing system including growing area of 3,800-sq. ft. and shed space of 2,000-sq. ft. not including land or structure:	$1.2 million
Total cost to get crops growing, distribution set up:	$1.6 million
Annual revenue:	$900,000
Annual salaries for 3 full-time-equivalent employees:	$120,000
Annual earnings before interest, taxes, depreciation and amortization:	$450,000

Source: Stephen Fane, CEO, Valcent, interview with the author, Sept. 2010.

Community Supported Agriculture

An urban farmer has a big leg up if he has customers who pay at the beginning of the season for a share of future crops. This is *Community Supported Agriculture* (CSA). In a CSA program, people buy annual shares in a farming operation in return for a weekly supply of fresh produce throughout the growing season. Not only is cash flow enhanced, but the customers are providing the farmer insurance by sharing the risk of crop failures. Often, CSA members also come out to the farm and provide free labor and build rewarding community links. CSAs in the city have the added advantage that buyers can often pick up their produce themselves, saving the farmer the cost of distribution.

Being Close to Cities Brings Business Opportunities

Financially sustainable, human-scale farms close to cities can feed on a web of business opportunities born out of proximity. The Intervale Center in Burlington, Vermont has a constellation of intertwined businesses:

Home Economics: Balcony Gardening at $5.75/Hr.

Mark Ridsdill-Smith writes online that he makes $5.75/hour harvesting only what he can grow in tiny spaces at his North London townhome: a 54-square foot northwest-facing balcony, six window sills (two north-facing) and a concrete patch outside his front door. That's after spending $303 and 170 hours to build and run his mini-garden complex.

In the 2010 season, he grew 145 pounds of vegetables worth $1,055. His five top-grossing vegetables were:

- tomatoes ($328)
- salad greens ($297)
- herbs ($153)
- runner beans ($107)
- zucchinis ($42)

That's a pretty good haul from a tiny space.

Source: verticalveg.org.uk.

Credit: Sally Cuttle, www.verticalveg.org.uk

Balcony grower Mark Ridsdill-Smith figures he makes $5.75/hour harvesting only what he can grow on tiny spaces at his North London townhome: A 54-square foot northwest-facing balcony, six window sills (two north-facing), and a concrete patch outside his front door.

Intervale Compost Products (the state's biggest compost operation); Burlington Electric's McNeil Generating Station; the Sugarsnap Café; the Stray Cat Flower Farm and Market; Intervale Conservation Nursery; Intervale Agricultural Development Consulting Services; and the Intervale Food Enterprise Center — among others. And that list doesn't even include the 13 private farms developed in the Center's Farm Incubator Program (estimated to provide 8% of the city's food — more than a million dollars of organically grown food produced for local consumption each year).

The McNeil Station generates most of Burlington's electrical power primarily from sustainably grown Vermont wood chips. Intervale Compost transforms the city's organic waste streams into compost and topsoil sold commercially in and around the city.

The same diversification of revenue sources is evident at Fairview Gardens, the 12.5-acre organic market garden now surrounded by freeways, tract homes and shopping malls near Santa Barbara, California. It sells not only food, but books, videos, DVDs and membership in its CSA program. It also offers cooking and gardening classes and apprenticeships.

Places like the Intervale don't pretend to be stand-alone businesses. They match earned income with foundation grants and charitable gifts — about 50:50 in Intervale's case. Being non-profit allows the Intervale to leverage revenue from its most profitable programs to underwrite startups and other initiatives. "Because we don't have to generate all of our revenues, we can build up enterprises, look to evolving systems and needs, try to understand what the obstacles are, and how to fill them, try solutions out, and develop something that is really functional," says Glenn McRae, the Center's executive director.[4]

Non-Profit/For-Profit?

Should the Intervale Center have been a for-profit? "I could argue either side of that," says its founder Will Raap. "I do think that because we were talking about becoming stewards of a very large portion of open space and public land, we had to be a non-profit entity. The city couldn't sell 200 acres to a private buyer." But, he adds, had the Intervale been a for-profit, it might have attracted private finance and been able to move more quickly on some of its business ideas.

Turning Vacant Liabilities into Farm Assets in Detroit

There are some cities that just might sell 200 acres to a private buyer for farming. Detroit is one of them.

John Hantz is a bold, bright Detroit businessman who has lived in Detroit for more than 20 years, refusing to flee to the suburbs like so many of his contemporaries. Instead, he stayed in the crumbling city and bought and renovated nine homes, including the immaculate estate where he now lives. During his many reverse commutes to the suburban headquarters of Hantz Financial Services, he watched the ongoing disintegration of his beloved city, where a gang sport is burning down abandoned homes. "I had plenty of time to think about it," he says.

The city of Detroit, a 140-square mile geographic colossus, has shrunk from a peak auto-boom population of over 2 million to around 900,000 today. Forty square miles of city property are vacant. The public school population has shrunk from 195,000 to 85,000, with population continuing to decline and unemployment climbing to over 20%. The city has a staggering debt load, triggering plans to cut off city services to properties outside certain boundaries.

Hantz's epiphany was realizing that Detroit was cursed with an abundance of empty lots. "We can't do anything until we get scarcity," he explains. "We've got to take large chunks of land out of circulation in a positive way."

No one wants to buy land that's going to be worth less tomorrow, he explained. Housing prices in the city are already down to the $15,000 range, with homeowners able to pick up adjacent empty lots for $1 if they'll just pay the taxes on them.

Hantz realized that the 200,000 tax-delinquent parcels of land owned by the city were a huge drain on city finances. "There's a difference between green space and vacant land. Vacant land destroys value, destroys community. The worst part is that it consumes the city's resources." At servicing costs of about $12,000 a year, "the 30,000–40,000 acres of abandoned land is a liability, not an asset. Carrying costs matter.

Over 5 years, that's $3 billion. If you had an asset that was going to cost you $3 billion over five years, you'd pawn it off on someone and keep the savings."

Driving to work with that dilemma rolling around in his head, he asked, "What would be a positive solution that people would want to live around?" His conclusion: Detroit is a perfect city for commercial farms.

So he teamed up with Michigan State University and the Kellogg Foundation to get some expertise. Hantz has pledged $30 million of his own money to assemble abandoned properties and warehouses and develop urban agriculture attractions that will remake Detroit as the urban agriculture center of the United States.

"I want this to be a city where people can come here and see all aspects of urban agriculture and leave excited."

He's looking at investing in three sites: one for a traditional farm growing fruits and vegetables; one for growing timber (such as pine, hardwoods, or Christmas trees); and one "like the Epcot Center or an auto mall," which would showcase advanced, futuristic indoor and outdoor growing systems. "We're a horizontal city," notes Hantz, "but most cities have to grow vertically."

"I'm raising $30 million over 10 years, mostly my own money. I'm counting on a 5%, maybe 7% return."

It's a strange, audacious vision. Hantz himself describes it as "so foreign, but self-evident to the rest of the world looking in."

It's definitely foreign to the prevailing culture of the exploding grassroots urban ag movement, raising the hackles of people like Malik Yakini, head of the Detroit Black Community Food Security Network. They operate a 2-acre farm, soon to grow to 7 acres, in the biggest park in the city — all staffed by volunteers. He's concerned that Hantz's proposal is an extension of rich white males treating Detroit's 82% black population as "objects that people do something to."

"They haven't engaged the Detroit community," Yakini says.

Not helpfully, Hantz counters, "I'm not partnering up with self-appointed people who claim to be speaking for the community. In business, people don't talk for other people. They put up or shut up.

"People ask me if I'm part of a movement. I am. I'm part of the 'I Live Here Movement.'" [5]

To accusations that this is just a speculative land grab, Hantz is un-repentant: "Of course it's a land grab. You need land to do a farm. And if there's a windfall, who better to get it than the person who took the risk into fear? If someone else wants to do this, I say, 'go ahead.'

"We have the backing of common sense. What do we have to lose?"[6]

Hantz's Ayn-Rand-infused approach to urban agriculture is never go-ing to sit well with more community-oriented approaches. It completely misses the vital self-empowerment payoffs of combining community farming with a higher social purpose, just as so many heavily-subsidized community projects miss the self-sufficiency of a more business-like ap-proach.

Detroit has vast areas of vacant land screaming for salvation, and a city government mired in deficit. It needs all the help it can get. There's acres of room for a variety of models to demonstrate the best in 21st-century urban agriculture—especially those that figure out how to combine a sense of community ownership with a keen eye on the bot-tom line.

Urban Ag Produce Still Skewed to the Rich

Making a living off urban agriculture usually means selling direct at the local farmers market, through a CSA, or to restaurants. Small urban growers and near-urban artisanal producers are still a long way from being suppliers to the bigger grocery stores where most people shop. The logistical challenges are still formidable.

So, the long-term sustainability of commercial urban agriculture de-pends on price-*unconscious* buyers at the farmers market while every-where else the number one determining factor in choosing what food to buy is still price. Even institutional policies to buy only local food, say for a university or school, fall apart if prices are too high. So how sustain-able is this model if prices of urban produce are too high for any except an exclusive group of elite buyers and a limited number of patrons at premium restaurants?

Is Added Nutrition Worth the Extra Price?

The strongest case for charging more for local produce is that it's fresher, more nutritious, and tastier. Thomas Pawlick, in *The End of Food*, got curious when a supermarket tomato refused to ripen or even rot when he let it sit for weeks in his kitchen. Then it wouldn't split when he threw it at a wall; it bounced back like a tennis ball. Contacting commercial industrial tomato growers, he found that of the growers' ten most valued characteristics of a great tomato (yield per acre, size, tolerance to shipping, color, and pest resistance are some of them), consumers' two most important ones were missing: flavor and nutrition.

Those just happen to be the main attractions of produce at farmers markets. Organic farmer Michael Ableman says he gives away about $400 worth of samples at the Saltspring Island farmers market every weekend. He does it because once people taste what he's got to offer, they want to buy it, even if it does seem expensive. They can literally sense the value in his produce that truck-ripened supermarket food can only mimic visually.

Nutritional analysis suggests that if you were paying per unit of nutrition, higher-priced organic and locally grown fresh food might actually be cheaper than its lower-priced competition at the supermarket. Most fruits and vegetables sold in Canadian supermarkets today contain far fewer vital vitamins and minerals than they did 50 years ago. The average potato has lost 100% of its vitamin A (important for eyesight), 50% of its vitamin C and iron (for healthy blood) and 28% of its calcium. Also gone is 50% of its riboflavin and 18% of its thiamine. Only niacin, of the seven key ingredients measured, increased. Similar results were found in 25 fruits and vegetables analyzed.[7]

There's a reason most food producers grow food that lacks nutrition and flavor. They can't afford to add costs when North Americans are spending only 11% of their income on food — and buy mainly based on price. The food producers who typically sell at farmers markets and through CSAs set higher standards for nutrition, ecological sustenance, fair wages, and pesticide-free growing, which results in higher prices for consumers and a perilous financial situation for the growers.

In B.C., even growers paying minimum wage ($8/hour) are paying a lot more than the big industrial farms pay the illegal migrants they often employ. Farms that pay a fair wage have a hard time competing.

Organic growing also requires more labor, especially when planting, weeding and harvesting is done by hand, as is often the case on small-scale farms trying to reduce their dependence on oil. A smaller-scale farm can't make up for a small profit per unit by selling large quantities. It's forced to make its money on a smaller number of sales — hence, higher prices, presumably linked to higher quality food.

Then, when crops are plentiful and big producers are dumping products into the market, small producers selling into mainstream stores are forced to match the low prices and take a loss or watch their produce rot.

"As a farmer, I want everyone to be able to access the food I grow," says organic farmer Chris Bodnar, "At the same time, I refuse to allow myself or my employees to live in poverty so that someone else can have cheap food. We live in a society with such abundance that there is little reason for people to go hungry. The inequality that results in hunger is a societal problem — it's not the farmer's fault."[8]

Conclusion

Farmers in cities have a lot of advantages that sweeten their financial bottom lines: proximity to high-end retail buyers, low-cost (in some cases, no-cost) distribution, more second-job opportunities, piped and captured water, fewer wild pests, and — the ultimate irony — access to free land. The surrounding customer base can also be tapped for cooking lessons, garden tours, setting up edible gardens, and selling seeds and garden accessories. Farmers markets offer the equivalent of a farm-gate mini-mall.

These advantages are compounded for small-scale yard farmers who focus on niche products, tight management and low overhead.

The external benefits generated by urban farming — creating green space, low-skill job opportunities, community bonding, better inner-city eating habits, diet education, community resilience, and brownfield cleanup — are often worth enough that someone else will pay for them. That's already the case in shrinking cities like Detroit, where land grants and tax breaks are helping it achieve its dream of being the urban farming center of North America.

While many would argue that the community benefits alone justify whatever subsidies are needed to make urban farming viable, finding a dependable formula for stand-alone financial success would add a flood of entrepreneurial energy to the food mix. Grants and subsidies are getting harder to find as governments reel with deficits and foundation assets shrink.

You have to wonder about the limits to the market for premium high-end niche products like purple carrots. How many cook-from-scratch restaurants are there that can afford to pay a premium for fresh sprouts every day? How many customers are willing to pay more for the fulfillment of buying fresh, local food direct from the farmer? If people knew that the prices of local organic food are not higher per unit of nutrient, they might happily support their neighborhood urban farmer. Looking ahead, new developments in aquaponics and tech-assisted indoor growing could well be the killer apps for affordable urban food security.

8

Economic Development through Urban Agriculture: Chasing the Local Job Dream

"I AM AN OKANAGAN [B.C.] orchardist," writes an anonymous farmer (signed in as "nlo") in the comment section of an online news service. "We need about 35 cents a pound for apples to make a living. When we get 35 cents, the price in the stores is about $1.50. Last year we (our industry) averaged 12 cents and lost a lot of money. The average retail price was still about $1.50.

"Retail concentration has happened so there will be very little [retail] competition; the big 3 (Overwaitea, Safeway, Loblaws) don't like competition. They hire ruthless people with MBAs who shop the world for the best deal; often the deal is due to the generosity of another nations' taxpayers; but it's very wrong to believe they 'pass on the savings.'

"The only thing that will keep farmers in this province alive is if our citizens will stop buying foreign produce. Then demand for B.C. produce will increase and we can demand a premium for our product so we can get our 35 cents; and it won't cost you [the consumer] any more. Maybe then we won't have to work until midnight and haul our workers around on the back of a tractor.

"Or we need a marketing board like the milk and egg producers, who, by the way are not subsidized but protected [from other countries' subsidized products]. US dairy producers receive direct cash subsidies, which is in reality a subsidy to their retailers, processors and exporters."[1]

Any discussion of reaping economic development benefits from urban and near-urban agriculture has to start with a decent bottom line for farmers. Can a stronger market for local food achieve this? Can it only be done with subsidies, supply management, import quotas and tariffs? This orchardist's comments illustrate how many farmers struggling to make a living selling locally are getting pummeled by cheap foreign — often subsidized — competition brought to town by vertically integrated retail and wholesale conglomerates. The good news is that in the aisles of our grocery stores, consumers are in the best of all possible worlds: they pay low prices for the widest variety of goods in history.

The dark side of that consumer dream world is that externalized costs such as soil erosion, water pollution and greenhouse gas emissions aren't charged back to the consumer. A study in the UK found that the real cost of a market basket of food would be 12% higher if the true cost of food miles in environmental and societal factors was included in the price. That's probably a low estimate. Writer/architect Carolyn Steel says in *Hungry City* that the true cost of a hamburger, charging all the externalized costs to the consumer, would be $200.

Just as consumers benefit from cheap imports, farmers who export their produce benefit from access to markets outside their own region, letting them profit from their comparative advantages (cheap water, great soil, lots of sun — whatever it might be). For now, relatively cheap oil prices grease this whole system and keep it going. Some of those exporting farmers who sign deals with the retailers' "ruthless MBAs" have to be making money.

How Stronger Local Markets Could Help Farmers

But just imagine if a region could divert a small percentage of the money it spends on imported food to support its local farmers? What if local consumers bought less foreign produce and bought at least some of their apples from local producers? That's a thought that's popping up everywhere, lighting up dollar signs in the eyes of regional economic development proponents as well as financially strapped farmers.

A study in Seattle (one of many similar studies) found that shifting just 20% of the food dollars spent into "locally directed spending" would inject nearly $1 billion into the region's economy each year. That's based on the assumption that when a farmer grows food for export, it only generates $1.70 in local economic activity for every dollar in sales. However, if the same farmer sells at a farmers market, each dollar in sales will generate $2.80 in local income.

Researchers looking at Detroit estimated that if 20% of fresh food purchased came from local sources, more than 4,700 jobs would be created, along with $20 million in tax revenues.

The economic impact of local procurement was measured in Portland in a study that gave school districts a bit of extra money to buy local food for school lunches. So instead of paying 30 cents for a serving of chili from a national distributor, they could afford to pay 34 cents to a local supplier. The local lunches cost 13% more, but for every dollar spent locally by two school districts, another 87 cents was spent in Oregon, adding up to a 1.87 multiplier. The extra $66,000 invested in more expensive local foods inspired an additional $225,000 in spending — a 241% return on the investment.

But where does protection for local producers stop? History shows us that restricting exports can create a protectionist spiral that will hurt all farmers who export, and hike food prices to all consumers. When one jurisdiction imposes a penalty on imports, its neighbor retaliates and exporting farmers are held captive to local markets. Protectionism also rewards inefficiencies, which adds to the prices that consumers eventually have to pay.

Under the extreme scenario of a strictly 100-mile diet for everyone, the local agricultural economy would be booming, but we'd be paying a lot more for a lot less interesting food. In many northern countries, most spices, sugar, coffee, black teas, citrus fruits, rice and any out-of-season fruit or vegetable would be out of reach. We'd be trading the vulnerability of diversified global supply chains for vulnerability to local upheavals — local floods, drought, pest outbreaks, water shortages and earthquakes.

True food self-sufficiency usually comes at the cost of high levels of protection for local markets. For Japan to achieve its official policy goals of relative food self-sufficiency, it has had to keep internal prices well above world market levels by restricting imported food. But it still has to import fertilizers and chemicals and feedgrains for livestock production.

Getting the Local Food Mix Right

Food security, not local food self-sufficiency, has to be our goal, which means coming up with local economic development policies that give us access to reliable, safe, diverse sources of affordable food locally *and* from outside sources. Achieving the goal of local economic development depends not just on growing food locally, but on adding value to exports produced locally. Having local processors who can make jam from fresh strawberries, or freeze and package them, adds more jobs than selling those strawberries fresh. It still starts with having enough local food available to add these new jobs.

Although the United States prides itself as the breadbasket of the world, in 2006, for the first time, the value of food imported into the United States exceeded the value of food exported from the United States.

Right now, most regions in North America are out of balance, depending far more on imported foods than local food — even when local food is being exported. Iowa, a top agricultural export state, imports about 90% of its food.

At least 60% of the fresh produce consumed in Toronto is imported from the United States, and a third of this arrives during Ontario's own growing season, competing with local produce. This amounts to $172 million spent annually in Greater Toronto to import fresh vegetables, many of which can be grown locally. Despite having more than half of Canada's most productive agricultural land, Ontario has a food deficit of approximately $3 billion.

In spite of the downsides of protectionism, stimulating local food supplies with local economic development policies is compelling for a lot of non-economic reasons. A stronger element of local food self-sufficiency in an otherwise import-dependent market adds to the resilience of a community. It protects against expected increases in transportation costs and greenhouse gas emission costs. It's a buffer against breakdowns in increasingly centralized global supply chains.

It builds community: "When we measure economic development solely in terms of 'Gross Domestic Product' at a national level, we forfeit a knowledge of our land, destroy the middle class, hinder entrepreneurship, and cause the demise of our rural communities," says Rob Marqusee, Director of Rural Economic Development in Woodbury County, Iowa.[2]

Patty Cantrell of the Michigan Land Use Institute sees the local food economy as a way to grow Detroit's entrepreneurial culture: "These people planting potatoes and starting new grocery stores with produce trucks going around neighborhoods are like the people in the Silicon Valley who were experimenting with software in their garages.

"These are the entrepreneurs who are going to remake our state and our city. They may not create big Fortune 500 companies, but their innovation, the jobs and businesses, the thriving neighborhoods, the creative culture that results is what will make a world class place. Detroit needs to create places where people want to be. This is a core part of that."[3]

Nations favor their own; individuals look after families and friends first. Why not cities and regions? Agriculture economic development expert Ken Meter makes the case eloquently: "What is economic development if it isn't feeding our children? The food system is very good at taking wealth out of our communities.... Local food may be the best path toward economic recovery."[4]

Local Food Multiplies Local Spending

Local economic development thrives on the multiplier effect: money spent on a local business circulates through other local businesses, multiplying its benefits to the community. The economic multiplier from spending a dollar at a locally owned business, like a local farm, is estimated to be 2–4 times the impact of a dollar spent at a business owned outside the community.

Locally owned businesses are more likely, because of proximity and familiarity, to use local couriers, office supply stores, mechanics, welders, marketing experts and other suppliers. When owners and local shareholders live in the community there's far more chance they will spend their profits locally.

Stimulating sales by farmers to their local markets offers some tantalizing economic benefits. Michigan State University did a study in 2006 that predicted that doubling or tripling the amount of fruits and vegetables sold by Michigan farmers to local outlets could generate up to 1,889 new jobs across the state and $187 million in new personal income.

Robert Waldrop, a 2006 candidate for mayor of Oklahoma City, used USDA data and analyses to identify $2.1 billion in economic activity in Central Oklahoma if Oklahoma County residents bought their eggs, poultry, meat, vegetables, flour, and milk and dairy products directly from farmers in the region.

In assessing the food economy of the Chesapeake Bay region, Ken Meter found that a 15% increase in local food purchases would bring in three times more dollars to farming communities than federal subsidies were bringing to the region.

Food Entrepreneurs Wanted, Encouraged

The city of Toronto is just one place that helps train entrepreneurs wanting to get into food-related businesses which will add value to the local economy. Adding value to unprocessed food is big business. The food and beverage processing sector is Ontario and Canada's third largest manufacturing sector, led by bakeries, meat processing and beverages. Two-thirds of the companies in the business are owner-operated, producing "fresh product" or serving specialty markets in the city.

To do this, the city works with the Toronto Food Business Incubator, an independent non-profit organization that offers its clients 24-hour access to a fully equipped commercial kitchen, along with training, field trips and mentoring. It partners with the city's economic development department to host free workshops in How to Start a Food Business, Basic Distribution Channels, How to Market your Product, and Food Regulation Guidelines, Pricing and Costing Your Products, and Preparing a Business Plan. Participants who are picked for a full program pay $1,000 for the first three months and $1,800 for the next three.

Portland's Food Innovation Center, located at Oregon State University in collaboration with the Oregon Department of Agriculture, is a comparable food business booster. Its mission is to bring products to market and advance regional food. One of its programs is a "Getting your recipe to market" competition where budding entrepreneurs test recipes and create business plans, with the winner getting guaranteed shelf space at the New Seasons Market.

The Economic Virtues of Organic

"Organic farming, to us, is economic development," says Rob Marqusee. "In fact, I think it's the least expensive, most productive way to spend dollars at the local level to increase quality of life. It's not only jobs, but people start eating healthier, and the community starts to come together over food."

Marqusee cites a study by Luanne Lohr at the University of Georgia showing that communities that have organic farms are better off than those with only conventional farms: "The [organic] farmer is better educated, younger, and contributes more to the local community.... Local food production has a much higher return per acre than the highly specialized industrial food system based upon large economies of scale. There's a conflict between local food production and a large economy industrial food system. You can't really improve the economics of a rural region without dealing with small farm and organic agriculture."

Woodbury County took action by providing a 100% property tax rebate for 5 years to farms that convert to organic, resulting in smaller farms, more labor, and higher income for farmers. They weren't limited to selling locally. Without that incentive, local farmers, average age over 60, weren't jumping at the opportunity to weather the 3-year turnaround to organics. The policy attracted a Wisconsin company that built a $40 million organic soybean processing plant.

Says Marqusee: "I sold it as zero up-front cost to the county. Potential lost revenue was $50,000.

"As a community, we're supporting our farmers and giving them a fair opportunity to serve our citizens and provide food at fair, competitive prices and make a decent living in the process. We spend $3 million a year on salaries to attract business to our county. You could take 5% of that and use it for micro-loans for farmers who will spend their money in our community.... This has to become a policy priority of your government — to value and respect small organic producers. Are you going to help your own people? Are you going to help people who want to get started in a business? I'm not trying to eliminate conventional farming, but right now the conventional farmers are completely subsidized."

Organic Farms Contribute More to Local Economies?

A study of counties in the United States with organic farms found that organic farmers are more likely to be female, young, hold a college degree, and be full-time farmers. In the study, organic farming, while only a small part of US agriculture, scored higher on nearly every indicator of economic, social and environmental benefits (except costs to consumers):

- The (mostly economic) case for organic farms: Organic farm price premiums are 70% to 250% more than conventional farm prices.
- Counties with organic farms have stronger farm economies, based on total sales, net revenue, farm value, taxes paid, payroll, and purchases of fertilizer, seed, and repair and maintenance services.
- Counties with organic farms have higher percentages of resident full-time farmers, greater direct-to-consumer sales, more workers hired, and higher worker pay.
- Counties with organic farms provide more bird and wildlife habitat and have lower insecticide and nematicide use.
- Watersheds with organic farms have lower runoff risk from nitrogen and sediment.
- Organic farming avoids social and economic costs such as pesticide poisonings.
- Organic farming provides community benefits without government intervention: customers paying organic prices cover more of the cost of producing socially desirable outputs, such as clean water.

Source: "Benefits of US Organic Agriculture," Luanne Lohr, Department of Agricultural and Applied Economics, University of Georgia.

Organic farming is also well-positioned as a defensive strategy against pending changes to taxes and regulations to reduce greenhouse gas emissions. Carbon taxes, cap-and-trade policies and higher energy prices will hit farming practices most dependent on fossil fuels. Organic farming has a lower fossil fuel dependence than conventional industrial farming. According to the Institute for Science in Society, existing organic agriculture and localized food systems mitigate 30% of the world's greenhouse gas emissions and save one-sixth of energy consumption.

Entry-Level Farm Jobs Help Disadvantaged Workers

The benefits of promoting organic and small-scale farms in rural areas are even more relevant to near-urban areas, where large-scale industrial farming isn't an option, and sensitivity to chemicals, pesticides and polluted runoff near where a lot of people live is much higher. The higher number of jobs on small-scale farms has a special appeal to cities hit with high unemployment.

"This is about growing jobs," says Will Allen of Milwaukee's Growing Power, Inc. "We can create thousands of jobs around small-scale agriculture." As someone who hires challenged youth to work in his hoop houses and compost-mixing yard, Allen also knows first-hand how accessible these entry-level jobs are to low-skilled people who don't have a lot of other job options.

I remember looking down on the rooftop garden on the Chicago City Hall, where workers recently released from prisons were raking and digging. Getting newly-released prisoners who lack education and work experience into the mainstream workforce is a major challenge — especially in the United States with its high number of people incarcerated. Jobs on urban farms are very accessible to these people.

Jobs on prison farms make the transition easier, but they're disappearing. The Canadian federal government recently decided to shut down farms in jails, thus eliminating this type of job training for inmates. One of the reasons given was that farm labor jobs are not the most desirable job options.

"Those farms were costing a net loss of $4 million a year," explained Canada's Minister of Public Safety Peter Van Loan in April 2009. "We felt that that money could be more adequately redirected to programs where people would actually gain employable skills, as virtually nobody who went through those prison farms ended up with employable skills, because they were based on a model of how agriculture was done 50 years ago, when it was labor intensive, and not capital intensive, as it is today. Almost none of those spending time on prison farms ultimately find employment in the agricultural sector."[5]

However, a representative of the National Farmers Union has a different view. Farming not only offers entry-level jobs, it also involves a lot of skills. Farm job training in prisons could provide a lot of economic benefits if it made inmates more employable. Dianne Dowling, vice-president of Local 316 of the National Farmers Union has said, "The [prison] farms are run on a very modern basis so the skills that the inmates are getting certainly would apply to modern farms.... In the Kingston area, The New Farm Project is encouraging farmers to farm in more sustainable ways and many of the people that are participating are opening up market gardens. So they are moving to a labor-intensive type of farming and a less capital-intensive one. So there is certainly potential for an inmate to come out of prison and to use farming skills, if not for a job at least in his own personal life: how to grow his own food, for example — if he had an opportunity to be involved in learning the gardening part.

"Anyone who has ever worked on a farm knows that you learn to work independently, you learn to take responsibility for things — particularly if you're caring for animals. If you don't get up and feed the cows in the morning, the cows go hungry. Most people are pretty sensitive to that not being a good thing.

"They learn equipment skills: how to operate and how to repair. They would, I'm sure, learn a little bit of carpentry and welding and plumbing and electricity. These things are all applicable to jobs in construction. Also, because they're processing the milk and the eggs at Frontenac Institution here in the Kingston area, they would get a certain amount of experience in food processing.

"We also feel that the farm program offers a big bonus in rehabilitation because we've heard from some of the inmates. They say things like working with the animals is like an anger management course because if you walk up to a cow angry, she's going to probably kick you back. You'd get immediate negative reinforcement for that.

"In a more positive way, just working with animals is very rewarding. We hear the inmates saying 'these are my calves,' 'these are my cows.' They really take ownership and concern about them."[6]

Kingston inmate Chris Parmer agrees. "I have worked on the Frontenac Farm for 2 years now where I started by driving tractors and cleaning the barns. I have worked my way up to working in the admin office as an Inmate Clerk. I do computer work where I log and print milk and egg orders for institutions in Ontario and Western Quebec. I track inventory and perform cattle counts in addition to maintaining a register of all cattle happenings every month. I do filing. I take calf pictures for registration purposes with the Holstein Association of Canada. I do computerized monthly roll-ups for institutional orders of milk and eggs and juice. This is just like working in the community because you start at the bottom and then work yourself up to a more advanced job.

"Working at the Frontenac Farm is a rewarding job for being in prison because you are treated like a real employee, not like a prisoner.

"Since working as a clerk at the farm I have learned many different ways of improving communication, listening, teamwork and my views or ideals. These jobs help offenders get up and go to work each day and be responsible in their choices. We come to a minimum institution like Frontenac to be able to work outside and be able to prove ourselves and to better our skills and have a better chance of returning back to society."[7]

Prison farms also strengthen the local farm economy. The two big ones in Kingston, Ontario, operate an abattoir that is used by other farmers; the prison farms are two of the biggest customers for local farm supply companies, providing vital infrastructure for other farmers.

Local Procurement Grows the Local Economy

Smaller-scale and organic farms producing food for the local market, trying to compete with the hidden — and sometimes not-so-hidden — subsidies for industrial agriculture, are turning to a powerful tool for generating local food sales. Institutional procurement that favors "local sustainable" food is a simple and powerful way to keep food-spending dollars in the community, and to meet consumer demand. Students at universities, for example, are starting to ask for local food in their cafeterias, which makes universities eager to provide it as a way to attract students.

Local procurement also delivers health and community-building benefits that reduce other public expenditures. It opens up a dependable market for local food suppliers too small to get into the concentrated funnel of corporate ownership that delivers most of our food. In 2005 in Canada, four grocery retailers controlled 78% of the market.

For the vast number of small-scale producers and processors, developing more and secured venues for selling locally is critical to diversifying their customer base. They simply can't produce the year-round volumes required to plug into the global supply chains that the big grocery retailers depend on to keep their costs down.

Local procurement strengthens farm businesses already in operation. This idea is in line with the standard economic development priority of retaining and expanding local business first. Whatever added costs result from local procurement need to be weighed against competing investments in local economic development that try to attract new businesses to a region. Local procurement can be an efficient alternative to conventional economic development, which has soaked up an estimated $50 billion in state and local subsidies (tax credits, refunds, abatements, bonds, low-interest loans, etc.) in the United States.

It's breaking out all over North America. The Illinois Local Food, Farms, and Jobs Act of 2009 established a goal for state institutions (hospitals, schools, prisons) to procure 20% of all food and food products from local farms or manufacturers by 2020, even if they have to pay a premium for it. Oregon allows its public agencies to pay up to a 10% premium for locally sourced foods.

The University of Toronto was the first institution to commit to buying a percentage of its food from sources ratified by Local Food Plus, a Toronto-based organization that has developed criteria for awarding a "Certified Local Sustainable" label. They define "local" as coming from

How to Become "Certified Local Sustainable"

Local Food Plus is a Canadian non-profit organization that aims to foster sustainable food systems by certifying farmers and processors as "Certified Local Sustainable" and linking them with local purchasers.

To win that label, farmers and processors have to:

- Employ sustainable production systems that reduce or eliminate synthetic pesticides and fertilizers; avoid the use of hormones, antibiotics and genetic engineering; and conserve soil and water.
- Provide safe and fair working conditions for on-farm labor.
- Provide healthy and humane care for livestock.
- Protect and enhance wildlife habitat and biodiversity on working farm landscapes.
- Reduce food-related energy consumption and greenhouse gas emissions through energy conservation, recycling, minimal packaging and local sales.

Source: localfoodplus.ca.

Certified Local Sustainable Harmony milk attracts customers looking for local food.

within provincial boundaries. Other criteria considered are production methods, labor practices, native habitat preservation, animal welfare, and on-farm energy use.

Lori Stahlbrand, the founder and president of Local Food Plus, found that the key to shifting institutional food service contractors to buying local sustainable food was to get their customers (such as universities) to demand that a percentage of their food come from local sustainable farmers and processors.

"We get better results working with big food service companies if the clients demand it," she told the Farm to Cafeteria conference in Detroit in May 2010. "Institutions can provide large-scale, stable markets for local sustainable food."

The few big corporate food service companies that dominate institutional food procurement in North America are not going to pioneer offering local sustainable (sometimes more expensive) local food if there isn't a strong market for it.

Local Food Plus is partnering with the University of Toronto to bring local sustainable food to its 70,000 students. Food service contractors agreed to spend 10% of the annual dollar value of food purchased on local sustainable food, with a 5% increase each year. By the end of the 2010–2011 school year, this should reach 25%.

But isn't such an arrangement in violation of the North American Free Trade Agreement (NAFTA), the Canadian Agreement on Internal Trade (AIT), and the Canadian Trade, Investment and Labor Mobility Agreement (TILMA) that prohibit protectionist policies?

According to a legal review requested by the Land Conservancy, the answer is "No": "There is simply no basis for impugning the validity of a local food procurement policy under either international or domestic trade rules. In the exceedingly unlikely event that such a policy was challenged under AIT/TILMA rules, that complaint would surely fail."[8]

Lori Stahlbrand backs that up from her experience setting up local procurement agreements for Local Food Plus: "For every argument that local procurement is blocked by trade agreements there's an answer. These agreements don't have to block local procurement," she says.

"For example, any good being resold to the public is not covered by the AIT. Since the food purchased by food service companies is resold, it is exempt."

Slow Money As Nurture Capital for Food?

Getting off the "fast, convenient, cheap" treadmill into the softer local economic benefits of "healthy, green, fair, affordable" local food is not easy in an economic environment where competitors are willing to take every possible shortcut to the biggest bottom line. From an investor's point of view, investing in the local economy is even more difficult with the recent entry into the food market of high-risk, high-return investors such as private equity funds.

Enter Woody Tasch, a Massachusetts-based investor-philanthropist-activist. Never mind waiting for economic development policies to stimulate a saner approach to growing good food. Tasch wants to harness the private market with a different set of reins. City and near-urban farmers would be at the front of the line for investments under Woody Tasch's Slow Money model (sympathetic with the Slow Food movement, but organized separately). His bold goal is to have "millions of Americans contributing tens of millions of dollars a year to be invested in local food systems, seed capital for the nurture capital industry." More specifically, he'd like to see "a million Americans investing 1% of their assets in local food systems...within a decade."

Tasch sees a strong economic case for diversification of food systems away from their challenged industrial underpinnings into more sustainable, local food sources. While promising long, slow returns to his investors in the 3–6% range, he also touts the non-monetary dividends of being part of healing the earth through local food production — what he calls the ultimate hedge fund. With a background in venture capitalism for socially conscious businesses, Tasch brings a curious mix of capitalism and philanthropy to his movement to build the Slow Money Alliance to "invest as if food, farms and fertility mattered... [and] connect investors to the places where they live, creating vital relationships and new sources of capital for small food enterprises" (slowmoneyalliance.org).

His first step is building a Slow Money Alliance—a non-profit mix that starts with "convening Slow Money Institutes and other events; incubating new intermediaries; collaborating with Slow Food and other NGOs; and publishing and communications." After that, presumably, money will start flowing directly to "small food enterprises, appropriate-scale organic farming and local food systems" out of a new "nurture capital industry—entrepreneurial finance supporting soil fertility, carrying capacity, sense of place, cultural and ecological diversity, and nonviolence." The "new intermediaries" being promoted include: "tax-exempt municipal bonds dedicated to developing local food system incubators and public markets; a private foundation that is organized as an investment entity, rather than a grant-making entity (with its assets dedicated to investing in local food systems); and a fund dedicated to supporting the expansion of the CSA industry."

How soon this will translate into easily accessible investments for qualified local food enterprises remains to be seen. And for investors who worry about simply throwing their money to the good-cause winds, it's not clear how Tasch's noble goal will avoid the nasty realities of starting any small private business: illiquidity, high failure rates, and lack of financial transparency.

One way to help keep food dollars in the local economy is to educate urbanites about local food sources through visits to local farms. Restaurants dedicated to local food are often the leaders in promoting local

---

Slow Money Starts with Slow Food

Slow Food's mission:
- To defend food biodiversity.
- To safeguard the environment and the land.
- To endorse sustainable agriculture.
- To protect small producers and their communities.
- To promote the gastronomic traditions of the whole world.

Source: slowfood.com

farm produce, helping to organize "open houses" at farms to showcase their produce. In the Vancouver area, a Slow Food chapter organizes annual bike tours of farms, many of which are contracted suppliers to local restaurants. On one trip in the Fraser Valley outside Vancouver, I cycled leisurely down country roads to stop at a herb garden specialist, a cheese specialty farm-gate store, a hazelnut tree orchard, a dairy farm, and an aquaculture operation growing Coho salmon in big tanks, with the wastewater fertilizing nearby watercress beds.

Farm Folk/City Folk has regular "Feast of Fields" days where restaurants set up sampler booths at one farm and showcase local foods which are also for sale. It's a bit like a farmers market for prepared foods — you meet the farmer, the vintner, the specialty grocer and the restaurant chefs, and go home with a new appreciation for what the local region offers and where to buy it.

Conclusion

Widespread craving for local food is a genuine force in the marketplace which is only going to grow as uncertainties multiply about the security and quality of imported food. As this chapter shows, the economic spin-offs from buying local food — especially if it's organic — have the potential to save struggling farmers and stimulate multiplier spending in the local economy. Global trade in food will always be with us. Without it, much of what we eat wouldn't be available and many farmers would be out of business. Many of the regional economic benefits from the food industry are based on processing food for export. But the new passion for local food is an economic lever that has the potential to ignite the economic benefits of buying local. A better mix of local and imported food is coming back within reach — along with economic benefits to match the environmental and social ones.

9

Rebuilding the Lost Food-Producing Infrastructure

M IKE LORENTZ, owner of Lorentz Meats in Cannon Falls, Minnesota, doesn't have a lot of time for farmers markets. Literally.
It isn't worth his time: "You won't make enough money to justify being
there. It's great for a hobby, you might even break even. But you won't
turn a profit." And, he adds, "if it isn't profitable, it isn't sustainable."

Caught between the giant mechanized slaughterhouses that process
thousands of animals a day and the small farmyard operations that look
after a few dozen home-grown animals a year, Lorentz found a way to rebuild a key piece of the agricultural infrastructure that's gone missing in
recent years. He built his own 10,000-square foot processing plant, got it
certified by the USDA, and is now able to process (by hand) cattle, bison,
pigs and elk. He found a financial sweet spot: he's just large enough to
meet the US Department of Agriculture's health and safety standards
and still compete effectively. Because of his relatively small size, he's got
the flexibility to service a variety of independent niche producers, and
he's able to help them connect with retailers and wholesalers.

Smaller-scale local food production in and around cities depends
on infrastructure like Lorentz Meats. As the food industry has become
more globalized, regional food processing, warehousing and distribution infrastructure has disappeared: the local abattoirs, juice factories,
cheese-making plants and packaging plants have been replaced by large,

centralized sites. Smaller food producers just don't have the volume to work with these large operators. Plus, they are often too far away to make their services affordable. Local businesses have been pushed aside by the efficiencies of economy of scale, cheaper labor elsewhere and safety standards that could only be met by large operations. How many small abattoirs can afford to meet the standard of providing an on-site washroom for federal food inspectors?

An Illinois study on growing the economy through local food production notes that livestock and poultry producers drive great distances and experience long waits at the state's few small meat processing plants. In most cases, large processors won't even handle small lots by local producers.

As the Metro Vancouver Regional Food Strategy notes, "minimal amounts of processing, like freezing, coupled with storage, would extend the shelf life of seasonally available foods while more extensive processing facilities would create new jobs and other economic benefits."

Getting local infrastructure right is key to building local food sources and reducing the carbon footprint of our food. It starts with having land available, as well as irrigation, suppliers of seeds, tools and machinery, composting sites, warehouses, loading bays, storage lockers, freezers, processing plants — and the people with the know-how to make it all work.

Waste from agriculture and food processing also has to be dealt with if we're going to rebuild our food-producing infrastructure. At the B.C. Innovation Council in Vancouver in September 2009, Dave Eto, vice-president of the B.C. Food Producers' Association, pointed out that waste from B.C.'s meat industry has to be shipped hundreds of miles to Calgary at considerable cost. "If we don't get local waste disposal capacity, we'll lose our meat industry."

Some cities (like Detroit) still have big public markets that are thriving food hubs surrounded by warehouses, processors and storage. Detroit even has a slaughterhouse at the Eastern Market. Having that hub in place is a big plus: "we are becoming one of the attractions for people wanting to get into urban agriculture," said Eastern Market Corp. President Dan Carmody at the Detroit Farm to Cafeteria conference in May 2010.

Infrastructure We Don't Need:
Does It Have to Be This Complicated?

"I can produce a gallon of milk from my barn for about $2.40 in hay, grain, amortized goat costs, and a tiny chunk of my mortgage payment," says Sharon Astyk, a writer, teacher and small farmer living in rural upstate New York. "Since my milk is mostly grass during the summer, that means with a reasonable markup, I could produce a gallon of milk for $3.50, and make a fair profit. That's not too bad—my local Stewarts is advertising milk for $3.80 per gallon, so I could sell a few gallons to my neighbors and offset some feed costs, without costing them more, maybe even save them some pennies. It also goes without saying that my goat's milk tastes better (sorry, but it does, and everyone thinks so), is organic, probably came from animals with better lives, and would be fresher than the milk in the store.

"My friend Judy, who runs a dairy, observes that it costs $9 for her to produce a gallon of goat's milk. Now why the difference? Why does it cost her $9, which isn't even remotely competitive and me $2.40? Well the main difference is that she had to get set up to sell her goat's milk. She had to put in a bulk tank, build a barn to specifications, put in the second septic system between the milk room and the barn septic, add restroom facilities (even though her house bathroom is three steps away), and pay $16,000 for a pasteurizer.

"As I'm adding up my costs, I don't have to count any of those things. I can amortize my steel milking pail and the quart mason jars I use, but that won't add but pennies. I can pasteurize my milk—after all, raising milk to a particular temperature and holding it there for a couple of minutes isn't rocket science, and a $4 dairy thermometer works fine, along with a stainless steel pot (let's not even ask whether I can sell it raw).

"Of course, the big difference is that Judy can legally sell her milk, and I can't. In order to sell milk, I'd have to build the milking parlor, get the bulk tank, run power to the barn, and buy the $16K pasteurizer. Never mind that for someone milking six does, this is ridiculous overkill—them's the rules. And look, my organic milk now costs $9 gallon—and gee, isn't that elitist, to think that ordinary people can afford organic milk!?

"Now I can hear the protests—after all, all this stuff exists in the name of progress and food safety, right? Well, the problem with that is that if you need all this stuff for milk to be produced safely, you have to first explain away the fact that the French are all still alive."

Source: "Is the Local Food Movement Elitist?" by Sharon Astyk, science blogs.com, Nov. 10, 2010.

The Granville Island Public Market in Vancouver provides shared cold storage for its tenants, covered by their rent. It's an important piece of retail food infrastructure, taking up 12% of the total space in the public market.

Some new inner-city food producers are building what they need anew: Will Allen's Growing Power, Inc. in Milwaukee took over an unused warehouse for its food distribution services. In Toronto, The Stop and FoodShare are similarly inventing a new infrastructure that marries low-income issues with agriculture and food. In one project, they've transformed the historic Wychwood streetcar repair barns into the city-owned Artscape Wychwood Barns — a 60,000-square foot multifaceted community center where arts and culture, environmental leadership, heritage preservation, urban agriculture, and affordable housing are all under one roof. At The Stop Community Food Centre's Green Barn, there's a greenhouse, a sustainable food education center, a sheltered garden, an outdoor bake oven and a compost demonstration site. The

Getting healthy food out into the community: At The Stop in Toronto, low-income people drop in for food, or get food boxes sent to them.

proponents of "The Stop" see it as a first step toward a network of publicly funded community food centers where food is grown, prepared and served, especially to people living in food deserts.

Costs Can Kill

Around the edges of cities, zoning codes can be overly simplistic in banning all industrial components. Often, all value-added agricultural industries and services other than crop production are characterized as "manufacturing," which is allowed only on industrially zoned lands. In the Vancouver area, speculation on industrial land is even more rampant than on protected agricultural land, so the price of locating agricultural services and value-added industries has gone up. Allowing farmers to parcel off a limited, less productive piece of their land for a farm-related industrial use like a welding shop or warehouse would be just as useful in promoting agriculture as a blanket protection of all agricultural land. For example, allowing refrigerated storage near fields could protect the quality of food from the moment it's picked.

Competing with the economies of scale available to centralized processors is a huge challenge for smaller producers catering to local markets.

"The middle pieces are what's often missing for small farmers who want to expand their businesses," says Janie Burns, a small farm entrepreneur from Canyon County, Idaho. "We can increase our supply, and we know that there is a demand for our products, but where do we process our foods and how do we transport and store them? Right now, most of those systems are designed to accommodate large-scale producers and buyers rather than small operations."[1]

There's a simple reason that smaller, more diversified food infrastructure has left town: cost. When the Waterloo region of Ontario studied how much food consumed in the region was locally grown in 2005, it found that only a tiny fraction of the food processed in the big local processing plants was locally sourced. Only 3% of the apples that were juiced, dried or canned at Golden Town Apple Products came from the region. "There's lots of buzz about a lack of processing facilities and a need to build new infrastructure," Peter Katona, the executive director of FoodLink Waterloo, told TheTyee.ca. "Nobody's still really looked at the root cause of why we lost our processing infrastructure, which is price. Farm labor wages in Ontario, not to mention high health and safety costs, are 25% higher than US wages, and 25 times higher than Mexican wages."

Ian Walker's company, Left Coast Naturals, makes organic snack foods in Burnaby, B.C. "To sell sustainable food, if it's local, especially, it's a fairly high price, so you have a limited market that you can sell to.... When you have that cap, that means you can only sell so much. But to build the infrastructure and the equipment, you need to have more sales. It's a bit of a chicken and egg issue."[2]

He'd like to see companies and organizations sharing the capital and operational costs of processing equipment, making it more economical to produce smaller volumes.

That's exactly what's happening at places like Intervale and Prairie Crossing. The Intervale Center in Burlington, Vermont makes a variety of equipment available to farmers, including a vegetable washing station, coolers, greenhouses, tractors and hand tools. The Farm Business Development Center at Prairie Crossing provides access to top farmland and infrastructure like packing sheds, greenhouses, coolers and equipment (tractors, tillers, hand tools, etc.). This is all in addition to providing start-up farmers with mentors, business advice, and access to consumers, wholesalers and retailers.

Woodbury County, Iowa, is one of many places that provide access to a commercial kitchen for local growers. The county partnered with community stakeholders to raise $100,000 to renovate a commercial kitchen for a local food/organic restaurant so it could also process organic salsa.

Giant Food Distributors Adapting to Local Food

Well-established, existing infrastructure *can* adapt to the drive for more local food. Sysco, North America's largest food service distributor (it has $40 billion in annual revenues) is realizing that buying local is a trend that's not going away. It has been running pilot projects to figure out how to overcome the complexities of buying from smaller local suppliers.

Rethinking its traditional operating premise of "fast, convenient and cheap," Sysco is hearing from chefs, schools and hospitals that they want to know where food comes from, who produced it, and how it was produced — right down to the family farm history and types of soils and working conditions. They want food produced in harmony with nature and neighbors, and with better taste, nutrition and variety than the usual mass market fare. The new test mantra is "romance, memory and trust," a slogan Sysco worked out in collaboration with the National Good Food Network, which itself has a mandate to get more "good food" (healthy, green, fair and affordable) to more people.

Working with local farmers in a 2008 pilot project, Sysco's Grand Rapids operating subsidiary found that by adding new local products, they boosted sales by 10%. They offered local alfalfa sprouts, pesticide-free hydroponic leafy greens, and twice as many varieties of Michigan apples as before — in all, there were 18 new products from 20 producers. Six of the farm suppliers were new Sysco clients, and all the farms involved were family owned and committed to environmentally sensitive practices. Sysco was able to ramp up local sales by adding "Michigan-produced" to their order sheets, and restricting sales of a particular item to local products when they were in season.

Sysco discovered they had to physically identify the local foods so food services operators could know which products were local/sustainable. They also found it was critically important to build strong relationships and promote an understanding of good food all along the value chain — from sitting around the kitchen table with the farmers, to educating food service suppliers *and* the people who would eventually eat the food.

As a result of this pilot, Sysco got 100% of Michigan State University's food services contract. A similar Sysco project in Kansas City added 76 new local family farm suppliers.

A similar initiative to Sysco's is fellow-behemoth Walmart's October 2010 decision to double the percentage of locally grown produce it sells in the United States to 9%. In Canada, where Walmart is just getting into grocery sales, it will buy 30% of its produce locally by 2013 — or 100% if it's available. (In the United States, "local" means from within the same state.)

"No other retailer has the ability to make more of a difference than Walmart," the retailer's president and chief executive, Michael T. Duke, told the *New York Times*. "Grocery is more than half of Walmart's [$405-billion-a-year] business."[3] Walmart is also spending $1 billion worldwide to help build the infrastructure necessary to achieve these goals. One of Walmart's goals is to save money by reducing waste and shortening supply chains — which should mean less spoiled food, longer shelf lives, and more profit for everyone. Walmart, too, is getting ready for higher oil prices.

While Walmart's shift to local food will certainly add business for smaller, more sustainable (but not necessarily organic) farms, it stops short of generating all the wonderful multipliers that depend on customers' money staying in the local community. Walmart's owners didn't make it into the world's top-10 richest list by leaving money on the local table. Local farmers supplying Walmart will have to be careful not to get drawn into the cutthroat supplier competitions that characterize other Walmart supply chains.

The mystery remains as to how these giant corporations will adapt to the subtleties — and possibly higher costs — of dealing with many small, diverse local producers. Saving money from rising transportation costs may be the key.

Enter the Aggregator: Someone Has to Pull It Together

When Sysco ran its pilot projects to boost local food in its distribution business, it identified the aggregator/distributor function as a key ingredient often missing in local food supply chains. Sysco frequently relies on third party aggregators to fill orders, someone who can source, consolidate and transport loads of products, as well as handle quality assurance and assume liability. To serve a big company looking for local products from new customers, the aggregator has the difficult task of finding local growers, then collecting and gathering their new products with unconventional packaging and sizes and making them fit into Sysco's systems. Sometimes that needs to include intermediate storage and repacking.

People trying to connect schools with local farmers and suppliers have run into the same problem: "If you don't have a cooperative or a group in the community where people from the schools can meet with farmers and work out what foods are needed and how to supply them, start one. Communication is key to making Farm to School programs work," advises Linda Samel, food service director for a Missoula County Public Schools District.[4]

Joel Salatin, the self-proclaimed lunatic organic farmer from Virginia's Shenandoah Valley, bootstraps his own distribution system: "All of us are struggling with efficiencies of distribution. Individual farmers have to work together and create food clusters where we aggregate our products.

"Unfortunately very few farmers are people people, good marketers, so we bring our products and other farmers' products together for Thursday and Friday pickups. We put one Polyface invoice on top, then separate invoices for the other individual farmers underneath. The other growers pay us 3% and they're thrilled to get the check up front from us.

"In Washington, D.C. they aggregate from 30 farmers for a Wednesday 8 AM cutoff. At noon they get pizza delivery drivers to collect it all. It's aggregated in a cool room from midnight to 5 AM, then, on Thursday morning those same pizza delivery drivers take it to the doorstep of the customers."[5]

Recent advances in technology, such as the online food hubs described in Chapter 6, will provide invaluable information for setting up a local distribution infrastructure. By sourcing each other online, producers and buyers can quickly identify each others' needs and be one step closer to identifying the most efficient way to set up ongoing distribution connections.

That's how the Oklahoma Food Co-operative figured out their low-tech, low-cost delivery model. Consumers place their orders online for fresh local food. The farmers are paid immediately, letting them know what they've sold. Once a month, pre-sold products are trucked to a central warehouse where they're sorted, packaged and delivered to 38 pickup sites across the state. The 20% markup charged by the co-op, partly to consumers and partly to producers, is about a quarter of the distribution margin in mainstream food businesses. This model is being copied in Texas, Idaho, Michigan, Iowa, Ontario and elsewhere (see communityfoodenterprise.org).

Having a shared central distribution plant has also been the key for three dozen mostly African American farmers in six rural counties in Mississippi to compete effectively. In their half-million-dollar plant, the Indian Springs Farmers Association sorts, washes, packages and then ships fresh fruits and vegetables. Most of the member farmers, in one of the poorest regions in the American South, concede that if it weren't for the co-op, they wouldn't still be in business.

In Portland, Oregon, New Seasons Market (NSM), a food retailing center, partnered with an organic producer cooperative, Organically Grown Company (OGC), to create a distribution system that benefits both organizations. The produce buyer for NSM contracts OGC to guarantee supply for the market's retail stores. They, in turn, generate demand for the cooperative's products. This has allowed farmers to scale up their production and create commercially viable crops for retail and direct sales. Consolidating transportation through this partnership also reduces costs.

In Chicago, FamilyFarmed.org got a clear message from local farmers that they didn't want to make cold calls on buyers, and the buyers wanted an easy way to connect with farmers. So in 2004, the organization Sustain launched the first Local Organic Trade Show with 50 farmers and hundreds of trade buyers showing up. The next year they added a consumer show. It has evolved into the FamilyFarmed EXPO, one of the largest annual local food events in the Midwest. Producers, distributors, retailers, restaurants and consumers network, learn from each other, and build marketing relationships (see familyfarmed.org).

In some places, particularly in the UK, local producer-buyer food hubs — "the missing middle of the local food infrastructure" — provide a variety of mixes of warehousing, distribution, packaging and marketing. One example is the Hornbeam in northeast London. It is a community café and environment center that houses a market for local sustainably grown food, a vegetarian café, a vegetable box enterprise, a fruit-picking project, and workshops and events. It's organized and run by its users, all of whom are volunteers (see hornbeam.org).

Home Delivery Services
Provide Customized Infrastructure

Local food home delivery services can add new dimensions to food distribution infrastructure: they can help cities to reduce traffic congestion and energy costs and meet their greenhouse gas emission reduction targets. David Van Seters is the former CEO of Sustainable Produce Urban Delivery (SPUD), a Vancouver-based company that sources local food, takes weekly online orders, and delivers to homes in Vancouver, Victoria, Calgary, Seattle, Portland, San Francisco and Los Angeles. Van Seters is a bright-eyed, visionary former accountant determined to make his difficult business work for himself, his customers and the planet.

"Growing more local food is only part of the solution to reducing food's carbon footprint," he says. "All our produce is local and 50% of it is organic. But getting that food to the consumer with a lower carbon footprint is a challenge if you have everyone driving to the local retail food store." A stickler for statistics and details, Van Seters has calculated that his trucks provide a 33% carbon footprint reduction compared to individual customers each driving their car to a grocery store.

His company buys direct from growers and ships directly to consumer's homes. It gives his customers the most direct connection to the farmer short of buying at the farmer's gate or at a farmers market. In each city, he has a distribution center where trucks from farms bring food to teams of workers who mix a variety of foods into custom delivery boxes that get driven to each household. Every box has a receipt with a message to the customer stating how many miles the food in it has traveled.

"When you add up the carbon footprint of trips to the store, the heating, lighting and refrigeration in grocery stores, the plastic bags, the hundreds of thousands of advertising flyers they mail out, our energy use per unit of sales is half that of a grocery store. As prices of fuel go up and carbon footprint becomes more of a factor, we benefit."

As regions get serious about reinventing infrastructure to meet hugely challenging greenhouse gas emission targets many have embraced, they'll be looking for local carbon offsets and carbon credits that could come from low-carbon operations like SPUD.

However, home delivery of local organic food runs up against the same barrier challenging other local food infrastructure: cost. No matter how much SPUD consumers like home delivery and local, organic food, they don't want to pay one penny more.

"Marketing in the food industry is all about price. Our products are fresher—they're all bought only when we get an order. We only buy bread when someone orders it. Nothing sits on a shelf. If we could price per nutrient we'd be an absolute bargain."[6]

People Too: Knowledge Has to Grow

Vanishing small farms and the farmers that go with them are leaving a knowledge gap that has to be filled if local food production is going to grow. An Illinois report sums it up: "Not only are there fewer Illinois farmers with the knowledge and skills required to produce diversified crops than there once were, integrated systems of technical support, mentoring and teaching do not exist in sufficient quantity to help farmers seriously consider these options."[7]

Currently, urban growers are typically low-paid and are often young people lacking business and marketing skills. Milwaukee-based Growing Power is one of many organizations trying to change that by educating urban farmers through local, national and international classes and workshops.

The Internet has done wonders for educating new and struggling farmers, with instant answers to technical questions, online courses, listserves and webinars on current issues. The Planning for Agriculture and Food Network (PAFN, planning-for-agriculture-and-food-network-pafn@googlegroups.com) is a great example.

But there also has to be ongoing research: the latest local pest and how to control it, new varieties, heritage seed preservation, and many other farming issues need researched, local solutions. In many places, the public agencies that used to produce this vital information have been cut back or cut out. Now, more research is being done inside agricultural corporate conglomerates and in corporately financed university projects.

The Intervale Center in Burlington, Vermont provides the full gamut of expertise needed by new farmers through its Farm Incubator Program.

Started in 1995, it gives small, organic farmers subsidized land lease rates and access to equipment and mentoring. "The Intervale is an incredible platform for young aspiring farmers to take a risk and launch an enterprise, and when they emerge from incubator status they are prepared to pay market rates to continue," observes Glenn McRae, the Center's executive director. "It has proven to be a great model for establishing viable sustainable organic farm enterprises" (communityfoodenterprise.org).

A newer Intervale program, Success on Farms, uses the same model outside the Center. Funded by the Vermont Housing and Conservation Board, it provides free, customized business planning and technical support services for growing farms throughout northern Vermont. The model has been successfully copied at Prairie Crossing's Farmer Business Development Center in Grayslake, Illinois.

In Canada, the McVean New Farmers project in the city of Brampton, Ontario, a partnership between Toronto and Region Conservation (TRCA) and FarmStart, is typical of a new wave of agricultural education aimed at a sustainable healthy and regional food supply that includes urban and near-urban farms. Kwantlen Polytechnic University in Richmond, B.C., uses "incubator farmland" donated by the municipality for a one-year training program with an urban, "human-scale" agriculture focus. Kent Mullinix, the university's Director of Sustainable Agriculture and Food Security, wants to see similar courses running all over the province. Nearby University of B.C. has a comparable eight-month Sowing Seeds sustainable agriculture practicum.

Lessons from Cuba: Share the Research

Economic desperation followed the disappearance of Russian oil money from Cuba in 1990. What came next was an agricultural revolution that was the result of a deliberate, integrated infrastructure buildup orchestrated by the government. It's fascinating and instructive to hear the former head of the Havana Ministry of Agriculture, González Novo, describe urban agriculture in exactly the terms used by locavores in the non-socialist world: "Production in the community, by the community, for the community...a way to bring producers and consumers closer together...to achieve a steady supply of fresh, healthy and varied products directly from the production site to the consumers."[8]

In 1991, the Havana city government exhorted people to use every available plot of land to grow food. They did — and they also found land to raise poultry, small cattle and pigs. A federal body identified best practices in various aspects of growing food (organically, out of necessity) and shared them with the country's 169 municipalities. The result is that produce from the urban farm is now cheaper than imports from bigger, rural farms.

Cuba's experience was the world's first nationwide coordinated urban agriculture program; it integrates access to land, extension services, research and technology, new supply stores for small farmers, and new marketing and selling organizations for urban producers.

Lessons from Cuba have to be tempered by the fact that Cuba's conversion to largely organic food self-sufficiency was driven by factors unique to that country: an oil-scarcity crisis, a strong dictatorial central government, and a US-backed blockade of many imports. In spite of all that, Cuba still remains a beacon in the world for its coordinated approach and impressive results. A study of 42 urban gardens in Havana found the average garden produced 60% of its household's produce needs, with savings from eating and selling food from these gardens equivalent to 40% of the average household salary.

10

Less "Waste," More Soil

Тhink of that bit of cheese that went moldy in the fridge before you could eat it. It either hardened up into a dry lump, or it grew a blue-gray coat of fuzz that screamed: "throw me out, now!" Not being a recommended addition to a rodent-free compost pile, it went into the garbage. Now, think of the embodied energy — all the handling, transportation and resources — that went into getting that piece of cheese into the drawer in your refrigerator. A cow somewhere had to be raised, fed, housed and milked to start that little lump on its journey. Its milk had to be cooled and shipped in a refrigerated truck or train to a cheese processor. There, it demanded more roofs, heating, cooling and handling; then it had to be packed and shipped to a central warehouse; then it went into another truck to the retail store; then you took it home in a car, or perhaps a bus. Then it had to be stored in your refrigerator that worked for days to convert electricity to cool air to shepherd that lump of energized milk into the state where it qualified as garbage. Even after all that, your cheese still requires more energy. It will be dumped into the back of another truck and rumbled off to a big compost pile or maybe an incinerator. Or, it may end up in a landfill where it will rot and vaporize into methane, a deadly greenhouse gas. That bit of cheese was only one tiny piece of a massive food-wasting frenzy that's embodied in rich-world food habits — a piece so hard to make, and so massively wasteful

133

to throw away. We all do this every day without thinking. Well, maybe we wince a bit.

Estimates of food waste in the food systems of the developed world are as varied and hard to trust as they are to ignore. Some examples: The Vancouver Food Policy Council estimates that 50% (1.8 million tons) of fresh food (mostly vegetables) "disappears" in Metro Vancouver before it reaches the consumer. A Canadian study in 2007 estimated that 38% of food available for retail sale was wasted.

One US study from the EPA says that between 4–10% of food purchased becomes waste before ever reaching a plate. Another says Americans throw away more than 25% of the unprepared food they buy, which comes to about 48 million tons of food waste each year. Two thirds of the losses were from fresh fruits and vegetables, fluid milk, grain products, and sweeteners (mostly sugar and high-fructose corn syrup). Some of these losses can't be avoided: diseased animals at the slaughterhouse, moldy bread in grocery stores, partly eaten entrees at restaurants. Many could be, though — with more frequent and efficient food recovery efforts. That would include charitable services that send trucks around to pick up marginal but still edible food for redistribution to social service agencies. Even if only 5% of all the edible wasted food were recovered, it would be enough for a day's food for 4 million people in the United States.

In Britain, one third of all food purchased is thrown away. One UK agency calculated that if we all stopped wasting food that could have been eaten, the CO_2 impact would be the equivalent of taking one out of every four cars off the road. And it's not just good food that's going to waste. Money is also being wasted — about $1,100 a year per family. Food is also a major contributor to every city's garbage pile: roughly 30% of all solid wastes are related to food consumption, half of it from food packaging.

Regardless of which figures you believe, a lot of food is wasted. Some waste is unavoidable, like rotten potatoes in a farmer's flooded field, but much waste is unnecessary, like misshapen carrots not deemed saleable only because of their shape or size, or food that goes bad in the fridge because too much was stupidly bought at a bulk discount sale.

UK Lessons in Cutting Waste

It's always better to prevent food waste than to find ways of disposing of it intelligently through better separating and composting. Wasting less automatically increases local food supplies. It is a bright spot on the food horizon that we can soon expect to see local food supplies increase on a massive scale. As a result of Walmart's new sustainability and buy-local initiatives, Walmart has stated that by the end of 2015 it will reduce food waste in emerging-market stores by 15%, and in other stores by 10%.

Food packaging waste is one cost that is ripe for cutting. The cost of excess packaging doesn't just impact retailers. It also adds greenhouse gas emissions and loads up urban waste disposal systems that everyone has to pay for. But defining "excess" is difficult. Grocery distributors point out that a shrink wrap around a cucumber adds four days to the shelf life of that cucumber. Eliminating that plastic would save some packaging waste, but it would also add food waste and greenhouse gas emissions.

In the UK, a fifth of household waste is packaging, and more than half of that comes from groceries. In 2010 in the UK, 29 major food retailers signed the Courtauld Commitment phase 2, pledging to improve on earlier successes in stopping the growth of packaging. That was part of their voluntary agreement in the 2005 Courtauld Commitment to improve resource efficiency and reduce the carbon and wider environmental impact of the grocery retail sector.

Between 2005 and 2009, they saved enough waste to fill "a queue of refuse trucks, bumper-to-bumper, stretching from Southampton to Newcastle [280 miles]." Now they plan to reduce the carbon impact of grocery packaging by 10%, reduce household food and drink wastes by 4%, and reduce solid and liquid wastes in the grocery supply chain by 5% by 2012.

The same UK organization works with individual companies to achieve these goals. Waste and Resources Action Programme (WRAP) did a waste prevention review at one of Europe's leading suppliers of frozen foods (apetito). It resulted in hooking up the company with an anaerobic digestion (AD) plant near its Trowbridge headquarters. The company now diverts all its food waste — meat, pastry and wet waste —

to AD treatment. In addition, apetito converted single-use cardboard packaging for food sent to hospitals and nursing home clients to recyclable crates. Not only are they reusable, but now, there's less damaged food because the new crates protect the food better (see wrap.org.uk).

Households waste almost twice as much food as food suppliers. An estimated 8.3 million tonnes of food is thrown away by households in the UK every year. WRAP also operates a very sleek website (lovefood hatewaste.com) to help educate consumers about how to avoid wasting food.

The Love Food Hate Waste campaign teaches better planning, better storage, and better understanding of food date labels. How many people know that "best before" dates tell us when the food will lose its peak quality but still be safe to eat? Potato chips, for example, might just be soft after that date; bread might be hard, but still provide nutrition. "Use by" dates are most important for foods that are highly perishable (e.g., meat pies) and thus present health risks.

David Van Seters of SPUD, the online order-and-delivery service discussed in the last chapter, points to the inherent waste required to stimulate higher sales in grocery stores. "Much of the food stacked up in grocery stores is decoration," he says. "There's a saying in the business: 'Stack it high and watch them fly.' People are less likely to buy food off a shelf with only a few items on it. So a lot of produce in those stores gets thrown away." By contrast, David is able to tailor his supplies to orders coming in, resulting in much less waste.

Recovering Wasted Food for Eating

There is an enormous amount of food that passes through the hands of a retail or wholesale distributor and ends up on a fast track to the garbage while it's still edible. More than a quarter of all our food supplies are lost by food services and consumers.

Although virtually every major modern city has a food bank that collects packaged foods and redistributes them, it's the unpackaged perishables that present the real challenges. Sadly, these are the very foods — fruits, vegetables and dairy — that usually have far more nutritional value than prepared, preserved and packaged foods. Hospitals, hotels and restaurants often have unexposed food left over after preparing what they need. Without any alternative, they throw it out. Lots of cities have food-gathering services that rescue this food and deliver it to needy people, but the logistics can be daunting.

"We pick up leftovers from hospitals, hotels, movie caterers, farmers markets and Starbucks stores," says Vancouver Food Bank CEO Cheryl Carline. "There's lots of good food we could be gathering if we had more refrigerated trucks and more warehouse space."

Another Vancouver organization, Quest Outreach Society, is British Columbia's largest food exchange program. It sends trucks around the city to collect bruised, blemished or dented packaged food, overstock, and mislabeled or near-expired products that would otherwise go to waste. Volunteers redistribute this food to those in need through a super-discount food store where prices are a third of normal grocery stores. Customers have to be referred by community centers, churches or social service agencies.

Farmers, too, lack alternatives for distributing excess food. In Metro Vancouver, as in many cities, there aren't a lot of processing options for cosmetically inferior or second grade produce. Where there are, farmers don't know about them or don't use them.

Online free classified sites are an excellent tool for reducing waste because they can link suppliers and buyers or charitable recipients. These sites help with food rescue by providing a venue for grocers, hotels, restaurants and even backyard gardeners with food they can't use to post what they have, while charities and organizations providing food to hungry people can post what they need. They also help farmers find buyers for food that otherwise would be composted.

Shared Harvest (sharedharvest.ca) is a good example of an online site with free ads for farmers, processors, grocers, distributors and the public (see Chapter 9 for more on foodhubs). It launched across Canada and the United States in late 2010. Timeliness is its strength for farmers. "If I can't find a market for the crop in a reasonable timeframe, the crop simply goes to the compost," says Abbotsford, B.C. farmer Andrew Arkesteyn-Vogler. "It is sad to see good quality fresh crops being taken out of the food supply simply because I don't have the time to find a

Picking Up Fallen Fruit

An artists' collective in Los Angeles has figured out a way to avoid wasting fruit in cities by taking fruit-sharing to a new level of sophistication (see fallenfruit.org). They've mapped neighborhoods in Los Angeles—and triggered similar maps in cities around the world—showing where anyone can find and harvest publicly available fruit. They even help homeowners plant "perimeter trees" strategically located to provide some branches that hang over the sidewalk for public access. The trees are cared for by the private owner; the public gets a piece. Nothing gets wasted.

spring: guavas, cactus
summer: apples, bananas, figs, grapes,
        nectarines, peaches, plums
fall: carob, persimmons, walnuts
winter: passionfruit, pomegranates
year-round: avocados, lemons, limes,
            oranges

take only what you need
say "hi" to strangers
share your food
take a friend
go by foot

NORTH

Credit: www.fallenfruit.org

FALLEN FRUIT OF ECHO PARK

Fallen Fruit, Echo Lake, Los Angeles: Map shows fruit available for public picking.

buyer. Shared Harvest helps me find that buyer!" Websites like these help quantify the gaps in the local food system infrastructure by revealing business opportunities for waste reduction.

Urban Food Scrap Composting Has Challenges

So-called food "waste" is a valuable resource in disguise — as is all "waste" when you consider that natural systems have no "waste" that isn't a resource for another cycle in the system. Food leftovers make up the bulk of the third to half of all household garbage that could be composted back into soil.

Returning composted food leftovers back to the soil is the ultimate "natural" solution, but in urban areas, it's an endeavor fraught with practical difficulties. It's hard to pick up food waste house-to-house and keep rats and pests away from it as it sits on the curbside. It's hard to keep out uncompostable plastics such as plastic bags, containers and other random undesirables that get into it. Food waste takes up a lot of space and can be smelly to process, and the resulting compost can have micro-impurities and other contaminants mixed in. For the purposes of making compost, gathering food waste only from restaurants and institutional kitchens is easier than going house-to-house, and it delivers more predictable content.

In many areas, the volumes of compost created are just too big. Farmers can only use so much. Some states use it to shore up the edges of highways, where it makes good bedding soil for stabilizing vegetation. International Composting Corporation in Nanaimo on Vancouver Island, B.C. tried to screen, bag and sell municipal compost in home improvement stores (under the R-Earth brand), but it was too difficult to orchestrate and they had to give up on it. Now they're doing bulk pickup sales and biogas production.

Some cities, like Modesto, California, have figured out a way to package and sell their compost. In Modesto, you can buy bags of "Mo-gro Pro" and "Mo-gro Magic" at the Senior Citizens Center. The composts include food waste and biosolids and are advertised as suitable for vegetable gardens.

Turning Food Waste into Biogas

Food waste buried in the landfill doesn't decompose the way it does in the open air; it does so much more slowly, eventually being converted into methane, which can be either a deadly greenhouse gas or a valuable source of fuel — if it can be captured. The United States has about 540 landfill gas energy projects that reclaim this methane, providing enough megawatts to power the equivalent of almost a million homes.

In Europe, biodegradable waste is being forced out of landfills. A European Union directive requires biodegradable waste going to landfills to be reduced to 75% of 1995 levels by 2010, and to 35% of 1995 levels by 2020.

Using food for generating biogas is common in Europe, and much simpler than trucking compost around. Separating food wastes from the rest of the garbage stream and creating methane from it in a digester makes economic sense; according to a Swedish study, biogas that comes from food waste produces 20 times more energy than is used in collecting the waste.

A pilot project in Los Angeles found that the value of biogas produced from anaerobic digestion of food waste was greater than the costs of processing and disposing of food waste. They concluded that biogas production from food waste makes good business sense.

The British food retailer Sainsbury's has started sending all its food waste from its Scottish stores to a biofuel refinery plant in Motherwell where it is converted into fuel for generating electricity. They've worked out that each ton of food waste diverted from landfill by Sainsbury's will generate enough power for 500 homes.

In the United States, more than 500 wastewater treatment plants, mostly large ones, operate anaerobic digesters, using their heat and biogas to operate the plants. Municipal engineers are looking at ways to build anaerobic co-digesters to treat sewage sludge and food waste together.

Just Grind It Up and Flush It?

For people in multi-family buildings, a food waste disposer under the sink (a.k.a. InSinkErator, garburator) is an easy way to divert food waste from a landfill — just flick a switch, grind it up, and flush it down the drain. In the United States, an estimated 60 million residential and half a million commercial food waste disposers are in daily use, diverting millions of tons of food scraps from garbage trucks and landfills. But breaking down their costs and environmental impacts is complicated. On one hand, if food waste is otherwise destined for a landfill — where it costs money to truck it to a dump, and it creates uncaptured methane — disposers make sense. A British study found that food waste disposers were cost-effective, convenient and hygienic, costing less and having a smaller global warming potential than curbside collection for centralized composting or landfill. As a result, Worcestershire County's "Sink Your Waste" initiative is directly subsidizing disposer installation as the preferred alternative to curbside collection.

In-home food waste disposers also make sense if the sewage treatment plant where the slurry ends up is generating biogas with the waste. In 2008, Stockholm lifted surcharges and restrictions on the use of disposers, the better to tap the biogas-producing potential of food wastes while at the same time using existing infrastructure.

On the other hand, however, if a landfill is tapping into its methane for power generation, adding food waste as a fuel source to the landfill can be a better alternative than sending it through a sewage treatment plant via your under-sink disposer. (That's not taking into account the cost of trucking these water-loaded wastes to a landfill, or the shrinking number of landfills.)

But, when ground-up, flushed food waste flows into a sewage treatment that *isn't* capturing energy or treating sewage beyond a primary level (filtering out the lumps), the extra organic carbon can add oxygen-consuming nutrients to the receiving rivers, lakes and oceans, with detrimental effects on ecosystems and fish stocks. However, in treatment plants that rely on bacterial decomposition as part of the cleaning process, the added organic carbon from food waste supplies an inexpensive and continuous source of carbon.

With all those variables at play, it's hard to give a definitive thumbs-up or down to under-the-sink food disposers. Given the trends in more biogas generation from sewage, fewer landfills, and escalating costs of trucking as fuel costs rise, under-the-sink disposers could well increase in popularity.

Composting Lessons at Milwaukee's Growing Power, Inc.

In Milwaukee, Will Allen's Growing Power, Inc. has a neighborhood composting operation that helps them grow healthy plants without fertilizers. Will Allen, 60, is a 6-foot 7-inch former professional basketball player and sales executive for Proctor and Gamble and KFC—who can't keep his hands out of the dirt.

"I'm a farmer first," he tells a weekend class of 80 people who are crammed into one of his 14 greenhouses in a working class neighborhood of Milwaukee on a freezing January morning. They're paying $150/day for a weekend course at the epicenter of the North American urban agriculture explosion. Allen has biceps the size of tree trunks hanging out of his cut-off hoody. Rocking back and forth to shift the weight on his battered knees, he strokes and pokes the moist black soil swarming with red wriggler worms as he repeats his lessons.

"They taught me at Proctor and Gamble that you have to hear something five times before you remember it. So, let's go over it again," he shouts. "What's the proper mix of nitrogen and carbon for healthy compost?"

"75% carbon, 25% nitrogen!" the group replies, enthusiastically.

"It's all about the soil," says Allen. He's a zealot about building healthy soil, seeing it as the foundation of high-value produce. He has sourced an unlimited supply of brewery mash from a nearby brewer, along with grocery produce that's bruised or past its "best before" date, wood chips to get fungus growing, old coffee grounds, cardboard and much else that is free and organic. In a ramshackle open area behind the greenhouses, volunteers and staff assemble composting bins out of old pallets; they pitchfork ingredients out of big separate piles into the pallet containers. Here's the lesson: Start with a layer of carbon for aeration—straw, cardboard, wood chips. Pile on some nitrogen—coffee grounds, old vegetables, brewery mash. Tamp it down by climbing onto the pile. Keep a rough eye on the mix: 75% carbon, 25% nitrogen, or 50:50 in the cold winter. Nobody's measuring precisely. Keep doing it until the bin is full. Leave for six months and let it cook to 120–150 degrees.

Composting 101: Workers at Growing Power, Inc. in Milwaukee demonstrate how simple it can be: Turn some pallets on end, wire them together, pile in the sawdust, straw and food scraps, stomp on it, turn regularly.

Later stir it up, then move it to another container and add layers of worms, leave it for another 3–4 months, keeping it moist, "like a mudball." Two feet of wood chips over raw compost will smother the offensive and dangerous smells of ammonia.

After three months, throw some food scraps on burlap on the top of the heap of worm-infested compost bins to attract the worms to the top. Screen them off with a 16-mesh screen, and you're left with a motherlode of worm castings and a bunch of worms ready to tuck into their next big load of freshly made compost. The castings sell for $2 a pound, or $4 for a plastic-wrapped bag the size of a small paperback book.

To make soil that isn't too rich, Allen adds ground-up coconut (instead of peat moss) and worm castings. The worm castings also go into porous cloth bags that steep 1–2 days in pails to make a "compost tea" that works as an organic fertilizer or dilutes 20:1 to make a spray-on fungicide and pesticide.

Do-It-Yourself in the Community

The simplest solution to recycling food waste is to treat it at home in a backyard composter. Like any environmental service that requires an infrastructure, composting is likely to be more cost-effective if it is decentralized. That's why many municipalities offer backyard composting bins at very low cost. But they only work where there's room for them.

Not everyone has a backyard. At McGill University, dedicated students get around this by strapping their compost pails to their bike racks and cycling them over to the university garden's compost pile. In Windermere High School in Vancouver, students can get physical education credits for riding their bikes and trailers to pick up compost from nearby elementary schools and seniors' centers and bring it back to their school garden.

Food waste can also be "treated" at home by feeding it to animals. Although few homes in North American cities have backyard livestock — or are even allowed to have any — where it is possible, kitchen scraps make great animal feed. One of the reasons pork is so popular in food-stressed Cuba is that pigs can feed off garbage. A chicken can consume approximately nine pounds of kitchen garbage a month. The municipality of Deist in Flanders, Belgium, gave 2,000 households a gift of three chickens each as an economic solution to the costly problem of recycling biodegradable trash.

How Cities Use Human Waste to Grow Food

One of the key lessons I learned from Will Allen's workshop is that good food comes from healthy soil — and that healthy soil has to be constantly replenished with nutrients. With that in mind, it's impossible to overlook the potential of the nutrients in human waste (urine and feces) to contribute to growing local food. Human waste is a vast, constant, dispersed source of valuable nutrients, present wherever there are people, with a long history of feeding plants and animals — except recently, in the developed world.

Most cities in the world design their waste systems to dispose of human excreta, not to recycle it, although recycling has been the habit in

China for millennia. Gennevilliers, across the river from Clichy, France, used to cultivate crops from sewage waste seeping in sandy soil. While at first greeted with skepticism, the produce from these lands was so full of nutrients that it was soon in demand from the top restaurants in Paris. They stopped doing it in 1980 due to rising land values.

Production of fish and, to a lesser extent, water vegetables (macro-phytes) in ponds fertilized by human waste has long been, and continues to be, practiced in many countries in Asia (India, Thailand, Indonesia, Vietnam, Taiwan, China), and in Israel and Africa.

Some of these ponds can produce up to six tons of fish per hectare per year. The East Calcutta Wetlands, consisting of 30 square kilometers of fish ponds, raises tilapia and carp in the world's largest sewage-fed fish production site. The Wetlands reportedly produce 22 tons of fish per day, treat 150 million gallons of Calcutta's wastewater and supply 10–15% of the fish consumed in Calcutta.

This kind of aquaculture is an achingly obvious way to treat waste and provide food for the city. Most importantly for the developing world, this relatively simple technology is inexpensive to construct and maintain.

Today's conventional sewage treatment plants in industrial countries mix industrial and domestic waste, which compromises the quality of the water coming out of them. Industrial wastewater can include every-thing from PCBs, pesticides, dioxins, heavy metals, asbestos, petroleum products and industrial solvents, many of which are linked to cancer and reproductive abnormalities. While some chemicals can be removed in treatment, enough remain to turn people off to the use of biosolids from treated sewage sludge for food production.

Sending sewage into waste stabilization ponds, where it is filtered from pond to pond over a few weeks, can produce safe irrigation water 1,000 times cleaner than what comes out of a conventional treatment plant. The downside is that these ponds require a lot more space than conventional sewage treatment, even though they cost about a quarter as much. Some industries are mimicking, at a smaller scale, the large and successful waste stabilization wetland in Calcutta that raises fish, processes waste and provides nutrient-rich irrigation water for farmers.

Industrial operators use open treatment ponds in garden-like settings to bypass sewage treatment plants and save costs.

Plants Like Urine

Human waste is where the remains of all the food we eat ends up. If we looked at all that waste a bit differently, we would realize that it is an incredible resource for a critical and dwindling element: phosphate.

All living things need phosphates. Humans get theirs from mined phosphate that goes into fertilizers. Most of the world's phosphate, of which 90% is used for food production, is in China and the Western Sahara. Just five nations control over 90% of the world's high-grade phosphorus, including China, the United States and Morocco. China's phosphate is protected behind a 135% export tariff. Currently, it is estimated that there is only enough phosphate left to be mined for a 50–100 year supply. The United States, the world's fourth largest repository, only has a 25-year supply.

Europe and India import all their phosphate. Production of phosphorus is expected to peak in 2034 and, unlike oil, there is no known substitute. Costs are already starting to rise because of transportation (oil) costs and growing expenses for extracting and refining lower-quality phosphorus.

As cheap fertilizer increasingly becomes a thing of the past, attention is turning to urine, which can be combined with organic sources like manure, feces and food waste to essentially replace the need for mined phosphate rock. All human settlements in all countries of the world have a urine surplus. Urine is sterile (it's even safe to drink), and it contains the key nutrients plants need — phosphorus, nitrogen and potassium — in the correct ratio. The World Health Organization already has guidelines for the safe use of urine as a fertilizer.

In a few places in Europe, urine is being separated experimentally as a way to save energy and water in sewage treatment; despite making up only 1% of the volume of wastewater, urine contributes about 80% of the nitrogen and 45% of the phosphate found in wastewater. By using "urine diversion" to get the heavy, sterile, productive urine away from pathogen-rich feces, it can be put to use as a fertilizer.

In Sweden, more than 135,000 urine-diverting toilets have been installed since 1990 — mostly in remote vacation homes. But experiments are ongoing in urban locations. Urine collected at the Cantonal Library in Liestal, Switzerland, using Swiss-designed NoMix toilets (men: sit down!), has been used to produce 20–30 liters a week of a pollutant-free liquid fertilizer ("Urevit") licensed by the Federal Office for Agriculture.

Although farmers are often very concerned about the micropollutants in urine (hormones and pharmaceuticals), there are some indications that this obstacle can be overcome. In the Netherlands, engineers are precipitating ammonium magnesium phosphate fertilizer out of stored urine at a treatment plant. Denmark has a urine separation project that works well enough that an organic vegetable farming collective called the Svanholm Gods is using it as fertilizer. A Vancouver-based company, Ostara Nutrient Recovery Technologies, Inc., has plants running in Edmonton, Portland, Philadelphia and London that extract phosphorus from wastewater and turn it into dry pellets that are used as fertilizer (see ostara.com).

After animal wastes on farms, cities are where the next-biggest supply of recycled phosphorus is, and where water and energy costs for traditional treatment are highest. These experiments are bound to continue, given the big upside of water and energy savings and phosphate recovery. And yes, men in the pilot projects really do accept sitting to pee!

Odorless, dry composting toilets work well to recycle human waste in individual homes; surprisingly, several years of waste can accumulate before these toilets need to be cleaned out. But they're not cheap — ranging from $1,000 to $6,000 per unit — and they require some ongoing maintenance. But the end product contains none of the detergents, solvents or cleaning products that sometimes contaminate mixed sewage, so it can be safely used for fertilizer.

There are many other alternatives out there. Where space is not an issue, waste can be diverted into (dedicated, artificially created) wetland ponds. In cities, waste collected from low-flush toilets could be used in biogas digesters to produce methane for powering buildings.

Treated human waste that is re-used as an energy source benefits food production as a whole by reducing the demand for biofuels made from grains and corn.

The Bekkelaget sewage treatment plant, which handles waste from 250,000 residents of Oslo, Norway, ferments sewage sludge to make a methane biofuel that's used to fuel 80 city buses. Oslo's engineers have figured out that if they also tapped Oslo's second waste treatment plant and added biofuels made from food waste, they could fuel all of Oslo's 350–400 buses. Even though it's 15% more expensive to buy and operate the biofuel-powered buses, compared to diesel, they're carbon neutral, emit 78% less nitrogen oxide, produce almost no fine particulates, and they're 92% less noisy. Those benefits are likely to encourage more cities to start using human waste in ways that lighten the demand for field-based biofuels.

Worms Work Overtime to Eat Food Waste

I was first educated about worms by my children's grade 10 ecology teacher, Mr. Raoul. To get the kids' attention, he loved eating live worms in front of the class. At the back of the class, pails of worms silently munched down food waste, generating a high-quality organic fertilizer through their slimy digestive tracts. In the garden, worms make the ground friable, help it to retain moisture, and provide it with nutrients. Compared to "normal" soil, worm castings have five times the available nitrogen, 7 times the phosphorus, 3 times the magnesium, 11 times the potassium, and 1½ times the calcium. (That's twice the amount of nitrogen needed for optimal growth; 7 times the phosphorus and potassium.) Worms could be a big ally in treating food waste and growing food in cities. In Hobart, Tasmania, the city sells worms to residents as part of its recycling program.

Having worms in your compost bin speeds up the creation of beautiful rich, black compost. Worms eat half their weight in food each day, so one pound of worms will eat half a pound of food scraps daily. The Kingdome Stadium in Seattle, Washington, used to feed a third of the stadium's food waste to 18,000 worms in 12 containers. They had no problems with odors or pests, and used the worm castings on the Kingdome's flower beds.

In Eugene, the University of Oregon organic gardening program teamed up with the university's grounds crew in 1994 on a vermicomposting experiment that turned yard waste and 2,000 pounds of daily food waste into a nutrient-rich soil-enhancing material that replaced the fertilizers the university used to buy. They did this without bins or special worm purchases. All they did was spread organic wastes on a half-acre site between rows of fruit trees and blueberry bushes; they relied on the worms that naturally occur in the soil. Every few days they would spread a thin layer of about 250 pounds of unused food from a local restaurant on the ground between the fruit trees. They would rotate the drops around the trees, each area getting a new load every 14 days. They'd sprinkle a thin layer of rock dust from a local quarry on top, along with grass, leaves and shredded branches delivered by campus ground crews, the city and private landscapers. The fruit trees and vegetables planted on the site thrived.

Conclusion

Reducing the vast amounts of food we waste is the easiest way to increase local food supplies. The food is already grown, and in some cases delivered and cooked. All we have to do is eat it all and stop throwing so much away. That takes education at the consumer level, as well as opportunities for easy access to alternate markets (for blemished or "abnormal" produce) at the producer level. New online exchanges are a good way to link previously separated buyers and sellers to make the most of everything that's grown. But they may only identify infrastructure gaps that still need to be filled with, say, a refrigerated warehouse, or a central distribution depot, or a place for packaging and pickup.

Truly inedible food and used food scraps have lots of untapped opportunities to be converted into compost to start the growing cycle all over. Cities are figuring out how to separate green wastes and make money selling compost made out of it. Worms are all too eager to help out. Chickens too. Urban farms are growing compost in decentralized locations. Kitchen scraps and restaurant leftovers are now contributing to biofuel production. That's better than letting them rot into untapped methane at the landfill, and it frees up fields for growing grains for food instead of for ethanol.

The greatest untapped waste stream is what comes out of animals and out of our bodies' totally self-sustaining, no-cost, 24/7 sewage treatment system, better known as digestion. All that waste is waiting for a more agriculturally beneficial place to land than in runoff from sewage treatment plants. It used to be a primary source of fertilizer before getting mixed with industrial waste in modern sewage systems. New technologies are turning it back into fertilizer.

11

Starting Young: Healthier Local Food in Schools, Colleges and Universities

I WAS RIDING DOWN Woodward Avenue in Detroit in a city bus when two school kids got on. They were probably sixth graders, and they were overweight — very overweight. Clutching Slurpees, they sat down puffing heavily and stared out the window as the bus pulled away. They were wide, those two kids, with big baggy jeans rolled up at the cuff and their hoodies hiding what must have been rolls of excess flesh. Then one pulled out a two-pound bag of peanut butter M&Ms and started eating it — all of it, small fistfuls at a time, chewing steadily but nonchalantly, saying nothing to his friend. He washed down each gulp of candy with a silent suck on the Slurpee. I kept waiting for him to put the partly finished bag back in his big front pocket, but it was not to be. Just a few stops later, the bag was empty.

I wanted to lean over and ask him if he knew what he was doing to himself. But I just watched, sickened about his prospects for a healthy life. For all I knew, this might have been the healthiest "food" he had eaten all day. Maybe it was the *only* food he had eaten that day. And really, it was no different from what millions of his classmates were doing every day, all day.

There's a pretty good chance a convenience store was close to his school, even though Detroit has had an ordinance since 1978 that forbids fast-food and convenience stores from being within 500 feet of a school.

Plus, I doubt one 500-foot trek would have stopped this kid, especially if the reward was a big bag of candy or a nice big burger.

The junk food industry likes this kid. It made this kid what he was that day. Fast-food restaurants tend to be clustered a short walking distance from schools. In Chicago, three to four times as many fast-food restaurants can be found within a mile of schools than if they had been distributed randomly. What's worse for the M&M boy is that if he were from a low-income neighborhood, his chances of being ensnared by a tempting fast-food offer would be higher. One study of fast-food restaurants and convenience stores within half a mile of public secondary schools found that as neighborhood income *decreased*, food outlet clustering around schools *increased*. The same study found that schools in African American areas had fewer retail grocery outlets within walking distance than schools in other neighborhoods.[1] In short, fast-food outlets and convenience stores like to be near schools, more so in lower income neighborhoods.

Does this necessarily mean the students eat more junk food just because these sources are nearby? Unfortunately, it does. Having easy access to junk food as they leave school undermines what students are taught about good nutrition when they are in school. Poor nutritional choices in the vicinity of schools have a strong influence on students' nutritional habits. Every day, a third of American children and adolescents eat fast food, which means they're consuming more calories, fat, sugar and sugar-sweetened beverages — and less fiber, milk, fruit and vegetables — than their peers who don't eat fast food. At most fast-food restaurants, young people order at least half of their maximum daily recommended sodium intake in just one meal.

Sure, many fast-food restaurants offer healthy options, but they don't promote them. The industry pushes kids' meal combinations, and less than half of one percent of these meet nutritional criteria for preschoolers.

Junk Food Marketing Aimed at Kids

It's the same inside the schools: students choose junk food when it's available inside school grounds. Researchers in Kentucky found that when children moved from elementary school, where the only source of food was the school lunch program, into middle school, where snack foods were available, they ate the snack foods instead. They started eating fewer fruits and non-starchy vegetables, and they drank less milk, replacing them with more sweet drinks and high-fat vegetables.

To get just a taste of an idea why, go to the M&M website and look at the promotions pitched at kids: tie-ins with popular movies, 50 games featuring M&M "characters," personalized lettering, customized colors, a 50-foot statue in New York City for the "create your own M&M character campaign," recipes for brownie ice cream sandwiches and dinosaur cake, and an enticing online community. Carrots aren't quite as much fun.

All of those M&M promotions are just a minuscule part of a whopping $4.2 billion that the fast-food industry spends on marketing, compared to a mere $6.5 million spent by the USDA's Center for Nutrition Policy and Promotion on healthy nutrition. So, for every $1 spent by M&M promoting brownie ice cream sandwiches with embedded M&Ms, a measly tenth of a penny is spent promoting better health and nutrition.

These fast-food campaigns are creeping ever deeper into kids' lives: preschoolers viewed 21% more fast food ads in 2009 than they did in 2003 (that's 2.8 TV fast food ads for the average preschooler every day); slightly older children viewed 34% more; and teens saw 39% more. Thanks to targeted ads for certain ethnic groups, African American teens watched 75% more TV ads for McDonald's and KFC than white teens did. (Meanwhile, Michael Pollan's book *Food Rules* advises us that one of the rules for healthy eating is to keep away from any food that's advertised on television.)

With web-based marketing aimed at kids as young as two on Ronald. com, it's not surprising that, in spite of what teachers might be telling them about healthy eating, kids want their parents to take them to McDonald's. Two thirds of parents in a US study reported taking their child to McDonald's at least once in the prior week, and almost half (47%) of them said the main reason they went was because their child likes it.

Say it again, kid: "Mmm I'm lovin' it." Slowly killing yourself has never been more fun.

Many schools are still offering junk food to students in vending machines and through fundraising drives for the same reasons convenience stores like to be near schools: they make money off it. In the case of school cafeterias, serving processed food saves money. Many financially strapped schools have scuttled their full kitchens and reverted to heating and refrigerating only—limiting menus to processed food prepared in a commercial kitchen somewhere else. With US federal lunch program subsidies paying a mere 90 cents for ingredients for a student lunch, and no federal funding at all for school lunches in Canada, many schools don't have much choice. Adding up the total $2.68 per meal cost (including labor and other non-ingredient expenses) for students in the United States, the annual spending on ingredients for students' school lunches is about the same as the fast food industry spends on marketing.

As data floods in recasting junk food from "fun and sweet" to "deadly and unsafe," schools and parents are feeling compelled to replace it with something healthier. In some places, like B.C., the province/state has banned school vending machines and fundraisers that sell junk food and soda. B.C. also requires schools to offer healthy choices in their cafeterias. But outside the school grounds, Girl Guide cookies and chocolate almonds are still a fundraising staple—sodium, sugar and all.

Since 1978, the city of Detroit has banned carry-out, fast-food and drive-in restaurants within 500 feet of the nearest school, citing exposure to "highly processed, minimally nutritious foods associated with unhealthy diets" as a reason. The ordinance has never been challenged, so presumably it could be adopted elsewhere.

What effect the ban has on kids' overall eating is hard to know. But it is known that having fast-food restaurants within a half-mile radius of a school results in fewer school servings of fruits and vegetables, more soda consumed, and more obese and overweight kids than in schools not as close to fast-food restaurants.

State, provincial and federal programs can support healthier eating in schools without resorting to bans. In addition to the junk food vending ban mentioned above, the B.C. government, through a non-profit partner, runs an educational School Fruit and Vegetable Nutritional Program for more than 1,100 schools. Through a distribution system worked out between local farmers, Overwaitea Food Stores, and Saputo, students and staff get one serving each of a new fruit or vegetable delivered to the classroom, twice a week, every other week for 14 weeks (aitc .ca/bc/snacks/). Everybody, starting with the teacher, takes a bite. The objective is to teach kids about local food, how to wash the food and their hands properly, and to discover new ways to get five servings of fruit or vegetables a day.

"When kids are exposed to new food in a peer setting, they will try it," says Lindsay Babineau, executive director of the B.C. Agriculture in the Classroom Foundation. "The teacher says 'this is a pear' and they eat it. Everybody has to put it in their mouth. There's been an absolutely phenomenal response to the program. Kids get very excited about discovering things they've never eaten before." The program supports what the schools' nutrition programs are already doing, but with real food instead of a demonstration plastic apple.

More Salad Bars Coming to Schools

In the United States, First Lady Michelle Obama's Let's Move campaign to end childhood obesity is teaming up with school food crusader Ann Cooper to get 5,000 salad bars into school cafeterias. Cooper had earlier partnered with Whole Foods to provide salad bars, worth about $2,500 each, to more than 500 schools in the United States. In addition to providing a rolling food station, preparation and serving gear, the program also provides training materials for teaching cafeteria staff how to run a successful salad bar program. One of the ingredients for success is simply locating the salad bar in the right place (see sidebar). Another B.C. program, School Community Connections, funds school kitchen renovations.

Ironically, some school districts won't take the salad bars because of concerns about food safety. In spite of the life-saving nutrition in salads compared to the sugary, sodium-laced, high-calorie alternatives, school officials are concerned that the standard "sneeze guards" on salad bars are above the children's nose levels, or that the kids might use their hands to pick up salad makings. (Meanwhile, food exports from countries with sketchy food safety standards are flooding into world markets with little or no inspection. In Canada, we import food from 190 countries, but we struggle to guarantee safety since only 2% of food can be inspected.)

Smarter Lunchrooms: Design It Right and Students Will Come

Draconian measures such as banning all junk foods from cafeterias can backfire: students just won't eat at school, or they'll go out to a fast-food restaurant to eat. There are lots of proven ways to encourage students to eat better without costly redesigns or expensive changes in menus. All it takes is adapting design and marketing techniques commonly used in restaurants and grocery stores.

Here's what Cornell University researchers tell us:

- Move vending machines away from the cafeteria.
- Putting healthy foods like broccoli at the front of the line instead of the middle increased healthy food sales by 10–15%.
- Changing names to "creamy corn" rather than "corn," "rich vegetable medley soup" instead of "vegetable soup"; using cool names like "X-ray vision carrots," "power peas" instead of "whole grain," "organic," "vegetarian" or "raw" increased sales by 27%.
- Calling a dish "food of the day" decreases sales.
- Offer choices. Given a choice between carrots and celery, students are more likely to pick one than if they aren't given a choice.
- Keeping ice cream in a freezer with a closed, opaque top significantly reduces sales.
- Encourage the use of trays. Students without trays eat 21% less salad, but no less ice cream.
- Shrink the size of bowls from 18 ounces to 14 ounces and students consume 27% less cereal at breakfast. The same with plates: putting the same amount of food on a smaller plate makes students think they're getting more value.
- Put the chocolate milk behind the plain milk and students will drink more plain milk.
- Putting apples and oranges in a fruit bowl rather than a stainless steel pan more than doubled fruit sales.
- Pulling the salad bar away from the wall and putting it near the cash register almost triples the amount of salad sales.
- When cafeteria workers ask each student "Would you like a salad with that?" salad sales increase by a third.
- Creating a speedy "healthy express" line for children not buying chips and desserts doubles the sales of healthy sandwiches.
- Accept only cash for soft drinks and desserts. Allow debit cards for other foods.

Source: SmarterLunchrooms.org

Schools Learning How to Buy Local

Local food isn't necessarily healthier, but when it's fresh produce it is, and it comes with all the community-building benefits of connecting better with local food providers. "When we started working on getting local food into schools, the outpouring from everyone was so positive and passionate," says Theresa Ramirez, from the Office of Food Service, Detroit Public Schools. "When people are calling me asking, 'What can I do to help?' I know I'm doing something right."[2]

The US Farm to School program links local farms with nearby schools. The number of schools participating went from just a handful in 1997, to more than 2,000 by 2008. The Farm to School Salad Bar program in B.C. links schools with local farms in urban, rural, remote and aboriginal settings across the province. Parents, students, teachers, elders and farmers roll up their sleeves and come into the schools to help prepare and serve the highest quality foods possible — local fresh foods from nearby farms (see phabc.org/farmtoschool). Everyone involved gets an education in nutrition, health and the local food system. In Detroit, produce sometimes comes from the parents themselves. "When you go into the community, you're buying food from people whose kids are in our schools," says Betti Wiggins, from the Office of Food Service, Detroit Public Schools.[3]

Who's Paying?

Finding the funding to get fresh local food into schools is often a challenge. Farm to School programs get good marks for contributing to students' knowledge, attitudes and behaviors toward local healthy food. They've been found to promote more consumption of fruits and vegetables and helped farmers' incomes (a little). But they don't always get passing grades for being financially self-sustaining.

USDA food service dollars are available to support some food production, as well as the purchase of seed and fertilizer for gardens that have an educational component. For public schools in Detroit, that's worth $31 million. In B.C., farmers themselves chip in through the Take a Bite of B.C. program that delivers B.C.-grown products to 33 school teaching kitchens. That food comes into the schools as a sort of teaching aid, but it ends up supplementing whatever else the school is spending on lunch food.

Farm to School programs may have a high initial price tag to set up in schools that don't have a kitchen or dining area. In B.C., schools may need as little as $2,500 to purchase a soup and salad bar unit or as much as $15,000 to set up a whole kitchen (counters, sinks, coolers, oven/range, dishwasher, etc.). Schools that use this initiative to get their first kitchens quickly discover that the kitchen becomes the heart of the school, with all the other benefits of sharing food such as learning, building self-esteem, and linking with the community.

Schools in B.C. make agreements with nearby farms to purchase their foods. The farmer sets the price for the food. Typically children pay $3 for a salad bar feast that contains six vegetables, three fruits, one protein and one grain. When compared to the cost of a fast-food meal with that much nutrition, it's a real bargain, which is something many parents appreciate.

When 150 children participate in the program, enough revenue is generated to pay for the food costs as well as a small stipend for the coordinator. The program is dependent on the generosity of volunteers — parents, elders, students and others — to prepare and serve food. Engaging and retaining volunteers is an ongoing challenge.

The best way to get fresh local produce into schools is through a local procurement policy. That's one of the goals of Michelle Obama's Let's Move campaign to end childhood obesity. "USDA programs should work to connect local farmers with schools and wherever possible to incorporate more fresh food into school meals," USDA Deputy Secretary Kathleen Merrigan told the May 2010 Farm to Cafeteria conference.

The obvious challenge of local procurement is that it can be more expensive. Many schools have struggled to understand if they're even *allowed* to pay more for local food. In lots of places, they already do. In fall 2004, the New York City school district, the largest in the United States, began to "reprocess" 14 of its top cafeteria recipes to make them healthier, tastier and fresher by including more ingredients grown in the northeast.

In 2006, Massachusetts allowed state agencies to pay a 10% premium above the lowest bid for local agricultural products as long as they weren't breaking any other state or federal laws. State procurement officers are free to award contracts under $25,000 without competitive bids, which is another way to bring local produce into schools.

In 2008, Washington State required its state department of agriculture to help get Washington products into schools by starting a Washington Grown Fresh Fruit and Vegetable Grant Program and revising food procurement and contracting procedures to make it easier to buy Washington-grown food.

In the United States, a 2008 breakthrough national school food policy allowed school districts to designate a geographic boundary for sourcing food, which effectively legalized making local food purchases a priority.

Finding good local food and getting it into school cafeterias brings on a whole new set of challenges. The Burlington, Vermont School Food Project was started in 2003, after three hurricanes in three weeks hit the city's traditional food sources. Today the city has a full-time farm-to-school coordinator. The two biggest challenges for Burlington's program are getting equipment upgrades in the schools and educating the food-serving staff. Some of the processing for school meals is done by volunteers at the high school, and then the food is sent out to smaller schools. The cost of the program is $1.15 per student per day — not much.

"The key to farm-to-school is having a distributor who can fill in when local gardens are lacking," advises Betti Wiggins. "You also need a partner who can broker relationships with 1,300 community gardens."

The EcoTrust online foodhub based in Portland, Oregon can provide invaluable links to farmers. "We keep hearing story after story from farmers who never imagined in a million years that they would be selling to schools," says Deborah Kane, EcoTrust's vice president of food and farms. "They thought that was a market that went away a long time ago as the nation commoditized the products that were being sent to schools."[4]

Schoolyard Produce Is Booming

While they will never keep school cafeteria shelves fully stocked, school gardens both improve students' diets at school and teach them how to eat better at home. Food literacy is a potent weapon in fighting childhood

Volunteers break ground for a new garden in a Detroit elementary school: "We've got to start teaching our kids about food in schools" says chef Jamie Oliver.

obesity and diet-related disease. Where better to learn it than hands-on, at school? In a world dominated by junk food, what more important topic could we be teaching in schools than healthy eating? British chef Jamie Oliver's famous TV scene showing elementary school children who were unable to identify potatoes, tomatoes, broccoli and beets was graphic evidence that many kids are totally unaware of the most basic elements of their lives: what they put into their bodies to survive. Schools are the default food education option. "We haven't really evolved schools to deal with the health catastrophes of America," says Oliver. "We need a revolution. We've got to start teaching our kids about food in schools, period" (ted.com/talks/jamie_oliver.html).

As more people come to understand this, school gardens have become a movement, popping up everywhere. The states of Texas and California, for example, encourage extensive programming in school-based gardening. The Edible Schoolyard (ESY), a program of the Chez Panisse Foundation, is a one-acre organic garden and kitchen classroom for urban public school students at Martin Luther King, Jr. Middle School in

Berkeley, California. In 2010 the foundation expanded the concept into New York City: at Arturo Toscanini School in Gravesend, Brooklyn, a state-of-the-art growing complex was built on a formerly asphalt-paved schoolyard. The school is in a district with the lowest percentage of green open space in Brooklyn. The 1,600-square foot garden will be covered with a sliding mobile greenhouse. Beside it will be a kitchen classroom where 30 students can prepare and share meals. Also adjoining will be a cistern that collects rainwater, solar batteries, a tool shed, a chicken coop, and space for compost and waste-sorting.

The example of gardens like this triggered a 2010 USDA initiative to pilot community gardens at high poverty schools, so students can learn about agricultural production practices, diet and nutrition. Students will be able to eat the produce at school, take it home, or donate it to senior centers. The USDA plans to follow up by promoting gardens at *all* K–12 schools.

"Learning where food comes from and what fresh foods taste like, and the pride of growing and serving vegetables and fruits through your own effort, are life-changing experiences," said Agriculture Secretary Tom Vilsack when he announced the program.

The biggest barrier to a successful school garden is stewardship. Who will look after it? Often it's a keen teacher, but to deal with the summer break, when most gardens are hitting their peak and need the most attention, a community partner works best. Some high schools in Richmond, B.C. have teamed up with seniors' centers. Community volunteers work alongside the students and keep the garden watered and tended during the summer months. Other schools "contract out" garden space to community-based organizations like Troy Gardens in Madison, Wisconsin, or Terra Nova Farm in Richmond, B.C.

At Terra Nova, elementary schools within walking distance of a central garden have their own plots overseen by paid staff supported by community grants (mostly corporate, now that the corporate community has started to understand the benefits of programs like this). An on-site chef in a commercial kitchen at the garden takes produce the kids have grown, cooks it up, and feeds it to them — along with a cooking lesson.

The Troy Gardens kids' program brings in 1,000 children a year to teach them about gardens and what grows in them. "Kids love eating vegetables they grow themselves," says Christie Ralston, who supervises many of the school visits. Not every child comes to grow things. "Some just revel in the chance to play in soil for the first time in their lives. They're happy just digging holes."[5]

In Vancouver, Environmental Youth Alliance, a community organization, sends in volunteers to help run what has evolved into an urban farm at Windermere High School. It's got a mechanized industrial composter in the school's courtyard (which is lined with fruit trees), 11 raised-bed gardens, a couple of vermiculture boxes, and a 320-square foot greenhouse that includes a fish-raising aquaponics operation. The students themselves have been running the farm and the composting operation, having built the greenhouse with supervision from a supportive principal and a teacher-sponsor. They get PE class credits for riding their bikes to nearby elementary schools to pick up food waste and leaves to feed the compost operation. They take the compost back to gardens at the elementary schools. The enthusiasm and sense of ownership built up around this school is so strong that 50–60 kids will come to the school on professional development days — typically seen as a holiday because classes are cancelled — to work in the garden.

The Windermere story is an example of what the research shows: school gardens not only educate kids about growing food, they also promote teamwork among students, they improve relations between students and the community, and, best of all, they're fun: kids like gardening. When they do it, their diets improve. One study of sixth grade students found higher levels of vitamin A and C, and more fruit and vegetable consumption among students who planted and harvested a garden at their school.

Keep It Simple: Gardening Without Gardens

Planting seeds in EarthBoxes is just one example of how schools can grow vegetables without a garden, at a reasonable cost ($30–$50 for each box). Earthboxes are plastic containers on wheels that have water reservoirs at the bottom of the box. There's an aeration screen over the reservoir, and a plastic cover fits over the whole box. Soil, dolomite and fertilizer are put in the box, then holes are cut in the cover and seeds or seedlings are planted. There's no wasted water, and all the fertilizer goes into the plants. It's simple enough for elementary school students to do their own planting. At one school, in Fort Vermilion, Alberta, students used EarthBoxes to grow corn, carrots, peppers, beans, peas and tomatoes.

How about Spuds in Tubs, promoted by farmers in the Fraser Valley, outside Vancouver, B.C.? Schools are lining up to get these into their classrooms.

"We have enough demand that we could have these in every classroom in the province if we had the money," says Lindsay Babineau, executive director of B.C. Agriculture in the Classroom Foundation. In the spring, 4 or 5 students share one tub, with each student planting their own seed potato ('Warba,' an early maturing variety). The tubs stay indoors until April, when it's warm enough to move them outside. The 'Warba' potato produces a harvest by mid-June, before school is out. As the potatoes sprout and grow, students record changes in the features of the plants — color, shapes, sizes and textures. Every time there's a good section of stem showing, they hill the soil around it. At harvest time, the students host a feast and learn different ways to cook potatoes.

"Once they get a chance to grow something themselves, kids are just beside themselves," says Babineau. "Kids are eating potatoes who have never eaten them before."

Here's one teacher's report on how it worked:

"We had our potato feast today and my 30 ESL students from Grades 1–6 came — ate and laughed together along with our principal. I separated the 500+ potatoes into small, medium and large sizes.

"The large potatoes I put in paper bags and labeled for each student (stapled the bags shut and told them to take them home before opening!). The other potatoes I boiled at the school and put in a crock pot to keep warm. On a buffet style table, there was a Russian potato salad, two types of chips and chocolate potato cake.

"The boiled potatoes were eaten with butter, salt, pepper, sour cream, chives and bacon bits. They were a huge hit. The pot was overflowing and within minutes nothing was left inside.

"Some students came back 4 or 5 times for more. The potatoes were more popular than the chips or the cake. The students enjoyed leaving with their 'goody bag,' potato journal, and the international potato cookbook that they had contributed recipes to.

"After recess, the grade 1's returned for their class with me and midway through, one little fellow asked when we could go visit the potatoes. When I reminded him that he had just eaten the potatoes, he became very quiet — I guess we all had become emotionally attached to the spuds!" (aitc.ca/).

At Waterville Elementary School in Oregon, students didn't need a garden to learn about vermiculture. A parent volunteer helped fourth grade students build five worm bins which they set on concrete blocks. They used these to experiment with the best way to raise worms and capture worm castings. They piled up shredded paper, pulverized cardboard, old corn silage and composted manure as bedding before adding six pounds of worms (donated by a local farmer) to each bin. Disregarding cautionary tales about meat and dairy odors, they added hamburgers, tacos, sub sandwiches, paper cups and napkins. Everything got eaten by the worms and was turned into castings.

Every day, students from second to fifth grade would take turns scraping food scraps off plates, weighing it, and taking it out to the bins. They would cover the new scraps with a layer of bedding. When it came time to collect the castings, students discovered the best way was to leave the lid off the bin, letting sunlight dry out the bedding. This caused the worms to migrate downward and leave the castings behind.

Conclusion

All over the developed world, parents, teachers and students themselves are realizing that healthier eating should start at home, but often it doesn't. Too often kids get detoured to the order counters of a voracious fast-food industry. It is left to the schools to rescue many kids from obesity, disease and a lifetime of unhealthy eating — as well as, in some cases, providing them with enough healthy food to get through the day. Schools are starting to clean up the food they offer in their own cafeterias and vending machines. They're doing it by purchasing fresh — often local — fruits and vegetables, incorporating better cafeteria design, and eating food grown on the school's own school grounds.

Government funding — even if it's just through local procurement policies — is essential to getting these programs off the ground and keep them running. In Canada, funding is sorely lacking at the federal level. Existing funding in the United States barely pays for the cheapest processed junk food.

But school gardens are springing up everywhere. They combine pedagogy and fun — and produce good food. Growing food — whether in a full-scale garden or in tubs and containers — also strengthens bonds with the community. Local farmers become local heroes when school kids realize what they produce.

"Agriculture has such a good story to tell, but farmers don't know how to tell it," says Lindsay Babineau. "They don't want to tell their story; they just want to farm. We tell their story in the classroom, and make them feel good about what they do."

Good learning, good health and good eating are impossible to separate. School gardens and indoor gardening projects are going to become as common as the school playground. When students turn the corner to fresh food, they're on the road to health. Schools have to be part of that transformation.

12

Farmers Markets and CSAs: Making the Most of Direct Sales

T HE MILLING PEOPLE and scattered tents at the Saturday morning Kitsilano Farmers Market in Vancouver give it the aura of a
festival-with-purpose — a row of pointed-top tents, makeshift banners
and portable generators, with the air sweetened by a group of friends
playing Celtic tunes on fiddles and guitars, their CDs propped up in
front of them. Richard the Pesto Man is heckling customers to come
to his booth to sample dill, cilantro, avocado, olive, sun-dried tomato,
blueberry, hempseed and "spicy skoogk" pesto. "Prepare to meet your
maker!" says the market's banner.

We check our bikes into the bike valet parking racks at the entrance
and take a ticket. The people handling food here are ruddy-cheeked and
wear cowboy hats, scruffy work shirts or branded aprons. Actual growers,
they come from places with names like Forstbauer Family Natural Food
Farm, Apple Lane Orchards, Fresh off the Boat, Garden Back to Eden,
Goat's Pride Dairy, Hui's Farm Specialty Mushrooms, T. and J. Bison and
Grains, Yarrow Eco Village Farm, Vlad's Apiary, and Kootenay Alpine
Cheese. It's like an outdoor trade show of local flavors and characters.
You can wander around just to learn about ancient grains, wild harvested
mushrooms or bee products, but almost everyone here is buying as well

as looking. It's like visiting a parade of farm-gate stands, sweetened with takeout coffee and local crafts.

Full experience shopping is typical of farmers markets. Not too many grocery stores have children's face-painting or corn-shucking competitions like the Greenmarket outlets in New York City. Most of the 49 neighborhood markets under its umbrella — "the nation's largest open air farmers market program" — feature events, festivals and educational campaigns.

The Kitsilano farmers market is a neighborhood place to load up with fresh local produce from farms I never knew existed — and all the food comes from within a few hours' drive from my home. I get to find out exactly where everything was grown. Battered scrapbooks and display boards show the fields and paddocks, hoop houses and dairies.

These boutique-style markets are springing up all over North America, but they're really an evolution of farmers markets that have been selling produce direct for centuries. Many are smaller variations of year-round, large-scale farmers markets that have been part of the local food retailing ecology for decades. The Atwater Market in Montreal, Detroit's Eastern Central Market, Granville Island Market in Vancouver and Toronto's Ontario Food Terminal wholesale market are just a few examples. Farmers are willing to get up at 4 AM to haul their products to these places because they can keep up to 90 cents for every dollar of sales — a lot more than the 18 cents they typically get when their food is sold through a traditional grocery store.

Buyers get an added do-good glow from knowing that much more of their average $32 in spending is going back into the local economy (and not into the cash registers of national chains selling imported products delivered by multi-national distributors). A study done in London found street and farmers markets are "major drivers of their local economies, attracting trade to and complementing other local retailers, and creating the 'social glue' that holds communities together."[1]

All that novelty and added value is getting a lot of media attention, causing some farmers to wonder why a segment of the market that sells such a tiny proportion of our food (less than half of 1% of total agriculture sales in the United States) is getting so much coverage.

Familiarity to urban media is obviously one factor that's helped push spending at farmers markets in Canada to an estimated $1.08 billion-plus in 2008, but there are two other reasons the media love farmers markets.

The first is that they're "a trend." Farmers markets are growing fast. Direct sales in the United States jumped 55% between 2002 and 2007. As of mid-2010, there were 6,132 farmers markets operating in the United States—a 16% increase from 2009, and more than a doubling over the past decade. The second is that they strike the same chord that lights up everything to do with local food: support for small farms and the local economy, fresher food, unique local flavors, neighborhood festivities, better health, and the opportunity to make a personal link with the farmers who grow the food you put into your body.

US Farmers market growth, 1994–2009

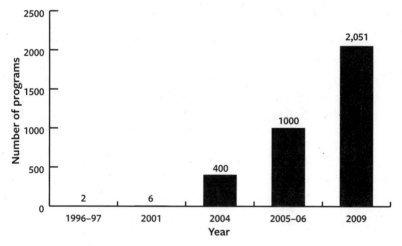

Source: National Farm to School Network

The allure of farmers markets makes them the #2 source of groceries for 62% of Canadian shoppers (after big grocery stores). Canadian farmers markets generate $2 billion in economic spinoff, though it's hard to say how that compares with jobs created by mainstream grocery sales. More than half the vendors interviewed in a Canadian study say that their participation in the farmers market created 1–5 jobs. With 95% of farmers market vendors coming back week after week, and some farmers markets having three-year waiting lists for vendor access, they obviously work for a lot of farmers.

Do Farmers Markets Really Cost More?

In spite of the well-earned hoopla and obvious customer appeal, farmers markets have their limitations. By far the biggest one is high prices — or is it just perception of price? Food at farmers markets is widely perceived to be more expensive than at conventional stores, in spite of studies by farmers market boosters claiming they're actually cheaper. Conventional wisdom says that farmers markets are just too expensive for the typical food-buyer on a limited budget.

Farmers markets have gallantly fought back with studies showing that organic products at farmers markets are competitive with other organic producers. While many farmers markets do feature premium novelty items like 50-cent purple carrots, the average prices at farmers markets can be below supermarket prices. A spring 2008 study by students of Prof. Stacy Jones at Seattle University found that the average cost per pound of all organic produce at Seattle's Broadway Farmers Market was $2.36, compared to $2.98 at the local QFC store, and $2.53 at Whole Foods. Two other studies comparing other farmers markets in the Seattle area came to the same conclusion: farmers markets have cheaper organic produce than mainline stores. But most people don't buy organic produce, so most buyers are comparing prices with conventionally grown produce, which is typically a lot cheaper.

A study for the London Food Commission found that prices for fresh produce in London's "street markets" were significantly lower than in supermarkets — by an average of one third.

A blogger in San Francisco was upset by Slow Food founder Carlo Petrini's statement that the prices at the San Francisco farmers market "were astronomical, twice or even three times as high as those of 'conventional' products." So she did her own price comparison. She took what she had bought at her last visit to the market and compared it with Safeway's prices. She was astonished to find that her list of 11 items that cost $23.40 at the farmers market were priced at $32.84 at Safeway, with only one organic item on the list (becksposhnosh.blogspot.com).

A more typical reaction comes from this buyer in Boston, who concluded that farmers markets were "boutiques for the well-off":

"Last weekend I went to the Saturday market at the Morse School in Cambridgeport. I saw some beautiful looking golden zucchini and bought some at $3/lb. On my way out of the market, I saw the same zucchini at another stall at $1.50. OK, my bad, I guess. Should have done more careful comparison shopping. But when I saw some equally gorgeous golden zucchini at Russo's yesterday for $.29/lb, I was amazed — and I started wondering why the farmers market prices were five to ten times higher" (chowhound .chow.com).

A bigger price comparison study in Edmonton confirmed the widespread opinion that farmers markets cost more than supermarket fare. A selection of goods that cost $1,045 at the farmers market were only $511 at the grocery store, almost half the cost.

But in New Zealand, a price comparison found the opposite: that farmers market prices were half the price of the supermarket.

There is no definitive answer to whether farmers markets are more expensive, because comparing one farmers market or one supermarket with another is like comparing, as they say, apples and oranges. Farmers markets can have wild price differences for the same produce at the same market. Or prices can shift based on seasonal surpluses, bulk buys or end-of-day specials. Supermarket prices vary the same way — way down when the market is flooded with seasonal produce or when they want to post loss-leader prices to get shoppers into the store to buy high-profit packaged foods.

The final answer on whether farmers markets are more expensive is elusive. Are we comparing farmers market almost-organic products with certified organic products at grocery stores? Are we putting a value on freshness and nutrition? Are we comparing the same produce at the same time of year? Do some farmers crank up their prices when they have a monopoly on a popular product at the market? Does price per pound really matter if 75% of farmers market shoppers are regulars, spending their $32 (on average) because they perceive value in meeting

If Only Customers Understood...

Why Watermelons Cost So Much At The Farmers Market

Here's how Chris Bodnar from Glenn Valley Farm (an hours' drive from Vancouver, B.C.) explains the prices he charges at farmers markets:

"Melon season arrived on the farm today and melons make me think of money. Prices, more specifically.

"Watermelons are a difficult crop, but well worth the effort when they grow well. They need heat, lots of water, weeding and more heat. We started growing melons two years ago as an experiment. When we sent a bunch to market for the first time, we had to figure out a price— we had no precedent.

"Once our costs were considered, we figured that we would have to charge the same price we have for our squash—$1.25/lb. This came as quite a shock to customers who normally pay $0.29/lb for conventional melons in the stores through the summer. After various comments about the price that first week, we discussed whether we needed to lower the price.

"So, consider this: each melon requires about 190 liters of irrigation water. It makes sense when you think of the primary ingredient of a watermelon: water. In fact, a number of customers noted that our price seemed rather high when most of the fruit is water (of course, they still line up to pay $3.00/lb for tomatoes that are 94% water and $2.50 for a bunch for spinach that is 92% water).

"Nonetheless, a large portion of the population doesn't blink an eye at paying $2.00 for half a liter of bottled water—that's four times what they pay for a liter of gasoline for their car. So what value do you place on 190 liters of water, especially when fortified with fiber and a great range of nutrients?

"Then I heard about watermelons in Japan. It turns out they are a delicacy. Many people in Japan have never tasted watermelons. They regularly sell for $200. Moreover, the first Hokkaido watermelons of the season are auctioned at an astounding price ($6,000 two years ago).

"All things considered, we figured that $1.25/lb was a heck of a deal for melons. The next Saturday morning I explained this to our customers waiting in line at the market. We sold out of melons in an hour." (glenvalleyorganicfarm .blogspot.com).

farmers and knowing their food is safe, fresh and local? Maybe farmers markets are more expensive only if shoppers limit themselves to calculating simple dollars per pound.

Making Farmers Markets Affordable

For many people, dollars per pound is the only calculation they can afford to go by, a reality that's recognized in the second half of New York's Greenmarket's mission statement: "Keep small farms viable and provide good food to all New York City communities regardless of income level." Many of Greenmarket's farmers markets target low-income customers: 14 of their 49 markets register most of their sales through food stamps, now known as SNAP (the Supplemental Nutrition Assistance Program) or WIC (the Special Supplemental Nutrition Program for Women, Infants and Children). About a quarter of the 6,000-plus farmers markets in the United States accept SNAP, but that's less than 0.01% of all spending at farmers markets. The WIC program, now in 45 states, provides supplemental foods, health care referrals and nutrition education at no cost to low-income pregnant, breastfeeding and non-breastfeeding postpartum women who are at nutritional risk. In 1992, the Farmers Market Nutrition Program (FMNP) was established by Congress to help WIC participants use farmers markets to get fresh, unprepared, locally grown fruits and vegetables, but fewer than a third of WIC recipients redeem their coupons for fruits and vegetables at farmers markets.

Getting US federal FMNP/WIC money into farmers markets isn't all that easy. Lots of low-income residents still don't know they can use their coupons at farmers markets. Even when they do, some see farmers markets as elitist foodie destinations that are often located too far away. Then there are the bureaucratic hassles for farmers using cash value vouchers (CVVs) and electronic benefit transfer (EBT) cards. Farmers getting these coupons first have to get authorized by a state agency, then they have to submit coupons to the bank or a state agency for reimbursement, and each FMNP recipient is limited to $30 in annual purchases. That can be a lot of paperwork for a few dollars.

Farmers markets have limited capacity to be significant year-round food providers (restricted hours, seasonality, range of produce). Even though 17,543 farmers, 3,635 farmers markets and 2,662 roadside stands were authorized to accept FMNP coupons in 2009, they only brought in $20 million in revenues across the United States. That's a relatively small amount, although it helps farmers a lot — for every dollar spent on FMNP, 83 cents went directly to the farmer selling the produce. Still, remember that it costs a farmer to pack a truck, drive it to the market, set up a booth and have someone there to sell. Lots of cities have tried to help boost low-income spending with matching dollar programs. King Portland Farmers Market in Oregon tripled SNAP spending when it got local businesses and individuals to donate to a fund that matched the first $5 users spent in food stamps.

A three-year project to boost low-income residents' spending in B.C. farmers markets, the first of its kind in Canada, was inexplicably cancelled in 2010. It provided $15 a week for 17 weeks in coupons to 3,000 low-income families and low-income pregnant women. The coupons could be used to buy fresh fruits, vegetables, meats, eggs, dairy or fresh cut herbs at participating farmers markets. It was tied in with cooking and skill-building programs.

Farmers Markets Struggle for Locations

As farmers markets grow in popularity, they struggle to find locations. Many are on temporary sites — church parking lots, closed-off streets, or vacant lots — that are hard to service because everything has to be set up and dismantled every week. Many cities are supportive, but they are scrambling to come up with regulations that allow expansions. Resistance can come from competing mainstream grocery stores that pay a lot more taxes than the average farmers market booth. In Philadelphia, farmers markets are allowed in certain commercial zones, but they're supposed to be in a completely enclosed building, which isn't how it usually works. So the city is working on new zoning regulations as part of an urban agriculture update. In some cities, markets need special permits every time they set up, and no permanent signage is allowed to let people know that they can find a farmers market at that location on weekends. And food inspectors can balk at certifying food as safe when it might be sitting in the sun all day.

A report conducted in London pinned down the other big challenges for farmers markets: a lack of investment, a shortage of wholesalers servicing street markets and farmers markets, a lack of support from some councils and a lack of status (as in signs, tourism promotion). The report said that farmers' and street markets attract shoppers to an area, which helps other stores, even competitors. The "vast majority" of retailers they surveyed near street markets were positive about the markets' presence. They found that people come to farmers markets mainly for quality and a desire to support farmers, whereas mainstream grocery stores depend much more on low prices to attract customers. A lot of markets have tight restrictions on non-food vendors, so neighboring stores that sell things other than food often benefit from the presence of a market.

As farmers markets grow, they get beyond the capacity of volunteer groups to manage them. In Philadelphia, a for-profit business has found a niche advocating for farmers and connecting them with consumers and markets. The most recent USDA study of farmers market managers found, not surprisingly, that year-round markets with paid managers, rather than those run by volunteers, are the most successful. It also found that markets that were at least five years old had higher sales per month and more sales per vendor than new markets. This could either point to a great future for new markets as they get more established — or maybe it's just that the longer-running markets got the best locations.

Some farmers markets have gone mobile in search of the best locations. Virginia-based organic farmer Joel Salatin is impressed with a converted school bus in his area that's like a mobile farmers market: "It drives up to offices and people come out and shop. This has taken off in popularity — just gone wild." Lots of cities have these mobile markets, as well as spinoff "pocket markets" in corporate lobbies, hospital foyers and random parking lots.

Beyond Farmers Markets:
Community Supported Agriculture

As farmers markets grow, finding enough farmers to sell at them becomes increasingly difficult. Some don't want to or can't afford to spend their weekends selling out of the back of a van. Many farmers don't like interacting with the public, however gratifying it might be to hear first-hand how much people appreciate local food. "There's a reason farmers live in the country," says Joel Salatin, an organic farmer who admits he's unusual in liking the lecture circuit. "They like the isolation and quiet, hard work away from city crowds." The new wave of young urban farmers stepping into the food supply chain may change that.

What won't change is the appeal of *Community Supported Agriculture* (CSA) as an alternative to farmers spending long hours at a stand in the farmers market. In this system, customers pre-pay for a weekly food box to be delivered to a pickup depot during the harvest months. The customers get fresh-picked produce from a farmer they get to know personally, and the farmer is paid up front, which is a cash flow boon. Once they've bought in, CSA customers go along with the farmer on the ride with uncertainty: if the weather's bad, they both lose. In most CSAs, everyone gets the same "share box." Sometimes a "member choice" CSA lets customers choose what goes in their pickup box. (If they don't make a request, they get a standard box of whatever the farmer has that week.)

Austrian philosopher and social thinker Rudolf Steiner gets credit for originating the concept in the 1920s. The concept took root in North America with two farms, one in Massachusetts and the other in New Hampshire; both of them started in 1986.

Woody Tasch, author of *Slow Money: Investing as if Food, Farms and Fertility Mattered*, describes CSAs as "the simplest, most beautiful, profound way to make needed changes. It's the ultimate beautiful outcome — scores of people investing directly, getting rid of as much intermediation as possible... This is about taking control of our money and getting directly involved in what we're investing in. It's not all about convenience."[2]

Especially suited to urban and near-urban markets, CSAs are becoming increasingly common. They are growing even faster than farmers markets. LocalHarvest.org, which claims to have the most comprehensive directory of CSA farms in the United States, lists more than 2,500, including 557 new ones that signed up in 2008, and another 300 in the first two months of 2009. The USDA 2007 Census of Agriculture started counting CSAs in 2007 for the first time and tallied a total of 12,549.

Will Raap, founder of the Intervale Center, estimates the CSA at his South Village Center in South Burlington, Vermont (the state's first and biggest CSA) needs 130 members to support one part-time farmer. Prairie Crossing's CSA, supported by residents in the Prairie Crossing agricultural subdivision and people living nearby, is the key to financial success for Prairie Crossing's biggest farm. It provides 60% of the $300,000 annual revenue of Sandhill Organics.

And Now, Community Supported Fish

The financial benefits of CSAs to farmers are well-illustrated by the CSA model used by "Skipper Otto," the retired high school chemistry teacher from Kelowna, B.C. described in more detail in Chapter 6. In his first year with a Community Supported Fishery (CSF), Strobel's revenue from a bin of fish went from $1,200 to $4,000. But the sweetest benefit is getting $50,000 in his and his partner's pockets before the season opens. No more maxing out their lines of credit before every season. Because he bases the number of members on the number of salmon they are certain they can always catch, that's real money in the bank.

Otto admits that even with the CSF covering his costs and delivering a small profit, the shortage of times when fishing is allowed means he can't make a living off fishing. He says that up north, where he fishes Skeena and Nass River runs up to the Alaska border, "most of us are old, semi-retired, just hanging on and hoping to qualify for employment insurance." But he agrees that the CSF "could turn it around for some of us, although not for the whole industry." Already he has been able to bring his old fishing partner Terry Mooney's catch into his CSF. Tuna and halibut fishermen who have heard about the CSF on the docks want to get involved, which would tap into customers waiting in line for memberships. While Strobel could hardly be classified as an urban farmer, one key to his success is having his group of urban buyers show up at the dock in Vancouver to pick up their fish every week.

What's Next For CSAs?

The first wave of CSAs were supported by passionate early adopters willing to readjust their lives to access fresh local food and become friends with a local grower. That sometimes meant showing up at a community kitchen depot or, in the case of one urban farmer I know, at his back porch on Thursday evenings. These were people committed enough to share the farmer's risk that bad weather might limit the harvest. They accepted the uncertainty — and excitement — of what might show up in the box every week. They also accepted the inconvenience of having to be available on pickup night, sometimes getting food they don't like, and taking as many trips to the CSA pickup as they might to a grocery store, but with only one part of their food order fulfilled on that trip. Need bananas and toilet paper too? Add another stop. Buyers also have to be able to afford a lump sum payment at the beginning of the season (usually $200–$300, but now as high as $600).

All those inconveniences suggest that CSAs will always have a limited market. But the CSA model can be widened without losing the local farmer/fresh food/buy-direct focus. Some CSAs have spun off pay-as-you-go "buying clubs," in which members can order food weekly, thus freeing them up from a full season's payment up front. That takes them off the financial hook, and yet still gives them access to wonderful fresh, seasonal, artisan products. Some people have worked around the up-front financial demands by forming bulk-buy clubs: members sign up and commit to their share of a group buy of a certain amount of flour, say, then pay for it when they show up to pick up their share.

Some CSAs reduce the farmers' hassle of sourcing separate depots by having a single storefront depot used by half a dozen or more CSAs. One of these in Vancouver had people coming in off the street and wanting to buy produce, so they've morphed into a retail store owned by the farmers, combining CSA pickups with off-the-shelf purchases. But the store has been struggling in the cutthroat grocery retail market, competing with other stores that specialize in retail sales. Will Allen's Growing Power, Inc. in Milwaukee has opened its own retail stores, confident that customers will pay whatever it takes to buy local fresh produce supporting local farmers.

In Philadelphia, a for-profit business run by a long-time local food advocate provides administrative support for CSAs and farmers markets for a fee. It operates 15 farmers markets and has a central website (farmtocity.org) that manages CSAs.

Some farmers think the next big thing will be multiple-farm CSAs, where a group of farms work together to provide a "full-service CSA" offering veggies, fruits, meat, dairy, grains and bread. This would give farmers economies of scale without losing the community connections and local smaller-scale production values.

One sign that CSAs are coming of age is that in 2010, for the first time, two of the six regional finalists in Canada's Outstanding Young Farmers' program were CSA farmers, and a third was a market gardener who also sells direct to the public through an on-farm program and U-pick enterprise. One of those finalists, Steve Cooper, offered this advice to fellow farmers contemplating the CSA model: "Market gardening is an art. Fifty years ago, there were all kinds of market gardens around cities — lots of people had those juggling skills of being able to grow a lot of things and have some ready for sale every week. That's why I call it an art, and that's why I say it takes time to learn your costs and crunch your numbers."[3]

Another for-profit workaround to shake off the inconveniences of the CSA model is special-order home delivery businesses. A company like Sustainable Produce Home Delivery (SPUD) takes online orders for products mostly sourced from local organic producers in seven west coast cities. Customers place their weekly orders online. They only pay for what they want, they get it local and fresh, and they don't have to leave home — SPUD delivers.

But not everyone has a shaded, secure porch where a delivery can be left if no one's home. And many people haven't got their week's meals planned by the 9 am ordering deadline the day before SPUD delivers. Some people like to make their own choices about what they put in their shopping cart — combining impulse buying with picking the perfect tomato, after giving it a little squeeze. I also think a lot of people get a buzz from the social interaction at grocery stores. It's a place to meet your neighbors and exchange glances — maybe even words — with strangers you'd like to meet. Especially for people who work at home or who are stuck at home, getting out to the grocery store can be a social outing.

CSA customers get this bonus when everyone picks up their produce at the same time. Sometimes the social scene is active enough to turn into regular group potluck dinners. That does not happen at grocery stores.

Conclusion

Direct sales are a great way to get fresh food to consumers with the biggest payback to the farmer. That's why farmers markets and CSAs are exploding. As they explode, their collateral impact expands, and with that comes a raft of new demands: permanent sites for farmers markets, better access to anti-poverty program food coupons, fewer bureaucratic hurdles, more convenience for the less-idealistic customer, competitive prices, CSAs that make home deliveries, and more winter produce.

It's all doable. Compared to growing our own food, getting it directly from a nearby farmer is the best way to eat healthier, support the local economy and find a new community connection to the soil that feeds us. Disenchantment with imported industrial food has re-ignited local food sales over the past decade and will no doubt carry farmers markets and CSAs to the next level.

13

Growing Community with Community Gardens

I ONCE HAPPENED UPON a community garden in Victoria, B.C., a provincial capital renowned for its gardens. Ever curious about community gardens, I strolled in and looked around. I had never seen such a neat, well-ordered community garden. Although these gardens typically express the various states of unruliness of their plot-holders, this one had little picket fences; there were no weeds in the pathways, and everything was neat and tidy. This even extended to the notice board, which in some gardens is nothing more than a scrawled notice on a piece of plywood saying "Please respect our gardeners. Don't pick what isn't yours." This garden had posted rules, notices and regulations, all evenly spaced and up-to-date. Meticulously typed minutes from the most recent meeting of the society's officers were posted. Citations for members who hadn't been properly attending their plots were listed in the minutes, along with a description of escalating penalties given in grinding detail.

As is usual in these gardens, there was someone around who loves to talk, even at 7:30 in the morning. A man tending his plot was glad to answer my questions. "This is an exceptionally well-organized garden," I commented. "That's because most of the gardens are used by former public servants with backgrounds in drafting legislation and crafting public policy," he answered with a wry smile. "We have an abundance of policy enthusiasm."

Every community garden has its own enthusiasms that reflect its community. The Eagle Heights Community Garden at the University of Wisconsin has gardeners who speak more than 60 languages among them. Gardeners can fill out application forms in four languages: English, Spanish, Chinese or Korean.

When I dropped by the community garden at the sprawling farm at the Intervale, in Burlington, Vermont, I spotted a policy enthusiasm of another sort. An older Chevy S-10 pickup was parked by the entrance, its tailgate emblazoned with bumper stickers espousing every progressive cause imaginable. As I wondered what the owner would look like, I caught the eye of an older man in shorts and a T-shirt, digging soil into a newly framed raised plot. In the tradition of everybody being friends inside a community garden, I started asking him questions, and he eagerly told me about his involvement, which had lasted two decades. I commented on the truck nearby. "That's mine," he said proudly. Then he introduced himself: "I'm Robert Kiss. I'm the mayor of Burlington."

Community gardens aren't new. They emerge in periods when people are threatened by food insecurity. Urban community garden food production has ebbed and waned in the United States in tune with food shortages caused by depression or wars. Detroit Mayor Hazen Pingree initiated "potato patches" to help Detroit citizens through the 1893 depression. During World War I the US federal government organized War Gardens. Work relief gardens and cooperative farms were created during the Great Depression of the 1930s. World War II brought the Victory Garden campaign to the United States, Canada, Britain and other countries. At their peak, Victory Gardens in the United States may have accounted for as much as 40% of the vegetable production in the country.

Britain's experience feeding its island population during World War II and through the privations of the post-war period (rationing was in effect until 1954) shows what can be done when people are mobilized. In this case, it was a battle for national survival, with memories of hunger from World War I still fresh for many people. As soon as war was declared in 1939, Britain set up a Ministry of Food to organize food rationing and help people make the most of wartime rations. A massive propaganda campaign taught Britons what to eat and how to eat. Food was considered a weapon of war. To waste food was to undermine the war effort.

The inefficiencies of beef production dictated more reliance on vegetables and fruits; pastures were plowed up to make way for food crops. By 1943, more than 1.4 million people had allotment gardens and were producing over a million tons of vegetables a year. Pigs became an important meat source. They were valued because they could be fed on food scraps. By 1943, 100,000 people had joined 4,000 Pig Clubs that shared the work of tending to herds of pigs. Instructional gardening pamphlets were mailed to all households, and the Women's Land Army was recruited to go out to the fields to grow crops. Fruit-picking was often organized by schools, which ran harvest camps as well. Boy Scouts and Girl Guides instructed children on how to properly pick fruit.

The result of all these efforts, according to *The Ration Book Diet*, was that "the war left us healthier as a nation than we had ever been before or have been since."[1]

Later in the 20th century, community gardens as we know them today began to spring up as part of grassroots urban movements, resulting in the establishment of the American Community Gardening Association in 1978, with members across the United States and Canada. Today's community gardens are a mix of private allotment plots and larger, shared gardens usually organized by a community group. The shared social experience of gardening is a big focus, but most gardeners are also interested in growing their own food. Typically, food is not grown commercially in community gardens, although some gardeners do sell their produce.

The four goals of the University of Wisconsin's Eagle Heights Community Gardens illustrate the range of interest of today's community gardeners: nutrition, recreation, education and community building.

Montreal is just one city with a proud explosion of community gardens. It has more than 100 gardens, each with an average of 30 parking space-sized plots. Sustainlane, the online "People-Powered Sustainability

Guide," ranked Minneapolis as the top US city for farmers markets and community gardens per capita (sustainlane.com).

Troy Gardens in Madison, Wisconsin claims to have the second-biggest community garden complex on the continent (after nearby University of Wisconsin's Eagle Heights, which has more than 500 plots and 1,000 gardeners. But it's been going since 1962). Troy Gardens' 327 good-sized plots (20 feet by 20 feet) are broken up into more than 30 different "gardens," which are all part of a wonderfully integrated 31-acre development that includes 30 units of co-housing, a five-acre farm providing produce for CSA members, and a five-acre restored natural area that's burned off every year. The co-housing residents are also worker-caretakers who keep their eyes and ears on the gardens. Many have their own garden plots and help as volunteers for work parties and special events. The rest of the work is done by five full-time-equivalent employees, 30-plus volunteer interns, and hundreds of other volunteers.

Acting Executive Director Christie Ralston showed me around the snow-covered site on a bright January day. She had her white wool hat pulled down low, and she smiled a lot as she talked proudly about what happened there when everything was growing. "This garden is a great equalizer," she noted. "When Mung women come here, they're speaking the common language of gardening, like everyone else."

Christie's gardeners speak English, Spanish, Mung and Lao. Some of her favorite visitors are the forensic mental patients who come here on day passes with a nurse. She also hosts teenage youths on day passes from a nearby jail. "They hate being out in nature, but when I give them hard, heavy work to do and they see results, they like it." The visitation programs connect visitors with nature through the gardens. For the younger kids, it sometimes means just digging in the dirt, never mind what kind of hole they're making. "I particularly remember one of the teenage boys tell me after we had done some sampling and pointing out different plants: 'I smelled things I had never smelled before.'"

Planting "Community" into Community Gardens

One of my first awakenings to the myriad benefits of community gardens was when the community police officer in a troubled neighborhood in

Vancouver helped get one started. She wanted a project for the homeless people hanging around the neighborhood. They embraced it eagerly — a chance to care for something, do something positive, to witness the fruits (actually, vegetables) of their labor. She said the only problem was that so many people wanted to water the plants all the time.

Community gardens contribute to safety by getting people into the street for hours at a time. "Eyes and ears on the street" make streets safe.

Gardeners love to talk about their plants, and community gardens can get conversations started. A friend of mine who started growing vegetables on the city-owned boulevard outside her house (encouraged in Vancouver and some other cities) said hardly anyone walked by without stopping to chat.

Another community garden in Vancouver is on an abandoned lot a block away from the highest-crime transit station in the city. It used to be littered with needles and condoms. Today, it's a proud little garden. Once when I went by, I talked to a gaunt, strung-out young woman. Her red nail polish was chipped, and she wore a black mock-leather coat as she squatted at the edge of a raised bed, carefully repotting vegetable seedlings in a zoned-out kind of way. She said she came to the garden and did these little tasks because it made her feel good.

You don't need a lot of skill to do something useful at a community garden, and you don't have to commit a lot of time to produce results you can actually see.

Another community garden in Vancouver's poorest neighborhood — home to the city's highest concentration of low-income housing and drug addiction — is a little oasis of green between two older buildings that are continually struggling for retail tenants. It has to be kept fenced off most of the time, but at least it's there, growing a bit of food, bringing a flicker of green pride to a destitute street.

Community Gardens Raise Property Values

The transformation of a blighted abandoned property into a community garden has a measurable economic impact. A study in New York found that opening a community garden increases property values ("a statistically significant positive impact") within 1,000 feet of the garden. And the impact increases over time. The biggest changes are in the most disadvantaged neighborhoods, and with the highest quality gardens.

A similar study in Milwaukee found that residents are willing to pay more to live near a community garden, driving up the market value of properties within a three-block radius of a community garden. That study went so far as to calculate the increased taxes to the city from the higher property values. They calculated that the average community garden contributes $8,880 in annual tax revenue to a city.

Other studies have shown that the presence of vegetable gardens in inner-city neighborhoods is positively correlated with decreases in crime, trash dumping, juvenile delinquency, fires, violent deaths, and mental illness. A simpler and more measurable economic impact of community gardens is the money saved in mowing and maintenance costs when a volunteer-run garden takes over space in a publicly financed park.

Health authorities concerned about soaring costs of obesity and diabetes love community gardens. They directly address the two main solutions to those epidemics: exercise and better diet. Research shows that urban gardeners and their families consume more fruits and vegetables, have reduced grocery bills, and supply culturally valued fruits and vegetables in ethnic communities. (To keep the money-savings in perspective, though, keep in mind this comment from a woman tending her plot in a beautiful seaside garden in White Rock, B.C.: "I'm certainly not doing this to save money—I spent as much on my organic bean seeds as it costs me to buy a big bag of fresh organic beans from Costco.")

Community Gardens As Political Power

Community gardens can also give new immigrants a chance to position themselves as local experts. In Montreal, a McGill University project called Making the Edible Landscape found that immigrants from India and Bangladesh came to community gardens with agricultural knowledge that enabled them to drastically increase a plot's yield (such as building trellises to triple available growing space).

Some disenfranchised groups see community gardens as a path to political power. "In Detroit, a lot of gardeners do it for political reasons — it's a slap in the face for agri-business, and a way to control their own food security," says Monica White, a sociology professor at Wayne State University. "Growing food is a way for African Americans to engage in a struggle for freedom. Resistance usually acts against institutions. With gardening, we take the initiative into our own hands."

Malik Yakini chairs the Detroit Black Community Food Security Network, an organization that operates D-Town, two acres of gardens in the largest park in the city, on land leased from the city for 10 years. Yakini, speaking at the Farm to Cafeteria conference in May 2010 said, "In most cities, community garden work is being done in black and Latino communities mostly by young white people with a missionary mentality.... We speak openly about white supremacy. We're unabashed advocates for self-sufficiency in the Afro-American community."

Self-sufficiency means food, and a study in Philadelphia showed community gardens grow a lot of it, even though most gardens are broken up into separately managed small plots, not geared for high production. All the same, a University of Pennsylvania research team found 220 food-producing community gardens in the city in 2008; an estimated 2.2 million pounds of food was produced, worth around $4.4 million. Most of it wasn't grown for sale: "The majority of gardeners in low-wealth communities distribute a significant proportion of their harvest to extended family, neighbors, fellow church members, and strangers who are hungry," writes Professor Domenic Vitiello.[2]

The Earlscourt Park Community Garden in Toronto is a consolidated community garden: a single 8,000-square foot garden that is geared to food production. Community members grow, tend and harvest more than 2,000 pounds of organic produce for use in The Stop's food distribution programs (for more on The Stop, see Chapter 9).

Finding Space for Community Gardens Isn't Easy

Even with all the well-known advantages of community gardens, finding space for them in crowded cities with competing claims on land is often a big challenge. Particularly vexing is security of tenure: who wants to build up a garden and then see it shut down?

Here's How

10 Steps to Starting a Community Garden

1. **Organize a meeting of interested people.** Determine whether a garden is really needed and wanted, what kind it should be (vegetable, flower, both, organic?), who it will involve and who benefits. Invite neighbors, tenants, community organizations, gardening and horticultural societies, building superintendents (if it is at an apartment building)—anyone who is likely to be interested.

2. **Form a planning committee.** These should be people who are committed and have the time to devote to it, at least at this initial stage. Choose a good organizer to be the garden coordinator. Form committees to tackle specific tasks like funding and partnerships, youth activities, construction and communication.

3. **Identify all your resources.** Do a community asset assessment. What skills and resources already exist in the community that can aid in the garden's creation? Contact local municipal planners about possible sites, as well as horticultural societies, community garden networks and other local sources of information and assistance. Look around your community for people with experience in landscaping and gardening.

4. **Approach a sponsor.** Some gardens "self-support" through membership dues, but for many, a sponsor is essential for donations of tools, seeds or money. Churches, schools, private businesses, or parks and recreation departments are all possible supporters. One garden raised money by selling "square inches" at $5 each to hundreds of sponsors.

5. **Choose a site.** Consider the amount of daily sunshine (vegetables need at least six hours a day) and availability of water, and do soil testing for possible pollutants. Find out who owns the land. Can the gardeners get a lease agreement for at least three years? Will public liability insurance be necessary?

6. **Prepare and develop the site.** In most cases, the land will need

considerable preparation. Organize volunteer work crews to clean it, gather materials and decide on the design and plot arrangement. Community gardener Velma Johnson, from the 3400 Flournoy Block Club Garden in Chicago, emphasizes the need to have a long-term vision from the outset for the future of the garden. "You need to look five years or more down the road when designing a community garden, and then work toward that vision. Chances are the garden is going to go through two or three transformations along the way, and it will be easier to work through and manage this change if you know what the garden is going to look like in the future."

7. **Organize the garden.** Decide how many plots are available and how they will be assigned. Allow space for storing tools, making compost and don't forget the pathways between plots. Plant flowers or shrubs around the garden's edges to promote good will with non-gardening neighbors, passersby and municipal authorities.

8. **Plan for children.** Consider creating a special garden just for kids—including them is essential. A separate area set aside for them allows them to explore the garden at their own speed.

9. **Determine rules and put them in writing.** Gardeners are more willing to comply with rules that they have had a hand in creating. Ground rules help gardeners to know what is expected of them. Think of it as a code of behavior. Some examples of issues that are best dealt with by agreed-upon rules are: Dues— how will the money be used? How are plots assigned? Will gardeners share tools, meet regularly, handle basic maintenance?

10. **Help members keep in touch with each other.** Some ways to do this are: form a telephone tree, create an e-mail list, install a rainproof bulletin board in the garden, or have regular celebrations. Community gardens are all about creating and strengthening communities.

Source: Adapted from guidelines of the American Community Gardening Association.

The most secure gardens are ones that have made their way onto public lands already protected from development — parks, schools and rights of way for power lines or sewer access. Park gardens often have to struggle against the argument that public land is being appropriated for private use by a self-selected group of gardeners. I understand this concern, but look at the result: volunteers will keep a portion of the park maintained, and they provide conversation, creative landscaping and interactive viewing for visitors who want to come into the gardens and visit and poke around. So who really cares?

Actually, one group who cares is park and school workers. Some of their unions see community gardeners as people who are taking over their jobs by providing volunteer labor. The same arguments can be heard when schools want to put in gardens. I know of one school where unionized staff insisted on being the primary garden builders, which cost the school's parents far more money than if they had been allowed to build the garden themselves.

The benefits of these gardens are so manifold and obvious that these turf issues will become irrelevant in the long run, especially if a garden has a wide enough coalition of supporters.

The city of Oakland moved in the direction of an Urban Land Trust when City Slicker Farms accessed $4 million in 2010 for acquiring land to grow food on. The funds were part of a $5.4 billion California state bond for projects involving water quality and access, park improvements, and natural resource and park preservation. Barbara Finnin, executive director of City Slicker Farms, described the grant as a game-changer: "It's painful to put big infrastructure in and not have the land for very long."[3]

Temporary Gardens Find New Homes

Community gardens deliver their biggest added value when they're sited in places that are not already green and protected — places like parking lots and abandoned industrial sites. This is where tenure gets tricky: demand for these lands evolves, and sometimes it's hard to justify keeping a farm going on valuable property. But what if the gardeners don't want to leave?

Davie Village Community Garden in Vancouver, B.C.: Local tax loopholes reward developers who build gardens on vacant sites.

In Vancouver, developers discovered that turning their vacant lots into community gardens while they waited for their next project to be ready could save them hundreds of thousands of dollars in city taxes. Putting a garden on a commercially zoned site allows it to be reclassified as public park or garden, resulting in an 80% tax saving — even if it is known that the garden is temporary. In one downtown property where a hotel parking lot was converted to an urban farm, the property owner is saving $132,000 a year in taxes. (Under Vancouver's tax policies, this money isn't lost to the city; it's parceled out among the remaining commercial property taxpayers.)

As a result of this discovery, developer-financed community gardens have popped up in prominent downtown locations to the delight of many. At least one has also disappeared as boarding goes up for a new residential tower — wiping out all the work that community gardeners contributed to the site (after they had lined up just to get a plot).

Given the realities of real estate land values in cities, this policy at least rewards developers for setting up gardens and managing some of them — however temporarily. For the community gardeners involved, even getting a temporary plot is obviously worth it. So how can these mutual interests of a stalled developer and an eager gardener be brought together?

In Britain, the Ministry of Environment, Food and Rural Affairs has introduced "meanwhile leases" that formalize temporary uses of public land for urban farms (and other uses). An organization called Meanwhile Projects is working across Britain "with landlords, agents, potential occupiers and local authorities to enable uses that benefit the community while something else is waiting to happen" (meanwhile.org .uk). In Bradford (UK), the developer of a stalled mega-shopping center is investing $480,000 in a temporary urban garden on a 10-acre site. A London-based charity called Global Generation has created novel mobile community gardens to deal with temporary access to land. They've converted "skips," the large construction rubbish bins, into mobile garden plots that can be wheeled around a site to keep it out of the way of cranes as the site gets built out. When it's time for eviction, they just move the skips to another temporary site. The trees and plants in the skips will eventually end up in rooftop food gardens on the completed buildings. At one 67-acre redevelopment site, Global Generation uses skip gardens to teach school children and adults about sustainable food-growing, crop rotation and waste reduction. (One skip with only a foot of soil can accommodate an orchard of five apple trees, two pear trees, two grapevines and many alpine strawberries.) One skip is covered with a plastic dome and wheeled up to nearby restaurants for the chefs to harvest fresh greens on the spot. Another is used for cultivating worms.

The Two-Block Diet Garden

Two neighbors in Vancouver have put together a new kind of community garden. It's made up of the backyards of residents in two city blocks. It started with a flyer asking neighbors if they had land available for growing food. Thirteen people showed up for a meeting. They started teaming up to plant and weed each other's backyards. That led to pot-luck dinners, a bee hive, some chicken coops, a shared greenhouse, a neighborhood compost operation, canning parties, and harvests two and three times bigger than they were before.

"We share tools, organize large purchases of seeds, compost and rentals together to lower fees," says Kate Sutherland, one of the organizers. "Each week we go to one person's garden to tackle a large project that would take a single person at least a day or two to do themselves. The results have been quite dramatic, visually and emotionally. We've all been blown away by how simple, effective and fulfilling this has been. We can't imagine going back to the way things were before our mini garden revolution."

Like so many community gardeners, she says the real payoff has been in the sense of community that's been created. "I lived on this block for 12 years and had never been inside most of my neighbors' homes; now I have been in all of the members' homes."

They've even produced a manual, *The Two-Block Diet: An Unmanual*. It includes the caution that "each neighborhood is different, and only you will know if things are going to work in your area" (twoblockdiet .blogspot.com).

Community Gardens Go Corporate

It isn't just Google, Yahoo, Sunset Magazine and Nature's Path that have corporate gardens these days. The trend to lunch-time weeding and organic food harvesting has now taken root at companies like Pepsico, Kohl's Department Stores, and the Toyota plant in Georgetown, Kentucky. On-site corporate gardens have become a fashionable new perk; some send food to food banks and some provide gardening education for the kids in the companies' childcare centers.

At Terra Nova Farm in Richmond, B.C., corporate groups are among the 1,700 volunteers who show up to help weed and plant the farm's big community garden. "We bring in corporate groups to volunteer on the United Way Day of Caring," says Arzeena Hamir, the coordinator of the Richmond Food Security Society. "They come in from London Drugs, Microsoft and Terasen Gas and mostly do weeding."

The fit soon becomes obvious: the groups get to work outdoors in an unusual situation outside their usual corporate hierarchy. They get some exercise and feel good about contributing to the community. They also come back as funders. Hamir gets half her funding from corporations. Sourcing funds is getting easier as corporations wake up to local food issues and see community gardens as a way to make a local philanthropic contribution that hits all the hot buttons: helping kids, living greener, improving diet, getting people active.

The next step for some corporations is branded sponsorship of community gardens, a move that has generated a certain amount of mud-throwing in the local food movement. Kraft's Home Farming Initiative to build 50 community gardens across the United States — and to put packets of herb seeds in select boxes of Triscuits — has some food advocates seething. Kraft set up the Triscuit-sponsored non-profit, urban farming.org, to oversee the project and stimulate web traffic. Writing in bostonlocalvores.org, Kristi Ceccarossi, a neighbor of the Triscuit community garden in Somerville, Massachusetts said she was "pretty repulsed by it." She found it "difficult to reconcile what could and should be a genuine community initiative with sponsorship from a corporation with about $50 billion in annual sales. Food giants like Kraft are largely to blame for the woeful transformation of our food system over the last 50 years.... I don't need the mammoth corporation that manufactures Velveeta to help me clear a bit of earth and prepare it for cultivation. None of us do."

In Vancouver, an offer from Hellman's, a Unilever company, for a branded sponsorship was flat-out refused by a community garden not keen on corporations enmeshed with the GMO-laced industrial food machine.

I'm as turned off as anyone by the prospect of an industrial food conglomerate trying to co-opt the urban food movement, but locavores are going to have to work this out: what are Kraft's options once it realizes it's causing the problems that created the local food revolution? Why not work with it to turn things around? The transformation of our food system at the community level will depend on the number of good-food partnerships that can be created. Growing Power, Inc. CEO Will Allen is adamant about this. He's quite prepared to work with any corporation that doesn't expect him to compromise his principles.

Do we want to feed more people good food, or don't we?

A community garden financed by Kraft or a property developer lacks the political purity of one financed by a neighborhood association. But it's better to have that "tainted" community garden than not to have one at all. We need every ally possible to get the food system turned around. If corporations want to join in, let's find a place for them. No one's forcing us to think any differently about Triscuits.

Conclusion

Community gardens satisfy so many needs in our communities that gardeners, police, seniors' centers, corporations and cities are lining up to be involved with them. They usually have other goals than simply providing food, but they invariably provide food. That's why they've been around since the 1800s, and why so many more people are getting interested in them in today's times of economic distress. So much the better that they also provide healthy activities, education and community building. Finding space for them is getting easier as their benefits become better known and flexible leasing arrangements become popular. Their reach is being amplified as corporations get involved, even if they're not always welcome.

14

Getting Food to
Hungry People

EFLECTIONS ON Thanksgiving Dinner at the Union Gospel Mission,
R Vancouver, 2008:

"12 more, down this way."

They get a cup, a bun, pumpkin-pie-and-ice cream puddle, plastic knives and forks, place mats with thanks to God and a volunteer's signature at the bottom.

"Is Richard here?" asks one young man, red-faced and greasy-lipped. "I want to thank him." Today he's just a signature on the place mat.

"OK another 12."

And they keep on coming.

Wet old shoes and torsos showing through the basement window up above us.

Pimpled, open-sored, red-and-white-faced girl, jerky in her wheelchair, folds up her mat, tells me she's kept each one for five years now. So young for four long years of this.

And still they keep on coming.

Heads down, draped in hand-out plastic ponchos.

"Bring in 6."

And still they keep on coming.

Stretched down the lane outside, soaking dampness from the sidewalk.

Toothless gums, hands mechanic-black with stains, heads capped in corporate marketing swag pulled out of gear bags, casually left behind.

"Bring in 18."

Natives, many. "Hey Morry, I'll meet you out back."

Missing parents up-country, missing school, missing jobs, missing a home, missing sick, dying, overdosing friends, now here among the exiles, scooping head-down gulps of turkey for survival.

"Hey, bun man, can I get another one? Over here."

Another 24 push in.

Rain pours outside.

And still they keep on coming.

The torsos shuffling past the window, fed in by what funnel of reserves and abuse and what broken home/wife/head? A man stares partly at me, more at internal demons dancing in grape juice cups and coffee.

And still they keep on coming.

The too-big-to-walk quack-quack lady in her brand new motorized cart that hooks the table.

Rounds of strong young guys with "strung out" written on their sorry faces, heads down to gulp, then quickly out.

"Cleaner, over here."

We slap the place mats down, signatures up, then napkins, then "Another 6."

And still they keep on coming.

From around the block, around the world, around the bend, comforted by angels here dispensing dignity and blessings — Mary, the Ismaili helper, Chinese Sarah from university, Erica coming with her jug when called.

Shoving, squeezing, sideways, in cramped space to let 12 more fill up the newly set up tables. One hour in.

And still they keep on coming.

Two thousand today, says the volunteer coordinator.

We feed and clear, rock vibes thumping through the wall that backs the worship hall where wet lines move inside.

And when they leave, take an orange for the road — and socks.

And still they keep on coming.

From dens and demons and homes with bed bugs, butting into line, pausing for this warm fresh food, then back into the dank bleak streets of Monday afternoon.

"Happy Thanksgiving," I say as one man leaves.

"Any day you're not in jail or on the street is one to be thankful for," he smiles back.

Hungry people populate every city in North America. Eighteen percent of children in the United States are living in "food insecure" households. According to the latest Canadian Community Health Survey, 11% of households with children in Canada are food insecure, meaning they don't have an adequate supply of good food. Thirteen percent of all US citizens — 38 million Americans — live in households where food security is an issue.

In Canada, 50% of the lowest income group were food insecure, half of those considered "severe," particularly single parent families headed by women, aboriginal people, and marginally housed and homeless people.

One way to look at hunger in our rich societies is to track food bank use. Food banks didn't exist in Canada until 1981; they were introduced as a short-term solution to a hunger emergency. By 2009 there were more than 900 across the country. In a typical month in 2010, 80,000 people in Canada used a food bank for the first time.

The food bank in New York City provides 400,000 free meals a day. Approximately 3.3 million New Yorkers experience difficulty affording food for themselves and their families, a jump of 60% since 2003. In the city of Toronto, food bank use is up 79% since 1995.

Between 2006 and 2010, the number of Americans getting food assistance at soup kitchens, food pantries and shelters jumped 46%. In just one year (2009), following a huge economic meltdown, food bank use in Ontario went up 19%.

What's worse is that many people's choice of food outside food banks leads to obesity and a host of other health problems. Thanks to the $1.6 billion spent every year by the food industry on advertising — almost all for salty, sweet and fat-laden food — families spend 22% of what little might be available for groceries on harmful treats, and only 12% of their grocery money on fruits and vegetables.

Families in B.C. on social assistance need to spend half their disposable income to cover the cost of an adequate supply of healthy food. With little money left to spend on food, low-income people often choose cheaper, unhealthy food with a high caloric value. That means fewer fruits, vegetables and dairy products. Families on low incomes first pay the bills to ensure a roof over their heads, heat in their homes, and transportation to work. Money for food is the most flexible part of their budget, so it's what gets cut to meet other needs.

Anyone who has even missed a meal or two knows that being chronically hungry leads to poorer physical, mental and emotional health. That's the pragmatic reason governments invest in getting food to hungry people. In the United States, the WIC program provides federal grants to states for health care referrals, nutrition education, and supplemental foods for low-income mothers and for infants and children up to age five at nutritional risk. It includes cash vouchers for fresh fruits and vegetables, which can be used at many farmers markets or roadside stands. The United States also has a school lunch program, however underfunded. Canada has no federal school lunch program at all.

Unfortunately, there's still a big gap between hungry low-income people and the "luxury" of fresh local food. "The immutable truth," says Kathryn Scharf, program director at The Stop in Toronto, "is that low-income people don't have money to spend on food, and local sustainable food costs more."[1]

Moving Beyond Emergency Relief

So what should a city do about all this hunger? Responding to the gap in services, the charitable sector has jumped in to fund food banks. Food banks can elicit huge public support because the cause is so immediate and close-to-home. But that doesn't mean they're the answer. Success is easy to measure if the goal is to prevent starvation. The challenge is to aim for the improved health outcomes and skills and personal resources that make food banks unnecessary. People living on welfare in B.C. can't afford rent, living expenses *and* good food — no matter how frugal they are.

Food banks are criticized for not explicitly aiming at putting themselves out of business. The argument is that not only do food banks perpetuate a demeaning dependency mentality among their recipients, they often do it with cast-off industrial food of dubious value; the worst-quality food is fed to those most in need, while donors glow in public kudos. I heard of one crate of energy bars delivered to a food bank by a donor. When one bar was opened, it stank of rancid peanuts. It was a year past the "best before" date on the wrapper. To their credit, food bank administrators constantly walk the tight line between getting enough food and finding food that's still fresh enough to serve safely. "If I get an offer of a bin of apples where some of them are a bit bruised, of course I'm going to take it," one food bank director told me.

A lot of food banks are as frustrated as their detractors with the growth in dependency on emergency feeding, and they are investing a lot of energy in "upstream" food security—helping people avoid the need to come to the food bank in the first place. Poverty reduction is the ultimate answer. People with decent jobs and incomes don't have to use food banks.

Giving everyone enough resources to buy their own food is the drive behind the USDA's 15 different programs that give people either money or coupons to feed themselves. The first US federal program to address food security was the Needy Family Program started during the Great Depression (it is now called the Food Distribution Program on Indian Reservations [FDPIR]). Then came the National School Lunch Program in 1946, then food stamps (the Supplemental Nutrition Assistance Program [SNAP]) in 1961. In 1972, the Special Supplemental Nutrition Program for Women, Infants, and Children (WIC) started providing food, healthcare referrals and nutrition education to low-income pregnant and post-partum women, and to children under 5. Then, in 1992, the Farmers Market Nutrition Program (FMNP) started giving WIC recipients coupons to use for buying fresh produce at farmers markets. Today these programs reach one in five US citizens at some time during the year, but much of the programs' focus is still on distributing surpluses from producers, not meeting the nutritional needs of recipients.

There are, however, lots of ways food banks and other community groups are helping low-income people become more self-sufficient. The

Food Bank for New York City uses a multifaceted approach, combining food distribution, income support, nutrition education, research and advocacy. In one program, food bank outreach staff work with low-income people to make sure they collect tax refunds and tax credits they're eligible for, so they can use the money to buy food.

In Toronto, The Stop covers the spectrum. It offers emergency food programs through a food bank and drop-in pickups, as well as community kitchens, community gardens, educational workshops, a speakers' bureau to help community members tell their stories more widely, a low-cost food market and an outdoor wood-fired oven. Its new satellite site, The Green Barn, opened in a redeveloped former streetcar barn in the Wychwood area of Toronto. It houses a large greenhouse, a kitchen, a demonstration garden, after-school programs for elementary school children, seedling production for local community gardens, vermicomposting demonstrations, cooking classes and catering. All this with accommodations for artists in the same building!

For those communities where that enviable scope of resources is out of reach, the key is to integrate as many of the main four food security elements at whatever scale can be managed: cooking, gardening, emergency food and civic engagement.

Not your average food store: Converted Wychwood Barn site in Toronto combines artists' residences, urban farming, food distribution and public education in a 60,000-sq. ft. multifaceted community center.

Community nutritionist Ellie Schmidt looks at food provision along a spectrum of choice. At the lowest end, people are given a fixed bag of food at an emergency food bank, or a plate of whatever is being served at a shelter. At the highest end, every type of food is available at all times. Her goal, she says, is to have wholesome food available once a day, every day, for everyone, by providing enough choices to suit individual needs.

Leaning off the edge of her seat, gesticulating with the passion and care that she extends to everyone who comes into the Dr. Peter Centre in Vancouver, she explains: "With some of my clients, their priorities are so out of whack they can't make eating a priority." For her, providing good food is a starting point for building relationships vital to healing the people with AIDS served by the center. Many just wouldn't eat the "perfect" diet prescribed by other registered dieticians. "If I have to put some sweet fruit into the yogurt to get someone to eat it, I'll do that. The College of Registered Dieticians would be appalled if they saw what I was serving to some people, but at least they're choosing to eat."

At Vancouver's Quest food store, which sells donated food to qualified recipients, customers can choose their own food. Putting even that level of power and control back into someone's life is a step to recovery and health.

Schmidt points out that getting good food into people's hands isn't enough. "They need to have a place to cook it and store it where it won't be stolen or eaten by rodents or bugs."

Another way she offers choice to the homeless is to help them deposit a portion of their welfare checks at their favorite restaurant or food outlet. Then they have the choice of not waiting in a soup kitchen lineup where they may feel threatened. "About 20% of the people I try that with agree to do it."

As people get their lives in order, they can move up to joining a community kitchen, or getting a plot in a community garden. People whose lives are in chaos need quality meals to get themselves stabilized before they can work on other problems.

Ellie Schmidt keeps emphasizing that there's no one answer to ending hunger. Everyone's needs are different.

Community Kitchens Bring Hungry People Together

Community kitchens, where a small group of people come together with a resource person who provides food and instruction on how to cook it, add another essential ingredient to reducing hunger: building community. Schmidt says when isolated people with multiple problems get together to cook, they gradually start talking to each other. "Then if someone doesn't show up, the group notices, and someone goes to find out what happened to the missing person. People start taking care of one another."

I'm reminded of a 1994 report on HIV/AIDS in Vancouver. Its title summed up the priorities for people in extreme need: "Something to Eat, A Place to Sleep, and Someone Who Gives a Damn." Truly beating hunger needs all three.

The origins of community kitchens may be Peru in the 1960s and 1970s. During that period, squatter settlements were exploding around city centers. Some residents started getting together to buy food in bulk, which grew into the women-led *comedores populares* (community kitchens) movement. By 2003, there were more than 10,000 of these kitchens, serving more than 3 million people across Peru. These too, grew beyond just food. One extension was a community development initiative that extended micro-credit loans from CARE to help women learn about financial management. The strongest kitchens expanded into self-sustaining, collectively owned restaurants.

In Canada, Montreal's Diane Norman is credited as the founder of the formal community kitchen movement. In 1984, she heard about Jacynthe Ouellette, a single parent on social assistance who had started cooking with her sister-in-law and neighbors to stretch her food budget. By 1986, Norman and Ouellette had teamed up to start Canada's first community kitchen in Montreal, an initiative that has blossomed into more than 1,400 community kitchens in Quebec and thousands more across North America. Since 1990, the Quebec Collective Kitchens Association has been promoting community kitchens made up of 4 or 5 members who pool their money, time and resources to regularly produce healthy meals.

The Vancouver Community Kitchen Project, as part of the Food

Bank, hosts workshops, FoodSafe courses and networking sessions for people setting up their own community kitchens. They also train community kitchen trainers. The same thing is happening on a larger scale with the New York Food Bank's CookShop education program. It provides hands-on workshops to more than 28,000 New Yorkers, teaching them how to adopt and enjoy a healthy diet on a limited budget. It also offers workshops to kids and their families in 1,300 elementary schools and after-school classes.

Joyce Rock is an example of why hunger can only be beaten with a *variety* of choices. "I wouldn't be caught dead in a community kitchen, slicing and dicing for three hours with strangers," she says. Rock is executive director of the Vancouver Downtown Eastside Neighborhood House, one of many social agencies in the tormented core of Vancouver that's home to many of the city's poorest, addicted, mentally and physically unhealthy people. "We go out with our official vehicles — shopping carts — and hand out bananas on welfare Wednesday [the day social assistance checks are handed out]. We ask people, 'Would you like to start your day with a bit of potassium?'"

Tall, scraggly haired and a non-stop talker, this former film-maker and writer sees food as central to her mission of engaging community members on the path to a better future. "Whenever I have to deal with someone in stress, I ask them to sit down, take some deep breaths, I offer them some water, and then I ask them 'have you had something to eat today?' Why would anyone assume that anyone's had enough to eat? Nobody in this neighborhood is eating three meals a day."

Her Neighborhood House office is on the corner of Hastings and Jackson, surrounded by social housing, amid the clashing currents of furtive drug dealers and sex predators on the prowl pushing against social activists dampening the poverty and dysfunction. A funky little garden sits in front of the barred window to Rock's ground floor office. Even the Neighborhood House has to keep its door locked.

A bowl of fresh blueberries sits on her desk, along with a box of Kleenex she uses to dab her eyes when her passion overflows into tears. "When you come in here for programming, when you walk in the door, there's always food — what we call substantial snacks. We make everything from scratch. Every day we have copious amounts of fresh fruit salads and dried figs and dates. We've got people eating nori — we tear it in strips and snack on it. We list on a white board everything that's in our food. We will never serve soup as long as it's metaphorically associated with materially poor people.

"When people come in for one of our programs with a Pepsi or chips or pastries, others will ask them not to bring them in here. The first things you lose when you're materially poor are privacy and choice, but your choice here is limited to eating healthy food. We have the right to tell people what not to eat if it impacts their health badly."

Food is central to the Neighborhood House's mandate. "Other people use art therapy; I use food," says Rock. "The majority of organizations here never had food as their mandate when they started up. People come in their doors and get served coffee whitener, Tang and no-name cookies."

The first goal of the Neighborhood House's Kitchen Tables project, backed by the Public Health Agency of Canada, the city of Vancouver, the Vancouver Coastal Health Authority, and local foundations, is to come up with nutritional and food quality standards. "We have to educate people, and work with the Food Bank to educate the corporate donors, to know that on behalf of nutritionally vulnerable people, with respect, we're collectively saying 'no' to a certain list of foods.

"There's a lot of control, power and emotion in food choices. When I say we don't serve white flour and white sugar, people get defensive. The poverty mentality is to take whatever is offered. Our belief is that anyone having decision-making power over what materially poor people are eating should have to come and eat what they're eating.

"Only in the last year and a half has it become OK to criticize the charity model of giving out food. We've got to push away from the conclusion that it's logical that we have food banks."

The Downtown Eastside Neighborhood House approach is to replace the charitable food model with "a sustainable local Downtown Eastside food economy, wherein residents have the living wage and affordable housing which enable them to exercise the choices implied by their inherent Right to Food." Given the burdens many of the Downtown Eastside (DTES) residents are living with, that's still a long way off.

Rock isn't waiting for people to come in the door or show up for one of the food bank's community kitchen projects to get them eating healthy food. The Kitchen Tables project goes to where the people are. A roving community kitchen visits organizations like the Chill Room (at Insite, North America's only supervised injection site for injection drug users), the Aboriginal Front Door, Oppenheimer Park, and the Vancouver Area Network of Drug Users storefront office. "We share the wonders of the humble blender and the unctuous, nutrient-rich smoothies which they produce," says Rock. "In a spirit of nutritional solidarity, we engage hundreds of low-income residents, for whom a traditional community kitchen holds no allure, in concise nutritional education.

"Our financial resources for this program limit it to one day a month and the day we chose is Welfare Tuesday [the eve of the issuing of social assistance payments]. It's a timely date as it reminds our neighbors that for between $15 for a second-hand blender or $30 for a new one, a blender is an item which could fit into their Single Room Occupancy hotel room." (For more on DTES Neighborhood House, see their website at dtesnh.wordpress.com.)

Beyond developing nutritional and quality food standards, the Kitchen Tables project has six other "food solutions" it's working on:
- menu and recipe development
- food procurement
- food preparation and processing
- food distribution
- engagement of professional support
- greening Downtown Eastside kitchens
  Source: potluckcatering.org

"Kitchen Tables is brain-dead obvious, doable and transferable, but it's a lot of work," says Rock. "If we looked at our neighbors as deserving the best healthy foods, so much would change."

How Providing Free Food Reduces Public Spending

The idea that everyone has a right to food, regardless of their responsibility for providing for themselves, sits heavily with those who think that such a "right" creates an incentive for dependency — not to mention

On Santropol Roulant:
Young, Green Meals on Wheels in Montreal

A traditional way of getting food to those in need is Meals on Wheels. Typically financed by a health authority, volunteers (usually elderly) drive ready-to-eat meals to people who are stuck at home. An inspiring post-carbon variation of the usual seniors-to-seniors Meals on Wheels program is Montreal's Santropol Roulant, the biggest of Montreal's 90 Meals on Wheels programs. Run by ten full-time staff (backed by foundation funding) plus interns and almost 1,000 volunteers, it offers bicycle-powered meal deliveries, serving 90 meals a day to 150 clients. (It also has a commercial kitchen, community bike repair center, a second-hand clothing store, an organic café, and a large-scale worm composter to recycle nutrients.)

"We use food as a vehicle to break social and economic isolation between generations and to strengthen and nourish our local community," says the organization's vision statement.

What's unusual about this meal-delivery program is the age of the volunteers and the source of their food. A typical Meals on Wheels program has seniors in their seventies doing the driving. At Santropol Roulant, the average age is 23. University students pedal around the neighborhood with custom-made backpacks that keep the food warm. All the meat they serve is prepped at their own kitchen and comes from two local farms, and a third of the produce comes from the Roulant's rooftop garden at nearby McGill University. The rest is surplus produce donated by nearby grocery stores and wholesalers. For the students (especially students learning English as a second language), it's a chance to learn more about Montreal, practice their language, get some exercise, and do some useful volunteer work. The seniors getting the meals have the bonus of getting regular visits from a young person.

huge social costs borne by taxpayers who fund that right without their consent. This is a variation of a "moral hazard": by providing food for people, they're encouraged to become dependent, knowing they don't have to take responsibility for feeding themselves. This is the primary concern of public policy-makers, who have to weigh compassion for needy recipients against respect for tapped-out taxpayers. Their reluctance to commit tax dollars to public spending on food has put the load on charities, churches and food banks. Unbelievably, almost no research has been done on connecting the requirements of people in extreme need (free fresh, quality food) with relief for taxpayers. Now that's changing, with research being done that adds a public cost-saving imperative to the moral and political imperatives of feeding people in need.

Dr. Karen Cooper has been studying the effects of proper diet on homeless people for the city of Vancouver. Her evidence shows that feeding the neediest people reduces public spending on police and emergency health services. Even before her final report was completed, there was no doubt in her mind that helping people out of homelessness needs a new mantra: "housing and food first."

"We should be feeding homeless people really good food, as much as we can get them to eat," she says, noting that on the strength of reduced police costs alone, feeding people afflicted with various combinations of drug addiction, mental illness and homelessness will save money. In many cities, a disproportionate number of police calls are to low-income housing projects looking after people with multiple disorders. The calls are triggered by fights, assaults, thefts, fires, overdoses and a lot of other crazy behavior. All those dangerous acts are exacerbated when people are hungry. Their bodily systems are out of balance, and stress levels are in the red zone. They are overwhelmed with as much anxiety about their next meal as their next fix — all for lack of minimally adequate nutrition. To think of feeding people as a crime prevention and drug treatment measure is to go to an extremely simple and obvious starting point. Feeding people gets strangely overlooked in the debates about methadone, detox centers, prescription heroin, emergency services, and all the other complications that beset chronically hungry people.

What if we focused on getting nutritious food to these people before anything else? Food is, after all, the biggest, most important "drug" we put into our bodies. What if we controlled it better? Karen Cooper says the cost of providing free food could easily be covered just by the reduction in police calls to attend to problems created by chronically hungry people. That's before adding the costs of fire calls, courts, jails, parole supervision, ambulances, emergency room medical services and disease, all fueled by malnutrition.

Cooper interviewed dual-diagnosed people (addicted and mentally ill) in shelters and in two low-income housing complexes in downtown Vancouver. When the housing centers started feeding everyone quality food twice a day, emergency calls for police and fire went way down. So did drug use. "Everyone tells me that when they're housed and fed, they lower their drug use. Usage keeps going down the longer they're in a shelter and getting food."

Even those of us not afflicted by severe hunger know how lack of food can add stress, irritability and short-tempered behavior to our lives. For a city that has North America's only supervised injection drug site, (founded on the premise that enabling safe injections is a first step toward stabilizing a user's health and preventing the spread of HIV/AIDS and hepatitis from dirty needles), the notion of starting with a healthy diet seems too obvious to state. But it has been overlooked in the chaos of rescuing people from various personal disasters.

"This is proving the obvious," says Cooper, "but people haven't been thinking about this or studying it. Data to prove this doesn't exist.... The best thing we could do for homeless people, their communities and our pocketbooks is provide wonderful food for them."

Donated poor quality, stale-dated industrial food loaded with sugar and sodium is not what she's talking about. "A person's blood sugar level is the biggest factor in poor self-control. If the brain's governor is starved of energy, you literally run out of energy for self-control." When glucose is low or can't get to the brain due to alcohol in the system, people are less able to control their attention, regulate emotions, quit smoking, cope with stress, resist impulsivity, or refrain from criminal and aggressive behavior.

This conclusion was also borne out by another study in Vancouver's poorest neighborhood that found that food affects mental status and behavior. "Increasing the intake of specific nutrients such as omega-3 polyunsaturated fatty acids and folate, has been found to improve mental health. Blood glucose may also play a role in self-control and therefore a low glycemic index diet may improve some behaviors."[2]

Just as important as access to food is access to fresh, clean water, which costs nothing once it's hooked up. Urine tests of drug users in Vancouver show that many are dehydrated. Thirsty people are just as edgy as hungry people. But the city removed public water fountains because they were being used for preparing drug injections.

Eating Well Is the Best Medicine

Karen Cooper found that when overweight people in shelters get quality, regular food twice a day, their weight goes down because they stop craving and eating junk food. Underweight people eating regularly gain weight. "Harm reduction leads to cost reduction."

A meal program at a social housing project run by the Portland Hotel Society in Vancouver found that feeding residents one good meal a day reduced 911 emergency calls by half. With three meals a day, 911 calls stopped. A network of doctors, nurse practitioners, dieticians and midwives in Toronto (Health Care Providers Against Poverty) uses provincial government "Special Diet Allowances" under social assistance regulations to arrange funding to overcome hunger.

There's a wealth of data to suggest that this is money well-spent. Healthy eating prevents chronic diseases among people of all ages, from pre-school children to older adults.

Until research like Karen Cooper's becomes more widespread, healthy eating will struggle for public spending dollars like all other preventive programs. It's hard to celebrate the absence of something (disease, hospitalizations, emergency police calls) as a measurable outcome of public spending. But just as spending on social housing for homeless people has been widely proven to be more cost-effective than leaving people on the streets, so too is spending on food being proven as a way to save costs.

Maybe this will one day translate into fresh, healthy food being a priority in hospitals. No doctor running a hospital would dream of having patients take irregular, low-quality pills, but the same hospital is willing to serve a brown steaming mush for dinner, ignoring patients' basic food needs. Ellie Schmidt says hospital food for her AIDS patients is typically so unappetizing that they regularly lose weight and become less healthy because they can't eat hospital food.

Money Isn't Everything

It's not just poverty that prevents people from eating adequately. San Francisco Food Systems identified other barriers to food security for low-income people: difficulties in getting transportation to grocery stores, lack of conveniently located quality food stores and farmers markets, and neighborhood crime (sffoodsystems.org). The New York City Food Bank estimates that more than 3 million New Yorkers in low-income neighborhoods lack access to affordable, nutritious food. Elderly and disabled people are further hindered by not being mobile enough to get adequate food when it isn't available near them.

Public health officials are now starting to see food security as part of the solution to cutting costs for treating diseases. "We want the food needs of residents to be planned for in all social housing," says Claire Gram, regional coordinator for Vancouver Coastal Housing. That could mean connecting tenants to neighborhood food programs or enabling them to cook or just heat up food in their rooms. One study recommends all social housing should offer tenants at least a fridge and a microwave, or else have staffed communal kitchens where residents can plan and cook together. Ellie Schmidt says that communal kitchens without staff and funded programming are a "disaster": food, utensils and cookware get stolen, and then the kitchens aren't used.

Zero Hunger Lessons from Brazil

The city of Belo Horizonte in Brazil — "the city that beat hunger" — is a place where all this knowledge about the importance of food has been turned into action. A state capital of 2.4 million in a metropolitan area of 5.4 million in southeastern Brazil, it stands out as the one city in the world that has made eliminating hunger a priority. It helps that it's in Brazil, one of the few countries on track to achieve the UN's Millennium Development Goal of eradicating extreme poverty and hunger by 2015. The country has a Zero Hunger strategy, food grants to families, a school meals program and a federal food procurement program.

Belo Horizonte's policy of food security as a right of citizenship, guaranteed by law, has resulted in food programs that reach 800,000 out of its 2.5 million citizens. The most obvious measure of success is a 60% decrease in child mortality in the decade after this policy was introduced in 1993. The number of children under five hospitalized for malnutrition went down by 75%, largely as a result of providing a nutrient-rich flour made of locally produced ingredients to mothers of young children (see ruaf.org). In 1995, one of the most visible campaigners for this initiative, activist Herbert de Souza ("Betinho") was voted the most admired Brazilian in a national survey (ahead of Pelé, the soccer player).

The Belo Horizonte municipal government starts with the premise that food security is a public good, and that the government is accountable to people who can't afford to buy food in the market. As in northern countries, the city manages federally funded meals in elementary schools and childcare centers. Belo Horizonte's food banks only supply charitable organizations and social agencies that prepare communal meals, not meals for individuals.

Four "popular restaurants" in different areas of the city serve 20,000 subsidized meals a day to anyone who shows up for the simple, frugal lunches and dinners during the work week.

A distinguishing feature of Belo Horizonte is the finessed mix of public regulation and private business. A variety of commercial farmers market-type outlets are licensed to set up at public locations. They are required to sell basic food items at low costs set by the city—up to 50% below market—but they can offer other foods at market prices. Workers' Convoy vans are required to serve low-income neighborhoods on weekends in return for being allowed to set up in profitable central locations on weekdays. In another market intervention of a sort, the city publishes information—accessible online and on bus-stop posters—showing the best prices on food items at dozens of commercial establishments.

A bus selling a subsidized monthly basket of 22 basic household products, including food, to registered low-income families visits low-income neighborhoods weekly or bi-weekly. The city only covers 2% of the cost of this program. Similar subsidized "Good Food Boxes" are distributed in cities in North America, including Toronto and Montreal. Compared to a food bank or shelter handout, these boxes come with guaranteed high-quality contents, and they give the recipient the dignity and responsibility of purchasing them — a step up on the spectrum of choice.

Conclusion

Hunger amid plenty remains one of the inexcusable conundrums of our time. In the United States, there's enough food available to load up eight dinner plates with food every day for every person, yet 13% of US citizens have to deal with some kind of food insecurity.

Hungry people don't suffer alone. Their ill health and hospital visits add costs for everyone. When hunger is combined with homelessness, mental illness or addiction, the added costs of police, hospitals, courts, jails and damage to social housing are far greater than they would be if good food were provided to everyone in dire need. Well-fed people don't fight as much as hungry people. They also heal faster and use fewer harmful illegal drugs.

Hunger is something everyone can understand, so it evokes generous support for charities running emergency food banks and food-serving community agencies. But those patch-work rescue missions shouldn't be mistaken for a long-term solution to hunger.

Cities that have really made headway in getting fresh food to hungry people are those that have embraced integrated policies that align charitable organizations, government interventions, and commercial food suppliers. They work simultaneously on handing out emergency food, building individual and community capacity for self-sufficiency, and changing whole systems of food distribution. They integrate emergency food with cooking, gardening and community engagement by moving upstream from take-what-you-get handouts to allowing people more choice, selling them subsidized Good Food Boxes, teaching them how to cook well at a minimal expense, and getting them involved in growing — or even gleaning — their own food. They also work at removing non-monetary barriers to food security: making sure public transportation connects low-income neighborhoods with grocery stores, bringing food vans to low-income neighborhoods, and ensuring social housing rooms have at least a fridge and microwave oven.

Universal access to enough quality food has to be seen as a basic building block of a healthy society.

15

Ending
Food Deserts

M Y FRIEND MARY counts herself as one of Detroit's luckier residents. She lives in a restored heritage apartment tower overlooking the Detroit River and Belle Isle Park. She has a local food store a block and a half away, and she passes a bigger, more upscale one on her daily drive from downtown to work. She has a car; she has choices. Her first choice is to go to the Eastern Market on Saturdays, a local food district where as many as 40,000 people come from all over the metro area to buy direct from hundreds of open-air stalls. The Market has been feeding Detroit since 1891.

Mary's day-to-day choice is to shop at a store three miles away; it's one of the few in Detroit that caters to a complete demographic range: from the senior executives who live nearby, to people who arrive with their own shopping carts. "I avoid the nearby food stores if I can," she told me. "There are always guys hanging around outside with those little bottles of beer. I'm never comfortable, although nothing has ever happened to me."

Later, when I called to follow up, she said she had stopped going to the local store entirely: "The store closest to me had a rash of pursesnatching in the parking lot in broad daylight. So I stopped going there."

Mary's less well-off neighbors in Detroit don't have that choice. Living in Detroit, they have fewer choices than almost anyone in North America when it comes to buying fresh food. A 2001 study by Phila-

delphia-based Food Trust found that Boston and Philadelphia had the
fewest supermarkets per capita, but Detroit is a strong contender for
food desert acreage.

Within Detroit's 139-square miles, there are more than 1,000 convenience stores that sell some kind of food, and 155 grocery stores, but no
big-name grocery supermarkets. In 2003, there were only five grocery
stores over 20,000 square feet. That's less than half the size of Walmart's
smallest Neighborhood Store format. Most of Detroit's residents live in a
fresh food desert. Roughly 550,000 people, or about half the population,
have to travel twice as far to reach the closest mainstream grocer as they
do to reach the closest "fringe food" location — a fast-food restaurant or
a convenience store of the type that features alcohol, cigarettes, lottery
tickets, snacks and a few tired fresh fruits and vegetables.

Detroit may be the worst city for food deserts, but it has many competitors. In 1990, the Dallas City Council commissioned a study of grocery stores in south Dallas, a predominantly low-income area, and found
only a handful of grocery stores, with none larger than 20,000 square
feet. In Chicago, more than 600,000 people live outside walking distance of a decent grocery store. As one Chicago food activist describes it,
"In my neighborhood, I can buy designer gym shoes, every kind of fast
food, junk food, all kinds of malt liquor, illegal drugs, and maybe even
a semi-automatic weapon. But I cannot purchase an organic tomato."[1]

In large areas of Toronto, it is difficult or impossible to find a grocery
store or supermarket within walking distance. In Montreal, 40% of the
population can't walk to a store with an adequate supply of fresh fruits
and vegetables. A 2003 study found that in three California counties —
Alameda, Contra Costa and Santa Clara — only 52% of residents lived
within half a mile of a supermarket. Those without cars were dependent
on buses running at 30- and 60-minute intervals in the evenings and on
weekends, which are usually the times when working families can shop.

Wherever there are extensive low-income neighborhoods, there are
food deserts. East Harlem has half as many fresh supermarkets as the
Upper East Side in New York (and double the rate of obesity). It's a pat-
tern that stretches across the United States. Nationwide, middle- and
upper-income neighborhoods have more than twice as many supermarkets per capita as low-income neighborhoods.

Fresh fruit in short supply: Not much choice in this Chicago neighborhood.

In place of big supermarkets with fresh meat, produce and dairy products, small convenience stores do whatever's required to make a buck. They load up on high-margin unhealthy snack foods, liquor and cigarettes. Sometimes they become de facto liquor stores, which then become magnets for crime, scaring away food customers. Because these stores don't get any volume price breaks from wholesalers, and they've got a captive market, what fresh food they do stock is typically more expensive than elsewhere, so it doesn't move as fast, it's not very fresh, and few people buy it. Meanwhile, the big stores in the suburbs not only have space for high-margin banks, pharmacies, delis and coffee shops, they can afford to keep fresh food prices down because of the large volumes they sell.

Food Deserts Ruin Health

Not being able to access decent food is synonymous with poor nutrition. Low-income neighborhoods are plagued by poor health from the high-fat, high-sugar, high-sodium snack foods so readily available in convenience stores and fast-food restaurants. When distances to grocery stores are shorter and distances to fast food and "fringe food" are longer, diet-related community health improves. As long as access to healthy food is difficult, people living in food deserts can expect to have greater rates of premature illness and death from diabetes, cardiovascular diseases, cancer, hypertension, obesity, kidney failure and other diet-related diseases. In Detroit, people living in neighborhoods with the worst access to fresh food have almost twice the rate of deaths from cardiovascular disease. This isn't necessarily all about the food they eat — or don't eat — but it's hard to deny a connection.

This isn't just a US problem. A study of 2,900 citizens in Edmonton, Alberta, came to the same conclusion: the odds of being obese were significantly higher where there was a preponderance of fast-food restaurants and convenience stores and an absence of grocery and produce stores.

Cars Drive Food Desertification

It's hard to believe food deserts could be so persistent and widespread when the harm they cause is so evident.

Given the choice, people living in food deserts would eat fresh food just as much as people living in the suburbs. Like my friend Mary, the ones who can afford to, drive to the suburbs to get it, leaving behind a potential business opportunity that never seems to materialize. Grocery stores abandoned the North American inner-cities in the 1960s and

1970s, following their more lucrative customers out into higher-income neighborhoods. In Detroit, it's been calculated that at least five new supermarkets could be supported by the customers who live in food deserts but shop elsewhere. But if those customers are too scattered, and if population is still declining, and the people left are spending less on food than higher-income residents, the business case for a new grocery store dissolves.

Cars are a big factor in food deserts. Many of the low-income food desert neighborhoods were built as car-dependent suburbs, where everyone was expected to drive to a shopping mall, so there was no need for scattered commercial development. "Infill" grocery stores never existed. Today, many food desert areas are low density, making public transit hard to justify. It's probably not a coincidence that Detroit, the ultimate food desert city, is both the most expensive city in the United States in which to own and operate an automobile *and* the world's top potato chip-consuming city.

More than a fifth of Motor City households don't own a car, but public transit isn't great, so a trip to the grocery store that involves a stroller, kids in tow, and waits at bus stops can be a major endeavor — and a further impediment to healthy eating. In West Oakland, California, another poor neighborhood where there's no large grocery store, one out of three people is carless.

When a major chain wants to assemble property to bring a big grocery store into a food desert, the difficulty of finding enough space for parking often blocks the way. And once someone has a car, they've always got the option of driving to a suburban mall to get groceries, undermining the business base of grocery stores within walking distance.

Crime and Groceries Don't Mix

Here are the major reasons cited by national retail experts in a *Detroit News* story on why brand supermarket chains avoid tough low-income neighborhoods:

- Net profits at supermarkets are 1–5% of revenue. If shoplifting by customers and employees costs 7–8%, the store is doomed to lose money.

- Security costs are high, something most suburban locations don't need. Shopping carts often disappear, at $300 per cart.
- Employees don't feel safe from robberies, thefts and assaults both inside and outside the stores.
- It's difficult to find qualified managers. Most prefer the suburban locations.
- It can be hard to find employees who can pass reading, writing and math tests along with credit, drug and criminal background tests. And there is a constant turnover of employees — "a human resource nightmare."
- Declining population: No national chain wants to move into an area that is losing population.
- Lower per-capita income means less expenditure on food.
- Racism and discrimination accusations. If the store raises its prices because of higher costs of doing business, it is often accused of gouging the poor.
- One well-publicized violent crime or armed robbery can cost the store 10% of its business. Three such crimes, experts say, and the store may as well close its doors.

  Source: "Grocery Closings Hit Detroit Hard," by Joel J. Smith and Nathan Hurst, *The Detroit News* July 5, 2005.

Yes, There Are Oases

Getting grocery stores to set up shop in neighborhoods where the market won't deliver profits can only be done if outside funding intervenes. Either that funding materializes, or we surrender to declining public health, disease, malnutrition and premature deaths. Wayne State University Professor Kameshwari Pothukuchi's extensive study on inner-city grocery stores found the majority of cities didn't have programs to get fresh food into underserved neighborhoods. In many cases, city governments and partners have worked hard to get a single grocery store into a troubled neighborhood, but Pothukuchi's look at 32 cities found that planners can waste a lot of time on such ad hoc interventions.[2]

Where planners and other city officials have looked at the bigger picture, with systematic and city-wide efforts, they've been able to gain some traction. This only happens where someone has been able to pull together high-level political leadership, skilled public agencies, and (often) partnerships with non-profits and grassroots advocates.

In Pennsylvania, the Pennsylvania Fresh Food Financing Initiative (FFFI), a public-private partnership set up in 2004, was the first state-wide financing program to get fresh groceries into underserved neighborhoods. It leveraged $120 million in state grants to make loans to 83 grocery store owners so they could open up new stores or renovate existing ones. The money was used for market studies, land acquisition, capital equipment, training and operating costs.

After being recognized as a model for effective government action by the Kennedy School of Government, the FFFI became the model for the $400 million federal Healthy Food Financing Initiative announced in 2010.

In 1994, 10 years before the FFFI, a program called Retail Chicago was able to attract grocery store development by simplifying city approvals and providing regulatory sweeteners. City staff helped with neighborhood and retail analyses, land assembly, and development approvals. The program involved non-profit Community Development Corporations (CDCs) and hung out the carrots of property tax abatements, low-interest loans, tax-increment financing, and bond financing in enterprise zones. It succeeded in bringing grocery stores into neighborhoods that were otherwise unattractive for business, and the city got paid back with the local sales tax revenues.

CDCs also helped bring new grocery stores to inner-city neighborhoods in Pittsburgh and Boston. Usually, a CDC will own and develop a retail site, then lease it to a private operator.

Non-profits have an important role to play in helping retailers develop local connections and customer loyalty in otherwise distrustful neighborhoods.

In Cleveland, Neighborhood Progress, a partnership of business, foundation, and community leaders, worked with CDCs to help Dave's Supermarkets, a local chain, open a 35,000-square foot store that offered 100 jobs in a neighborhood that hadn't seen that level of private investment in 25 years.

In Rochester, the city worked out a deal for Tops Markets to build five new stores, including one in the underserved neighborhood of Upper Falls. That store went into a shopping center developed by the Rochester Economic Development Corporation.

In New York, the New York Food Retail Expansion to Support Health (FRESH) program, modeled on FFFI, demonstrates what can be done by using zoning incentives. The FRESH program gives developers extra residential space if their development includes a food store that devotes 30% of its retail space to perishable fresh or frozen foods. It also eases parking requirements in pedestrian-oriented neighborhoods and allows larger grocery stores to be built in light manufacturing zones without reviews and special permits.

Chino went one better, becoming the first city in California to include public health in its urban plan, enshrining in its land use policy the goal of ensuring that healthy food is available in all neighborhoods. It is now city policy to fast-track permitting for grocery stores in underserved areas. It's still too early to tell how that added legislative clout will lead to more results than, say, Philadelphia's sustainability plan goal of bringing local food within a 10-minute walk of 75% of residents by 2015.

Just Say No

Some cities have flexed their legislative muscles to block unhealthy food options. This doesn't cost anything and works to create market openings for healthy food. The Chicago Supermarket Ordinance of 2005 forbids supermarkets that close down from preventing other supermarkets from opening in the same location. The only exception is the allowance of a three-year restrictive covenant on a site if the original supermarket relocates within a half mile of its vacated premises.

In Los Angeles, a 2008 moratorium on new stand-alone fast-food restaurants in certain low-income areas became a permanent ban in 2010. The intent is to give people more food choices by encouraging sit-down restaurants, full-service grocery stores and healthy food outlets to move into these areas. "This is not an attempt to control people as to what they can put into their mouths. This is an attempt to diversify their food options," said council member Jan Perry at the time of the unanimous council vote. Stand-alone fast-food restaurants can't open within half a mile of existing restaurants in the fast-food saturated area that encompasses 800,000 residents. It may take a while for measures like this to open up a market niche for alternative food outlets, especially if the incentives of friendly zoning and easy permitting aren't in place.

The city of Arcata in northern California has a novel approach to the problem. That city has frozen the number of "formula restaurants" at nine. The only way a new fast-food restaurant can come to town (and then only in certain business districts) is to replace an existing one.

Farmers markets, while still fringe players in the overall food retail picture, are surprisingly effective in injecting community-based fresh food into food deserts. The US Farmers Market Nutrition Program (FMNP) distributes $1 million in FMNP vouchers in Brooklyn, Upper Manhattan and the Bronx. This is enough to stimulate the creation of numerous farmers markets. Philadelphia is seeing an upsurge of farmers markets in low-income neighborhoods. The Food Trust, a non-profit, runs 30 farmers markets in greater Philadelphia that accept food stamps as well as FMNP vouchers. Another 25 communities in Philadelphia are on a waiting list to get their own farmers markets. Still, these markets are only open once or twice a week in scattered locations, and most shut down during winter, so they're a useful, but limited, solution.

Freshening Up the Corner Store

Yes, the ultimate solution to food deserts is more supermarkets in underserved areas, but in the meantime, many cities are looking creatively at the assets that are already in place: the corner stores. Low-income neighborhoods often have a corner store that serves as the de facto grocery store (though they sell little or no fresh food). The rent, insurance and labor costs are already being paid; they're usually in high-traffic locations; the proprietors know something about food, and they have enough management expertise to run without subsidies. Could these corner stores be converted into fresh food stores?

A lot of cities are looking for the key to unlock this asset. Several have found it — or, more accurately, them. Detroit Fresh Food Access Initiative, organized by the Detroit Economic Growth Corporation, includes a program to makeover "party stores." They've recruited 20 stores, mostly in needy areas. Consultants provide advice to the owner on what fresh food to carry, in-store marketing materials, nutrition brochures, connections with wholesale distributors, and outreach to let residents know that fresh produce is now available in their neighborhood.

"We bought a fridge for one store, and we're planning health fairs in some stores," explains Kameshwari Pothukuchi, who is working on the project.

"If stores are interested, we provide them with basic advice — about suppliers, shelves, where to locate the products. Stores already offering some fresh food did better. Some stores would make orders in the first ten days of the month when food stamps were coming in. We provide information about pricing, but we don't tell store owners how to price.... The distribution network is the hardest. That is the big barrier."[3]

In Oakland's Fruitvale district, California Food Policy Advocates approached School Market, a 1,300-square foot 7-day-a-week convenience store where snack foods were the best-selling item. Their objective was to help the owner sell more fresh produce and dairy products. After coming up with $7,000 to pay for a refrigerated display rack, façade improvements, start-up inventory and marketing, the store became an important source of fresh produce and other nutritious foods. The Advocates listed five reasons for success:

- help from a seasoned consultant with extensive hands-on experience in produce markets
- a willing owner who wanted to increase fresh produce sales
- space available in the store
- a strong existing base of customers who also shopped at larger supermarkets
- enough customers within walking distance
  Source: Ed Bolen and Kenneth Hecht, "Neighborhood Groceries: New Access to Healthy Food in Low-Income Communities," California Food Policy Advocates, January 2003.

In London, 17 convenience stores are being given a "fruit and veg makeover" as part of the Buywell Project. This includes appointing a member of the store's staff to champion fresh fruits and vegetables and connect with the larger Change4Life better eating campaign. The program is based on a pilot scheme run by the Department of Health in the northeast of England, which produced an average 40% increase in sales of fruit and vegetables.

Two types of independent grocery stores are successful in fresh food-deficient neighborhoods. One is the specialty store that has a focused selection of high-quality perishable fresh foods for frequent shoppers who buy in small volumes. The other is the ethnic store that specializes in food for a particular ethnic community, usually recent immigrants with low incomes. Either way, there has to be an experienced, well-capitalized and dedicated entrepreneur at the helm prepared to work 12–15-hour days.

People who have worked on corner store makeovers come back to some of the same policy recommendations we've heard elsewhere: governments have to provide grants, tax breaks, easier or low-cost loans, streamlined processes, technical assistance, and easier access to vacant land. They also need to build food access into the requirements for a rezoning or development permit — new developments that want rezoning have to provide a food store to get it.

Food Without Mobility Is Not Enough

Owning a car actually has a greater effect on access to fresh food than living close to a grocery store. So, another way governments can help with food access is to enable people without cars to get to existing grocery stores. While establishing grocery stores within walking distance is the ideal, providing bus service through food deserts to the nearest supermarkets is also vital. While they work on getting permanent grocery stores into underserved neighborhoods, many cities are sending mobile grocery vans into the heart of food deserts. In Toledo, Ohio, the Mobile Market Program has been running since 1984; it sends a grocery-store-in-a-van to housing centers for seniors and disabled people once a week. Volunteers help deliver groceries to homebound residents at some of the stops. Designed to break even, it gets a $15,000/year subsidy from United Way. Its scope is limited: only 150 clients a week.

Baltimore has a program that eliminates the need for fancy vans in getting food to food deserts. The city's first "food czar," Holly Freishtat, set up a virtual supermarket arrangement with two libraries, the health department, and Santoni's Supermarket. Each of the participating libraries is at least a mile from the nearest supermarket. Customers come in to the libraries' computers and order groceries online, paying with cash, credit, checks or food stamps. The next day, they come back to the library to pick up their groceries, with delivery costs subsidized by the Baltimore City Health Department. The program required $60,000 of federal stimulus money to get it going.

Another approach is New York's Green Carts program that licenses mobile food carts that sell only fresh fruits and vegetables in underserved neighborhoods. Set up in 2008, the plan was to have 350 carts in Brooklyn and 1,000 vendors city-wide, but by mid-2010 only 84 had been licensed in Brooklyn — with mixed results for the vendors. The ones in areas far from local grocery stores do better, especially if they have a food stamp machine. Grocery store lobbyists accuse these carts of cannibalizing local stores and undermining already-imperiled local economies.

"I agree with having more fruit and vegetable vendors, because it promotes health," one vendor told a *New York Daily News* reporter. "[But] it's not a business that makes a lot of money." He said he was putting up with selling vegetables while he waited to get what he thinks will be a more lucrative license to sell hot dogs and ice cream.

Unfortunately, New York's mobile perishable foods carts are burdened by many health and safety regulations. One of the most onerous is the requirement that carts be stored overnight in a place inspected by health officials. It took New York three years to get its program going.

In general, high set-up and regulatory costs push most mobile vendors to higher-market, high-traffic locations (if a city allows them to be there).

Conclusion

Waiting for the market to deliver healthy foods to shrinking neighborhoods with low incomes and high crime rates is going to be a long wait.

Crime, fear and shrinking markets scare supermarkets away. Cities that are making progress are the ones partnering with grocery retailers, neighborhood groups, funding organizations, Community Development Corporations and commercial lenders to entice grocery stores back into abandoned neighborhoods, or strengthen ones that are already there.

It's not easy. Successful cities have used various combinations of inducements, such as grants, tax breaks, zoning incentives, and low-interest loans. They have also used prohibitions, including banning fast-food restaurants and preventing restrictive covenants on former grocery store locations.

Some cities are making some headway by converting corner snack stores so they can sell more fresh produce, or by allowing mobile vans to bring mini-farmers markets to people who can't get to grocery stores. Full-fledged farmers markets accepting food stamps and Farmers Market Nutrition Program vouchers are growing and helping, but in a small way. In any city, frequent bus routes to major grocery stores are a big step forward.

Public spending to make fresh food accessible in food deserts is increasingly justified on economic grounds by the savings in health care costs from skyrocketing diet-related diseases.

16

Is Local Food Safe?

W HEN AN OUTBREAK of *E. coli* in Minnesota that sickened at least eight people was traced to raw milk coming from the Hartmann brothers' dairy farm in Gibbon in spring 2010, the debate between freedom and food safety broke out again. Michael Hartmann argued that his unpasteurized milk didn't cause anyone to get sick, so he continued selling it even after state officials told him to stop until the farm cleaned up its act.

Once again, the freedom to eat and drink what we want clashed with the reality that someone else is deciding what is safe for us. As more people look to local food for sustenance, a lot of us want the freedom to make our own decisions about eating something grown by a neighbor. Public health officials, however, have an obligation to protect us whether we like it or not. In the Hartmann case, the brothers' customers may have disliked the state's intrusion into their relationship with their milk-seller, but no one wants *E. coli* poisoning.

In Wisconsin, a state famous for its cheese, a bill allowing direct sales of raw milk to consumers made it all the way to the governor's desk before it got killed because of its "loose standards" — and a lot of lobbying from the state's $26-billion dairy industry.

In the Hartmann case, four people ended up in the hospital, including a two-year-old who got a potentially lethal condition that can lead to kidney failure. Minnesota law allows direct sales of unpasteurized milk if it's sold on the farm where it's produced. Since the Hartmanns were delivering to drop-off locations, customers didn't see what the Minnesota health investigators saw: "the extreme buildup of manure on virtually every surface in the dairy barn," according to evidence presented to the court. The milk house ceiling was water damaged and crumbling. It was covered by thick layers of cobwebs and dust; there were dead flies and live flies in abundance, dead animals, rodent droppings, chickens in the milking parlor, rusty and corroded equipment, and milking equipment stored in a sink.

This is a case where local food advocates had to acknowledge that industrial food isn't the only threat to food safety. A lot of locavores prefer local food because they don't trust the safety of imported industrial food from unknown places handled by a lot of unknown people. At least with local food there are fewer people involved, and there is a much greater chance that consumers can get personal knowledge about the farms where their food is being grown.

There's good reason to be concerned about supermarket food: the vastly bigger scope of the industrial food system means much bigger consequences when something goes wrong. In 2010, between 400 and 500 million eggs had to be recalled due to salmonella contamination after 1,900 people across 14 states got sick. A year earlier, a peanut recall affected nearly 4,000 products. In 2008, a record-breaking 143 million pounds of ground beef got called back, including some distributed through the National School Lunch Program.

In Canada in the same year, 22 people died and hundreds of people fell ill from *Listeria* in tainted meat from Maple Leaf Foods cold cuts.

The US Centers for Disease Control and Prevention report that food pathogens are responsible for 76 million illnesses a year, 325,000 hospitalizations, and 5,000 deaths.

But is local food grown in and around cities any safer? It certainly has its own dangers. A community garden in Montreal had to be shut down in 2006 when food being grown in it was found to have metal contamination. It turned out that the garden (and four others in the city) was built on a former dump site. No one was paying a lot of attention to soil composition when it was built in 1984.

Eli Zabar, who built rooftop greenhouses to supply his restaurant and gourmet food warehouse in Manhattan, had problems with raised beds made of pressure-treated wood, the kind that's prohibited on certified organic farms because of potential arsenic, chromium and copper contamination from leaching.

One study of residential soils in areas contaminated by lead found that in a typical array of vegetables, fruits and herbs, lead was transferred from the soil through the root to the stem and leaves of garden crops. Lead comes from paint and leaded gas residues, making soil near highways more prone to have a lot of lead in it. Lead is especially dangerous to children and infants, causing brain and nerve damage, but it can also hurt adults, causing high blood pressure, hypertension, nerve disorders and muscle and joint pains.

Lead is less of an issue in fruits. But root vegetables are another matter. Because significant amounts of lead can accumulate in some roots, eating root vegetables grown in questionable soils is not recommended. But concerns about the safety of urban food should be kept in perspective. A study in the UK found that food grown on 92% of an urban area in West Midlands was only minimally risky to the average person, although "highly exposed people and highly exposed infants" faced potential hazards.

The lesson from these risks is simple: if in any doubt about what's in your soil, get it tested. Growing crops like sunflower and spinach and digging in copious amounts of compost can help remove lead and other toxic metals, but testing provides certainty. It costs less than $30 to get soil tested for toxic metals.

Air pollution is more of a problem above the soil than in it, but fruits and vegetables growing in polluted areas are safe to eat as long as they are washed. Growing crops indoors in a greenhouse is even better protection from air-borne pollutants.

Where soil contamination from petrochemicals is a concern, exposing the soil to sunlight, fresh oxygen and microorganisms from compost helps break down many harmful compounds into harmless carbon compounds.

Ken Dunn, at City Farm in Chicago, likes to play it safe after more than four decades of urban farming. "Almost everything in urban areas is contaminated to some level," he says. His solution is to grade and compact bigger urban plots, then lay down an impermeable four-inch layer of local clay that he sources at construction projects. On top of that he loads 24 inches of uncontaminated compost, which he controls by making it with kitchen scraps he collects from restaurants. Ironically, city safety concerns about composting required City Farm to shut down its one-acre row composting site and truck all the farm's food waste 80 miles to a commercial composting operation. Composting with food waste that includes meat and dairy is a safety issue when it attracts rodents.

A good way to ensure soil safety is to use raised beds (without pressure-treated wood!) filled with imported, clean soil and compost piled on top.

Will Allen at Growing Power, Inc. in Milwaukee has a formula for starting beds right on top of pavement: Start with 10–16 inches of wood chips laid down on the asphalt. Then add a 24-inch-tall mound of composted soil, 36 inches wide. To start another row, make an 18-inch path between rows with chips and old newspapers, then repeat. Allen says plant roots don't go looking for bad soil when they're surrounded by rich compost.

Larger-scale cleanup of big abandoned lots is beyond the capacity of most urban farmers. Toronto is working around that problem by getting and sharing better information about soil conditions on prospective urban farm sites. Toronto Public Health's Environmental Protection Office is putting together a soil-contaminant protocol to assess the potential risks in various uses of soil, so the city can better identify lands suitable for urban agriculture. The next step would be to assess soil being removed from construction sites and banking it somewhere for delivery to urban farms in need of good soil.

Industrial Safety Standards Hurt Small Producers

Efforts to ensure that safe food is coming out of big industrial farms are always in danger of trampling on smaller producers who can't meet compliance costs. In Canada, changes to federal meat inspection standards for abattoirs effectively shut down local meat production in many areas. The costs and loss of product identification that comes with shipping livestock to distant, centralized slaughterhouses caused some smaller meat producers to pack it in. Some are re-entering the black market in sheer defiance of regulations; others are counting on a more understanding application of rules intended for large operations (such as providing separate washrooms for inspectors). It's hard to justify the same extensive regulations for shorter local food supply chains as for big international importers and exporters.

The 2010 shutdown of the Estrella Family Creamery in southwest Washington illustrates the impact of safety regulations on smaller producers. Estrella's award-winning hand-crafted cheeses were enjoying national and international accolades when Food and Drug Administration inspectors seized all its cheeses. They had found *Listeria monocytogenes* in the creamery's products, although no illnesses had been linked to Estrella cheeses. The owners are facing the loss of their farm, unable to convince the FDA to help them overcome the problem rather than seizing everything in what the family calls a "Gestapo-like" way. A bigger, better-capitalized operation could much more easily rebound from a hit like this. Estrella is fighting back in court, forbidden to sell a lot of the cheese it had produced.

Unfortunately, *Listeria* is dangerous no matter where it enters our food system, so there's no justification for letting small producers off the hook. In 2010, when FDA inspectors found *Listeria* in 102 soft cheese samples, half of the 24 farms where it was discovered were artisan producers. But what if a pathogen is present in such small amounts that no one gets ill? The FDA's zero-tolerance principle for certain dangerous bacteria could shut down most artisan producers even though the actual danger to consumers is minimal. The level of risk is far greater in large national operations than in small operations, just based on the number of people exposed to the products.

Libertarian organic farmer Joel Salatin has a more cynical take on food inspections: "The reason local food is expensive is non-scalable regulations that discriminate against small producers," he told an

audience in Vancouver. "This is the ugly truth of the food police. The industry fears food freedom. If we had it, we'd drive them out of business.
The bureaucracy is there to protect the status quo."

New Federal Food Safety Act Won't Hurt

The Estrella seizure was one of many that is leading to more flexibility
in federal safety regulations. Most local food boosters agree that the US
federal Food Safety Modernization Act passed in late 2010 is a long-
overdue upgrade to food safety — the first since the 1930s — that won't
kill smaller producers with red tape. It has more realistic standards for
small farms and mom-and-pop producers that sell directly to consumers
via venues such as roadside stands, farmers markets and community
supported agricultural programs.

Illusory Safety

Food safety is a much bigger issue than simply checking for contaminated food that causes illness. What about excessive soda consumption
that causes diabetes? Excessive sodium consumption in snack foods that
causes heart disease? What about the antibiotics used in livestock production (more than are consumed directly by people) that are breeding
resistant superbugs?

Then there's the haphazard nature of inspection: 98% of the imported
food eaten in Canada isn't inspected. Canadian food importers aren't
required to provide documentation that traces a primary food source
to its origin. Only with the new Food Safety Modernization Act will US
imported foods be subject to the same standards as local food.

When it comes to fresh local produce, contamination is a low risk.
"Most of the stuff at farmers markets has been deemed a low hazard
food," says Vancouver Island Health Authority Officer Doug Glenn. "If
people wash and cook their foods, there is little chance for bacterial
infections."

"Food safety is entirely subjective: junk food is OK, but homegrown
chicken is not," says Joel Salatin. "Food safety is all about faith in the
person inspecting."

Amid all that capriciousness about what gets inspected is a simple
truth: local food can always be traced to its source, so it offers a

greater chance for the consumer to know if the grower can be trusted. Consumers understand this. In a July 2010 poll, 77% of Canadians said they were either "very" or "somewhat" concerned about the safety of the food they eat, up from 66% in 2007, according to an Ipsos Reid poll conducted for Postmedia News. Another 87% trust food that comes from Canada more than food that comes from abroad. In return for that trust, almost 70% of the people polled said they are willing to pay more for Canadian food than imported food, and 85% of respondents said they make an effort to buy locally grown and produced food.

The best protection against unsafe food is knowing where a particular food item comes from, how it has been grown and taking personal responsibility for eating only what's safe. That's not always going to be possible, but it's a lot more possible with food grown closer to home. The inspectors just can't cover all food. As Joel Salatin has said, "If I don't have the freedom to hurt myself I don't have the freedom to help myself."

Conclusion

Food grown in contaminated soils in and around cities, especially root crops, can be unsafe to eat. Urban food growers should have their soil tested, or they can avoid the issue by using raised beds with fresh, safe compost. Air-borne pollutants from city-grown food can be washed off.

Smaller local producers are just as capable of producing contaminated food as large producers, even if their impact is limited. However, new US food and safety laws have exempted small direct-sale operations from stringent national standards, accommodating small-scale producers who can't meet zero-tolerance standards.

Consumers prefer local food because they perceive it as safer. They have a better chance of knowing how local food is grown than they do with imported food. Most imported food isn't inspected, and the primary source of imported products is sometimes unknown.

17

What We Can Do: Systemic Changes, Personal Choices

I CAN REMEMBER MY IMPATIENCE at an early meeting of the city of Vancouver's relatively young Food Policy Council. Discussion swirled endlessly around wording for a food charter, and about how we should do an assessment of the entire regional food system before making any moves. The people around the table who had been at this for many years insisted on starting with the Big Picture.

"Can't we just do something?" I wondered, sometimes aloud. "We're just a municipal government. We can't transform all agriculture from this basement meeting room in Vancouver City Hall."

As I was to learn, we were both right. Quick wins are important, as in the city's move to add 2,010 new food-producing community garden plots in time for the 2010 Winter Olympics. But so are Big Picture visions. Cities can do a lot, but their actions always come in the wake of federal, provincial, state and regional policies "trickling down" from above. Vancouver eventually got its food charter and its food system assessment, but it still has to work through policies coming down from above.

Puzzlement among municipal Food Policy Council members is legitimate. What governance structures and policies will hasten the production and wider consumption of more local fresh food? How much

239

can be left to the marketplace? What can governments do, faced with
shrinking revenues? What's the role of NGOs, community groups, and
individual citizens? Does it make sense to have a single agency in charge
of food, like the Ministry of Food in the UK during World War II?

Food system planning has to work in a world where many people
trust the market to deliver what they value most. The line between the
world of planning, regulation and subsidies and the world of consumers voting with their dollars is never clear. "The market," represented by
free-enterprise farmers, equipment suppliers, distributors, wholesalers,
retailers and others, has been amazingly successful in delivering abun-
dant, cheap, not-always-good food to those who can afford it. But it has
only been able to do that in a world of subsidies, protectionism, publicly
funded research, supply management, land use restrictions, and freedom from huge external costs like soil erosion, water depletion, runoff
pollution, and health care.

The market isn't concerned about national security, but as cities wake
up to the realities of protecting food security, national security and resilience kick into the discussion. Nor does the market price unrestricted
agricultural land with any concern for ensuring a city can stave off dire
food shortages if its external food supply chains are broken. The market
can't be responsible for educating obese people about healthy eating, or
improving public health by making sure fresh food stores are located in
areas where low-income people can't sustain a profitable grocery business. The market doesn't care about biodiversity or vulnerability from
monocultures.

Government intervention, planning, and rules and regulations are an
inevitable part of the necessary fix to our broken food system. Governments and planners have to step in to support essential services where
the private sector is unwilling to invest. But investments have to be based
on outcomes beyond a single (financial) bottom line.

Political tensions over, for example, whether government or families
should provide school lunches will influence what's politically possible.
Some communities are more open than others to government intervention. Every city has to work around those tensions. The best way is to
have a clear vision.

When cities look up to senior layers of decision-makers, they find themselves staring at complex and often disjointed policies, rarely meshed to achieve affordable, accessible fresh local food in cities. At the international level, the Food and Agricultural Organization, the General Agreement on Tariffs and Trade, the North American Free Trade Agreement, the World Trade Organization, the World Bank and other international agreements and coalitions lay the framework for a predominantly global food system that ends up being dominated by large corporations that are fed by subsidies.

At the federal level, the mixed messages continue: the Agriculture Department wants volume; the Health Department wants nutrition; the Social Services Department wants low-income people to have access to food; the Education Department wants school lunches; the Environment Department wants less pollution, more biodiversity and reduced GHG emissions; the Trade Department wants exports; the Economic Development Department wants local jobs; the Defense Department wants security; and — everywhere — the lobbyists want to protect their clients' interests.

Belo Horizonte in Brazil is one city that has done a good job of getting healthy food to hungry people and stimulating a local agricultural industry at the same time. But they could not have done it without the backing of their federal Plan Against Hunger. The Plan aligned federal departments around food under the National Council for Food Security. The city took the same approach, centralizing all decisions about food security and making it a priority.

Other governments have made similar moves — with equally impressive results. Norway adopted a food and nutrition policy in 1975 to encourage a healthy diet, increase reliance on local food, and promote agricultural development. Within two decades, fat consumption dropped from 40% to 34% of total calories, and deaths from heart disease fell, likely influenced by healthier diets. Finland had a food policy in the 1970s that led to decreases in the consumption of saturated fats, a doubling of vegetable consumption, increases in fish and fruit consumption, and coincidentally, a 55% decrease in men's coronary heart disease.

Of all the national food-related concerns, health is the likeliest driver in unifying federal food policies because it involves the biggest costs and has the biggest impact on the largest number of people. The US Healthy, Hunger-Free Kids Act of 2010 is an example: it aims to improve school meals, support farmers through Farm to School programs, address sky-rocketing obesity rates, and feed more hungry children.

Reducing greenhouse gas (GHG) emissions is another federal-level issue closely linked to food. Growing, processing and delivering the food consumed by a family of four in the United States requires more than 930 gallons of gasoline a year, about the same amount needed to fuel the family's cars.

In the European Union, 30% of GHG emissions from consumer purchases come from buying food and drinks. Estimates from the Food Climate Research Network in the UK suggest that almost one-fifth of that country's GHG emissions come from food and drink. In British Columbia, half of the agricultural GHG emissions are from animal production, with another 17% coming from off-gassing from manure. In short, reducing GHG emissions has to involve changing what we eat, how it's grown, and how it's distributed. Expect more federal campaigns aimed at reducing the amount of meat we eat. Then expect resistance based on anti-protectionism. When Sweden tried to get EU countries to agree to reduce meat consumption and promote locally produced foods and sustainable fish in 2009, it was called out for contravening EU free-trade principles. Government interventions in the economy that provide for food are accepted by the World Trade Organization — but only if they are classified as anti-poverty programs.

Food Links to National Security

Other dangers from our unsustainable food system and related dietary imbalances are starting to surface at the federal level. The need to guarantee a country's food supplies has never gone away, but today's growing insecurity of supply is reviving attention to that need. As well, the lack of awareness of the economic significance of the food sector, partly due to the absence of a "food department" in government, impedes economic development based on food.

The UK, which had a Ministry of Food during World War II, now has a national food policy. Called UK Food 2030, it integrates all the food-related government ministries for the first time since the 1940s. Food security is part of that agenda. By 2030, the plan is supposed to ensure food security, in part, "through strong British agriculture and international trade links with EU and global partners, which support developing economies" (defra.gov.uk).

Neil Currie, general manager of the Ontario Federation of Agriculture, likes to tell the story of meeting the equivalent of the deputy minister of agriculture from Sudan. "Sudan doesn't have food. They have subsistence farming at best. But they have a national food strategy because they value food. They know they need to plan for it because it's not always there."[1]

As food shortages loom around the world, many believe the next wars will be fought over food and water. The best protection against world food conflicts is local, regional and national food self-sufficiency.

Some less obvious national security issues related to food imbalances are also starting to surface. More than a third of uniformed men and women in the United States do not meet the Army's weight standards — another reason food system reform could become a defense priority.

Realizing the need for a national food policy for Canada, no fewer than six organizations are working on one. The Canadian Federation

---

The UK's National Food Policy, *UK Food 2030*, Has Six Goals

- Encouraging people to eat a healthy, sustainable diet
- Ensuring a resilient, competitive, profitable food system
- Increasing food production sustainably
- Reducing the food system's greenhouse gas emissions
- Reducing, reusing and reprocessing waste
- Increasing the impact of skills, knowledge, research and technology

Source: defra.gov.uk

of Agriculture, heeding reports from the Metcalf Foundation, is working with representatives from across the agri-food spectrum — from producers to consumers — to come up with a 15-year National Food Strategy. The federal Liberal Party is working on what it calls "Canada's first comprehensive National Food Policy." The New Democratic Party wrapped up two years of consultation with its 2010 report, "Food for Thought," which calls for a national food policy, with local food production set as a priority. The Conference Board of Canada, a private research organization, has launched a three-year, $2 million Centre for Food in Canada. The project is financed by agribusinesses and targets a business and government audience. The Canadian Agri-Food Policy Institute, partly funded by government, is also working on a national food policy.

And from kitchen tables around the country, The People's Food Policy Project is a pan-Canadian network of citizens and organizations that is creating what it calls Canada's first food sovereignty policy (peoples foodpolicy.ca).

In the United States, food policy is mostly determined by the US Department of Agriculture Farm Bill — its most recent incarnation being the Food, Conservation and Energy Act of 2008, which directs $288 billion in spending. This gives federal government planners a heavy hand on the tiller of the US food system, steering it mostly with massive subsidies for selected products and producers (including, unfortunately, biofuel production). US federal funds available for community food projects, farmers markets, and alternative food systems are "a drop in the bucket" when compared to continuing support for more conventional agricultural programs, according to long-time community food researcher and advocate Professor Kameshwari Pothukuchi.

Every aspect of the Farm Bill has implications for cities and near-urban lands — nutrition programs, commodity programs, conservation, rural development, trade, value-added food enterprises, and air and water quality enhancement. A 2010 project in Cleveland demonstrates how cities can use federal money to change direction toward more sustainable urban food sources. The Cleveland Urban Agricultural Incubator pilot project is the conversion of a bleak half-acre vacant property into fruit and vegetable production for profitable sales to local schools, restaurants and farmers markets. Out of the $1.1 million budget, $740,000 is coming from a US Department of Agriculture program that normally helps farmers and ranchers in rural areas.

USDA Deputy Secretary Kathleen Merrigan has been open about getting rural development program money to support local and regional food systems. In a 2009 memo she wrote:

> "I would like to play the role of matchmaker...to help USDA program administrators...build local and regional food systems.
>
> "Imagine an NGO receiving USDA grant money to construct a community kitchen where farmers drop off produce and families join cooking classes that teach about healthy eating while everyone prepares fresh, nutritious meals to bring home.... Imagine a community using USDA money to construct an open-sided structure to house a farmers market.... Imagine a school using USDA loan money to set up cold storage as part of a larger effort to retrofit the school cafeteria to buy produce directly from farmers and return cooking capacity for school lunch."

Merrigan then detailed how to use USDA funding for the kind of projects being developed by First Lady Michelle Obama and her food policy team. The funding can be used for such projects as improving school lunch infrastructure, creating farmers markets and Farm to School programs, and conducting cooking classes.

The USDA's own Community Food Projects Competitive Grants Program gives out $5 million for projects that get food to low-income people, promote local food, build local food infrastructure, or create innovative local food marketing.

The Greening Food Deserts Act working its way through Congress is another move by the USDA to finance the food-producing capacity of cities and increase the availability of fresh food in underserved neighborhoods.

With a community garden and farmers market at the White House, the tide is definitely turning to US federal recognition of the importance of strong local and regional food systems.

In Canada, Toronto public health officials have targeted three federal legislative changes they think will do the most to improve public health related to food safety and diet: funding for school lunches (Canada is the only G8 country without such a program); compulsory limits on trans fats and sodium in food; and a ban on food advertising to children. When I think about how a ban like this will discriminate between healthy and unhealthy foods, I am reassured of its fairness by invoking author and food activist Michael Pollan's rule for eating: "Don't eat anything you see advertised on television." I have yet to see a TV food ad where the food isn't processed and/or loaded with fat, sugar or sodium.

Los Angeles's prohibition of new fast-food restaurants in South Los Angeles is an example of a city stepping up to use legislation to improve public health.

It can also happen at the county level. In 2010, to break the link between unhealthy food and prizes, Santa Clara County in California banned toys that come with high-calorie children's meals in restaurants.

Bans and taxes are tough politically, but they work. Thirty-three states have taxes on sugary carbonated drinks (the top source of calories in the American diet). The evidence of the taxes' effectiveness is in the millions spent by soft drink companies to resist them — or prevent them, as happened in Washington State in 2010.

Researchers in Australia spent five years trying to figure out what changes would produce the most measurable cost-effective impact on living longer and healthier. Their conclusion: increasing taxes on tobacco, alcohol and unhealthy foods, and setting mandatory limits on salt in just three basic foods — bread, cereal and margarine.

Kelly Brownell of the Rudd Center for Food Policy and Obesity says a tax on sugary, unhealthy food is the only solution to obesity that doesn't cost money: "The harm from obesity is approaching the harm from tobacco. A tax worked with tobacco, why wouldn't it work with sugary drinks? Government has to be involved or we won't solve this."[2]

What States and Provinces Can Do

The New York State Council on Food Policy, set up by then governor Eliot Spitzer in 2007, is one example of what states can do to advance food security. The Council makes recommendations to the governor on state regulations, legislation and spending to coordinate the state's food policies. It also promotes New York agricultural products, especially locally grown and organically grown food.

The 21-member Michigan Food Policy Council didn't have any funding for the recommendations in its 2006 report, but it set the framework for farmers market expansion, direct-to-consumer food sales, agricultural-processing "Renaissance Zones," attracting supermarkets to underserved neighborhoods, and expanding urban and school gardens.

A shortage of local food is currently the biggest obstacle to improving local food security and consumption. States and provinces have policy levers that can make a big difference in changing the situation. They can use those levers to protect agricultural land, institute local food quotas in state institutional food procurement, and bring in labeling and marketing to promote local food businesses.

The New York Department of Agriculture and Markets is an example of how states promote agriculture and local food. Its Agricultural Districts program provides preferential property tax assessments so farmers can afford to keep their land in production. It supports community gardens, school gardens and educational farms, even requiring vacant state lands to be made available for community gardens. Its Farmers Market Nutrition Program provides coupons for fresh produce at farmers markets to people in need. The Agricultural Districts program also provides financial assistance to municipalities to purchase development rights that protect working farms. And it promotes the sale of New York-produced food and food products. It even posts an online guide to farms that sell direct to the public.

States and provinces are also the jurisdictions that can do most about getting healthy food to the most marginalized — and saving the public the cost of dealing with malnutrition. When people beset with mental illness, addiction, poverty and homelessness are fed healthy food, they're less violent, their health improves, their drug use declines, and their pull on costly emergency health services and police and court time goes down.

What Cities and Regions Can Do

When the city of Vancouver started to take on food issues by creating a Food Policy Council, I'll never forget the city manager's response: "Please don't make feeding Vancouver a new line in the city's budget," she pleaded.

Today, Vancouver City Hall, like those in San Francisco, Baltimore, Portland, and a growing list of other cities, has converted part of its front lawn into a community garden.

Sometimes by default, the job of coordinating food policy has fallen into the lap of civic governments. In many cases, like Toronto and New York, this is because access to healthier food can reduce health costs borne by the city.

San Francisco's City Hall food garden: On-site demonstration food gardens are evidence of cities' commitment to food security across North America.

It's hard not to lump food in with other services traditionally supplied by municipal governments. "Access to healthy, low-cost food helps assure the health, safety and welfare of citizens every bit as much as other services that city governments provide, such as clean drinking water, protection from crime and catastrophe, sewage treatment, garbage collection, shelters and low-income housing programs, fallen-tree disposal, and pothole-free streets," says Darrin Nordahl, author of *Public Produce: The New Urban Agriculture.*[3]

But this hasn't meant cities are going it alone, taking on all the expenses of reforming food policy. As Belo Horizonte did in Brazil, cities are learning to partner with other public agencies (especially health authorities), NGOs, universities and

Chickens Are Everywhere

One of the things Seattle did to celebrate its Year of Urban Agriculture was raise its urban chicken limit from three to eight (even more are allowed on urban farms). In spite of ongoing bans in some cities like Toronto and Boston, backyard chicken-raising is back in hundreds of cities across North America. Chicken laws—mostly allowing them—for several hundred North American cities can be found at http://home.centurytel.net/thecitychicken/chickenLaws .html. Regulations are all over the map: from "pet" hens only, to manure management requirements and "crowing" bird prohibitions. More cities are now allowing bees, with Cleveland (one beehive per residence) upping the ante to allow residents to raise pigs, sheep, goats and geese on one-acre-and-larger properties.

community groups to improve food security in projects like community kitchens. In Cleveland, the city has been partnering with Ohio State University on a 12-week summer entrepreneurial urban agriculture course.

Cities' ultimate power is having the last say on how land can be used, and urban agriculture needs access to land. Montreal's success with expanding community gardens is closely linked to its policy of allowing urban agriculture in its parks. Montreal's Permanent Agricultural Zones cover 4% of the city's lands, addressing the ongoing challenge of finding permanent sites for urban farming. (See Chapter 4 for more on converting urban and suburban lands for growing food.) As cities make it possible, community gardens will become as commonplace as swings and playgrounds in city parks.

As part of its Year of Urban Agriculture in 2010, Seattle now allows "urban farms" and community gardens anywhere in the city, with some limitations in industrial zones. Residents can sell produce they grow in their backyards, and farmers markets can set up in more areas of the city. Building owners can get height limit exemptions to build rooftop greenhouses for food production.

Cities also have the power to promote food security with free water for community gardens, local procurement policies, opportunities for neighborhood composting, and buses to get food desert residents to groce stores and other food services.

(run agencies like health authorities and school districts have a huge le to play in making food healthy. Schools and post-secondary institutions control nutrition education, research, technological innovation, procurement policies, even vending machine contents.

Tax Breaks for Urban Gardens?

Rural properties typically get tax breaks if they produce a certain amount of agricultural produce. But letting food-producing city properties pay less tax for growing relatively small amounts of food is dangerous for financially starved cities. The city of Victoria, B.C., allows urban agriculture as an acceptable home business occupation ("a permitted secondary use in residential zones") but it was careful to attach a rider to the change: high-grossing urban farms on residential lots would still pay residential tax rates.

Meanwhile, developers in Vancouver are eagerly building community gardens to exploit a tax loophole. When a commercially zoned property is converted to a garden in Vancouver, even if it grows no food, its tax classification changes to "recreation and non-profit." One prime vacant commercial property in downtown Vancouver, a former gas station, was converted by its owner to a community garden.

Citizens love its funky charm and bursts of color. Nearby residents line up for plots. The development company that paid to set up the garden (and provide garbage removal, water and soil) got a $212,000 annual property tax reduction. In Vancouver, that shortfall is distributed among other commercial taxpayers, so there's no reduction in money flowing to the city. Discovery of this tax break has resulted in eight new gardens in downtown Vancouver, including a serious urban farm on a hotel parking lot.

Most of these farms and gardens exist month-to-month, and most of the landowners are getting far more in ta breaks than they're investing in the garden.

Sole Food Farm: From hotel parking lot to working farm in Vancouver's inner-city.

While these gardens have been delightful additions to the cityscape, there's no requirement that they produce food. A more deliberate tax policy aimed at making permanent food-growing sites would make more sense.

Woodbury County in Ohio has a smart tax policy: it offers a 5-year rebate to farms that convert to organic. The goal is the creation of permanent smaller farms with higher incomes and more local job opportunities.

Planners Picking Up on Food

City planners are only recently waking up to food as an urban planning responsibility. "Food is a sustaining and enduring necessity. Yet among the basic essentials for life — air, water, shelter and food — only food has been absent over the years as a focus of serious professional planning interest," says the 2007 American Planning Association's (APA) *Policy*

Guide on Community and Regional Food Planning. That publication was considered a breakthrough in legitimizing food system planning in the United States and Canada. At the 2009 APA annual conference, food sessions were sold out. "Cities' sustainability plans wouldn't have included food 10 years ago. Now it's recognized in many," says Jerry Kaufman, urban planning professor emeritus and chair of the board of Growing Power, Inc. in Milwaukee.[4] In a recent survey of America planners, 70% said food systems and healthy eating were a high priority for them. Food is part of climate protection plans in cities like Kansas City, Missouri. Chino was the first city in California to include public health in its urban plan, which promises to ensure that sources of healthy foods are available in all neighborhoods.

Food Policy Councils to the Rescue

In the absence of over-arching national food agencies, cities, regions, states and provinces across North America have jumped in with purpose-built food policy councils. The first one formed in Knoxville, Tennessee, in 1982. These councils work to bring together the scattered public and private food decision-makers to discuss food issues, coordinate efforts, propose policies, and run or support local programs. They alert governments about how their actions are affecting health, nutrition and food access. They've been mainly responsible for pushing food policy into the political mainstream.

In New York, the Food Policy Council brought together the Department of Agriculture and the Department of Health to implement the new WIC program (USDA Food and Nutrition Service's Women, Infants and Children food subsidies) to make it possible for farmers to accept the new cash value vouchers.

In Kamloops, B.C., the Food Policy Council's success in linking the city, school district, health authority and other key organizations resulted in Kamloops being the only city in Canada to show a decline in food bank use in the early 2000s. The Council coordinated everything from fruit tree gleaning to running community gardens to operating greenhouses and conducting horticulture training courses.

There's no blueprint for Food Policy Council success. Most of them are shoe-string volunteer operations, with no staff or only a part-time staff person. A quarter of food policy councils in the United States have no funding at all. At the state level, the better-endowed half are government agencies. Most state food policy councils have appointed members. At the county and local level, most are completely independent of government.

These councils typically start with a food system assessment and a community food charter, then go for a specific "quick win" (an inventory of available urban land, getting electronic benefit transfer equipment into farmers markets, negotiating for new food-producing plots, etc.). To be effective, a Food Policy Council has to find a way to get government decision-makers to buy into its work—whether it's through a city council resolution, having an elected official on the council, getting government funding or even just getting a government-donated place to meet. Sometimes a Food Policy Council will choose to be overtly political to get to where it wants to go: the Detroit Food Policy Council explicitly attacks what it sees as structural racism in the food system in that city. By asserting more control over food systems, these councils start communities down the path to food sovereignty.

A lot of food policy councils feed into the Community Food Security Coalition, one of the more effective advocacy groups lobbying for fresher, more local and regional food (foodsecurity.org).

Markets Move Mountains of Food

While there's a vital role for the public and NGO sectors in creating food solutions, private-sector leaders who "get it" know they too have a huge role to play. "We can create more change in three years than 30 years of public policy," says Loblaw Companies Executive Chairman Galen Weston. Loblaw is the biggest private-sector employer in Canada (they own Real Canadian Superstore, Extra Foods, No Frills, and other grocery stores), so when they make a move, it makes a difference. In 2010, Weston announced that Loblaw would shift to Marine Stewardship Council-certified seafood and source all fish and seafood products (including all products that contain seafood as an ingredient) from sustainable sources by 2013. Loblaw is doing this because buying sustainable seafood is increasingly on the mind of consumers — an example of how changing what food we buy is the most powerful lever under every citizen's control.

A more dramatic example of a big player making a difference is Walmart's 2010 announcement that it will embrace local food as part of its focus on sustainable agriculture. By deciding to double the percentage of locally grown produce it sells in the United States to 9%, and in Canada to 30%, by 2013, the multi-national mega-store will trigger huge change in the direction of local food security in North America.

Restaurants are also responding to consumer demand for more local food (the top restaurant food trend in 2010 in Canada), making restaurants the most lucrative markets for local farmers. Restaurants dedicated to local food — and able to charge premium prices for spectacular flavors — not only support local farmers, they also educate their customers. "If you wanted 300 people to eat sustainable food tonight, it takes a lot of effort to convince them to buy it and cook it at home," says Vancouver chef Robert Clark. "But all you have to do is convince one chef, and everyone who comes into that restaurant will eat it."[5]

The Vancouver Convention and Exhibition Centre has had a local food sourcing policy since the mid-1990s, the better to impress customers with fresh food that reflects the region. And, as discussed in Chapter 9, we know that even giant corporation like Sysco will go through the pains of sourcing local fresh food if its customers demand it.

The "Buy Fresh Buy Local" (BFBL) movement was launched in the United States in 2003 by the FoodRoutes network (foodroutes.org). There are now 73 BFBL chapters in 40 states promoting local produce — often in partnership with businesses, such as restaurants that feature local food.

In Pennsylvania, local food eaters complement the BFBL campaign with their own Good Food Neighborhood website to support local food and network with other local food supporters (buylocalpa.org).

In Ontario, Local Food Plus (LFP) is shifting markets with a campaign (buytovote.ca) to get people to pledge that they'll shift $10 a week to buying food with LFP's "Certified Local Sustainable" label. They've calculated that if 10,000 Ontarians took the pledge, the environmental impact would be the equivalent of taking 1,000 cars off the road, and the economic impact would be the creation of 100 new jobs.

The more consumers insist on fresh, local food, the more businesses will spring up to supply local seeds, test soil, package and sell compost, manage temporary-use leases, supply local processing, grow indoor greens, develop farm-centered subdivisions, invest in technological innovations — and a lot more. Foundations like Kellogg, Metcalf, McConnell and Liberty Prairie are investing in pilot projects and prototypes, but opportunities for self-supporting enterprises will only grow as demand for local food grows. Consumers alone have that power.

Community Groups Make Change

Local Food Plus is one of thousands of community-based organizations seeding changes in the food system. Usually they're out ahead of government. In the UK, a blogger chastised the government for trying to recreate what community groups have already done to find free land for local food production through websites like Landshare (landshare.net) and Spareground (spareground.co.uk): "I was rather surprised to hear of the Government Scheme when the exact schemes needed to maximize space are already in existence. It would be more beneficial if these locally based garden-share schemes were publicized throughout the UK rather than re-hash what is already out there under a Government name" (guardian .co.uk).

Getting vacant backyards into food production is just one of a multitude of changes that can start anytime through community or individual initiatives.

Community and non-profit groups are also essential for pushing change past the powerful vested interests protecting the unsustainable status quo. The Community Food Security Coalition (foodsecurity.org) has been especially effective with its Farm to School program. Since 1996, it has been rallying national and regional agri-foods organizations to overcome hunger and food insecurity and bolster small farmers. Slow Food (slowfood.com) promotes small-scale and sustainable production of quality local foods around the world. Global Eco-Village Network (gen.ecovillage.org) and Transition Towns (transitiontowns.org) have broader agendas for transforming the way we live, including the creation of a more sustainable local food production system.

Changes to the food system are coming from everywhere — governments, non-profits, businesses and individuals — because the need for change is so obvious in so many places.

What can you and I do as individuals? We can start by voting with our forks — shifting to more fresh, local foods and less meat, and being more mindful of what we eat and how we eat it. Some of us can grow some of our own food, and learn more about how to preserve it. We can get together with local groups and work on the small wins on the road to the big vision. We can join other parents in getting rid of junk food in our kids' schools. We can join any number of national groups pushing for bigger systemic changes. We can support politicians at all levels who are scrambling to keep up with the urban food revolution. We can patronize farmers markets. We can shift to grocery stores and businesses that sell sustainable local food that adds jobs and diversity and resilience to our food supplies.

We can recognize that the road to a better food future goes through the gray zone of compromise. No one organization, no one program, has The Answer. We have to learn to live with possible contradictions and less-than-ideal solutions: chickens next door *and* corporate logos on community gardens; organic *and* industrial food; local *and* imported; volunteers *and* paid workers; handouts *and* paid Good Food Boxes; private businesses *and* neighborhood co-ops; vegetarians *and* meat-eaters.

Government has its role, but all deep change starts with changing our own thoughts and actions. We each make daily choices about what we eat, and we each have the power to change those choices. Governments, corporations, farmers, grocery stores, school cafeterias and restaurants all respond to the aggregated demand of individual people. When we change, they will too.

Conclusion

Cities have to work around the political pressure that comes from those who want to continue to rely entirely on the market system to solve our food problems. Cities also have to find ways to work with the burden of numerous international laws and treaties that encourage exports and global trade by larger corporations.

Coherent federal policies like Brazil's Plan Against Hunger and the UK Food 2030 plan are examples of how federal policies can be aligned, especially around goals like reducing hunger and promoting better health. Federal greenhouse gas emission targets also have to include changes to the food system to be effective. National security in a time of food and water shortages is another big driver for a federal food policy.

Cities have to plug into federal and state/provincial policies to achieve the goals that growing numbers of food policy councils have laid out. These councils have become the local unifying force for steering changes on the ground in cities. Bans, taxes and prohibitions have a role to play at all levels. So do partnerships with community groups and NGOs. Cities' biggest lever is their power to decide urban land uses like where urban farms can locate, and whether buildings can add rooftop greenhouses without extra permits. Cities and counties can also adjust taxes to preserve near-urban working farms, covert them to organic, or create new farms and chicken coops inside cities.

While public policy changes are essential, consumer pressure on big private-sector food producers and retailers — even restaurants — can trigger immediate widespread changes, as evidenced by Walmart's new emphasis on buying local food.

Ultimately, all these changes start with individuals making daily choices that lead to accessible, affordable, healthy, fresh, sustainable food for all.

References/Sources Consulted

Chapter 1: What's the Matter with Food?
American Planning Association, "Policy Guide on Community and Regional Food Planning," 2007.
Arieff, Allison. "Agriculture is the New Golf: Rethinking Suburban Communities," *Good* online magazine, April 18, 2010.
Baker, Lauren et al. "Menu 2020," Sustain Ontario — The Alliance for Healthy Food and Farming, metcalffoundation.com.
Brown, Lester. "The Great Food Crisis of 2011; It's Real, and It's Not Going Away Anytime Soon," *Foreign Policy* Jan. 10, 2011.
Dirt! The Movie. Common Ground Media, Inc., 2009.
Food and Agriculture Organization of the United Nations, fao.org.
FOOD, INC. A film by Robert Kenner, A Magnolia Pictures Release, 2009.
foodroutes.org/mission.jsp.
Hill, Holly. "Food Miles: Background and Marketing," attra.ncat.org., 2008.
Holden, Ronald. "What America Buys at the Supermarket," Crosscut.com. Sept. 12, 2010.
Hume, Gord. *The Local Food Revolution, One Billion Reasons to Reshape Our Communities*, Municipal World, Inc., 2010.
Kimmett, Colleen. "A Tale of Two Farmlands: Growing the Local Bounty in Ontario and B.C." TheTyee.ca., Oct. 22, 2010.
LAUNCH, promotional video, Water forum hosted by NASA, USAID, March 2010.
Lee, Marc et al. "Every Bite Counts: Climate Justice and B.C.'s Food System," Canadian Centre for Policy Alternatives, Nov. 2010.
Millennium Ecosystem Assessment. *Ecosystems and Human Well-Being: Synthesis.* Island Press, 2005.
Pauly, Daniel. "The End of Fish," *The New Republic* Sept. 28, 2009.
Pfeiffer, Dale Allen. *Eating Fossil Fuels: Oil, Food and the Coming Crisis in Agriculture.* New Society Publishers, 2008.

Pinchin, Karen. "Growing Plants Indoors No Longer Rooted in Sci-Fi," *Special to Globe and Mail* Oct. 20, 2009.

"Power Hungry: Six Reasons to Regulate Global Food Corporations," Action Aid International, actionaid.org.

Marqusee, Rob. Director, Rural Economic Development, Woodbury County Iowa, speaking online at a Certified Organic Associations of B.C. conference, Kamloops, B.C., March 2010.

Scott Kantor, Linda et al. "Estimating and Addressing America's Food Losses," ers.usda.gov, accessed Nov. 7, 2010.

Shore, Randy. "MD's Sound Warning About Antibiotics in Feed," *Vancouver Sun*, Sept. 11, 2010.

slowmoney.org

Steel, Carolyn. *Hungry City, How Food Shapes Our Lives*. Vintage, 2009.

The Greater Philadelphia Food Systems Study, Delaware Valley Regional Planning Commission, 2010, dvrpc.org.

Vancouver Sun. "Ready-to-Eat Salads, New Pathogens Fuel Rise in Contaminated Produce," Aug. 7, 2010.

Weber, Christopher and Scott Mathews. "Food-Miles and the Relative Climate Impacts of Food Choices in the United States," *Environmental Science and Technology* Vol. 42, No. 10. 2008, pp. 3508–13.waterland.net

Chapter 2: Past Forward to Local? Let's Be Real

Born, Branden and Mark Purcell. "Avoiding the Local Trap: Scale and Food Systems in Planning Research," *Journal of Planning Education and Research* 2006 26:195.

Canadian Federation of Agriculture (CFA) in partnership with Meyers Norris Penny (MNP). Telephone surveys from August 2006 to Feb. 2007, in "The Economy of Local Food in Vancouver," vancouvereconomic.com, Aug. 2009.

CRFA Canadian Chef Survey, Canadian Restaurant & Foodservices Association, 2010.

Crouch, David and Colin Ward. "The Allotment: Its Landscape and Culture," in Carolyn Steel, *Hungry City, How Food Shapes Our Lives*. Vintage, 2009.

Donkersgoed, E. "Locally Grown Food and Near-Urban Agriculture: Challenges and Opportunities, Toronto: Food for Talk Seminar Series, York University, March 2008.

"Feed the City from the Back 40: A Commercial Food Production Plan for the City of Toronto," toronto.ca.

"Feeding the Cities: The Role of Urban Agriculture, Food and Agriculture Organization," fao.org, accessed Jan. 16, 2011.

Follmer, Max. "Japan's Weekend Farmers: City Dwellers Dig It in the Dirt," takepart.com, accessed Dec. 27, 2010.

"Food for Thought: The Issues and Challenges of Food Security," Provincial Health Services Authority, Canada, 2010.

Halweil, Brian and Danielle Nierenberg in "Is There Now an Opportunity for a Viable Small-Scale Sustainable Agriculture to Emerge In Brisbane, Australia?" by Stuart Brown, June, 2008, spinfarming.com.

"Interest in Old-Time Canning Gets Cooking," *Vancouver Sun* Aug. 7, 2010.

Ipsos Reid poll, "Canadians See Many Benefits Of Locally Grown Food," Dec. 2006.

"Local and Fresh Foods in the US," packagedfacts.com, May 1, 2007.

Nabham, Gary. "From the Field, to the Campfire and Kitchen: Stories of Where Our Food Comes From," garynabhan.com.

Nasr, Joseph et al. Scaling up Urban Agriculture in Toronto: Building the Infrastructure," Metcalf Foundation, June 2010.

"NewsNotes," May-June 2010, Vol. 35 No. 3, maryknollogc.org.

Philpott, Tom. "From Motown to Growtown: The Greening of Detroit, grist .org, Aug. 2010.

Pirog, Rich et al. "Food, Fuel, and Freeways: An Iowa Perspective on How Far Food Travels, Fuel Usage, and Greenhouse Gas Emissions," Leopold Center for Sustainable Agriculture, June 2001.

Roberts, Paul. "Spoiled: Organic and Local Is So 2008," *Mother Jones* March/ April 2009.

Severson, Kim. "The Rise of Company Gardens," *New York Times* May 11, 2010.

Smit, Jac and Rachel Nugent. "Sustain, City Harvest: The Feasibility of Growing More Food in London," in CPUL, p. 67.

"We be Jamming," *Globe and Mail* Sept. 5, 2009.

Weber, Christopher and Scott Mathews, in "Food for Thought, The Issues and Challenges of Food Security," B.C. Provincial Health Services Authority, 2010, phsa.ca/populationhealth.

Chapter 3: Preserving Rural Agriculture Land for Food Production

Campbell, Charles. "Forever Farmland: Reshaping the Agricultural Land Reserve for the 21st Century," David Suzuki Foundation, 2006.

Carty, Tony and John Ferguson. Norwegian Koncession Act 1974, no.19, 13th May s.7,14, cited in "A Comparative Study of Land Purchase Standards in Scotland and Western Europe," *Power and Manoeuvrability: The International Implications of an Independent Scotland.* Q Press, 1978.

Curran, Deborah and Tracy Stobbe. "Local Government Policy Options for Preserving Agricultural Land," prepared for Metro Vancouver, April 2010.

Gillis, Mark Herbert. "An Analysis of Landowners' Attitudes Towards the British Columbia Agricultural Land Reserve," MA Program Planning, 1980.

"Greenbelts: Local Solutions for Global Challenges," globalgreenbeltsconfer ence.ca, accessed Jan. 17, 2011.

Heimlich, R.E. and W. Anderson. "Development of the Urban Fringe and Beyond: Impacts on Agriculture and Rural Land," 2001, ers.usda.gov, accessed March 23, 2011.

Kimmett, Colleen. "A Tale of Two Farmlands: Growing the Local Bounty in Ontario and BC," TheTyee.ca., Oct 22, 2010.

Krauter, Bob. "Farmland Loss is Real California Concern," American Farm Bureau, Feb. 28, 2000, fb.org.

McKeown, David, Medical Officer of Health, City of Toronto, speaking at Local Food, Lessons from other Communities, Vancouver, Oct. 2010.

Michigan State University. "Loss of Agricultural Capacity Due to Urban Sprawl," msu.edu, accessed Sept. 2010.

Preutz, Rick. beyondtakingsandgivings.com/tdr.htm.

rockies.ca/programs/cocs.htm.

Robbins, Mark. Interview with the author, Sept. 2010.

Stump, Jeff. Conversation with the author, Sept. 2010.

Seltzer, Curtis. "Loss of Farmland: What Does It Mean?" April 30, 2009, landthink.com, accessed Sept. 2010.

The Greater Philadelphia Food Systems Study, Delaware Valley Regional Planning Commission, dvrpc.org, 2010.

thinkfresh.rockyview.ca/.

Truelsen, Stewart. "Why Farmland Preservation?" American Farm Bureau, Oct. 7, 1996.

Tsur, Somerville. UBC Sauder School of Business, public presentation to NAIOP, April 2010.

Yearwood-Lee, Emily. "History of the Agricultural Land Reserve," Legislative Library of B.C., Aug. 2006, llbc.leg.bc.ca.

Chapter 4: Converting Urban and Suburban Lands for Growing Food

Ableman, Michael. *Fields of Plenty: A Farmer's Journey in Search of Real Food and the People who Grow It.* Chronicle Books, 2005.

Baker, Linda. "Up on the Farm: Vancouver, British Columbia, Hatches a Program That Brings Food Cultivation into Town," posted May 22, 2008, MetropolisMag.com, accessed Oct. 2010.

Curran, Deborah and Tracy Stobbe. "Local Government Policy Options for Preserving Agricultural Land," prepared for Metro Vancouver, April 2010.

"Deconstructing Dinner," Kootenay Co-op Radio CJLY in Nelson, B.C. July 2, 2009, deconstructingdinner.ca.

Deitz, Paula. "One of a Kind: Tokyo; Rice Paddy In The Sky," *New York Times* March 7, 2004.

Greenaway, Twilight. "A Walk In the Ag Park," August 11, 2010, civileats.com.

Monocle, issue 25, volume 3, July/August 2009, monocle.com.

neighbor-space.org, accessed Oct. 2010.

omlet.co.uk.

Pawlick, Thomas F. *The End of Food: How the Food Industry Is Destroying Our Food Supply — and What You Can Do About It.* Greystone Books, 2006.

Teulon, Ward. Interviews with the author.

"Using Zoning to Create Healthy Food Environments in Baltimore City," prepared for Baltimore City Food Policy Task Force, by Seema Iyer and Anne Palmer, Harrison Institute For Public Law — Georgetown University Law Center, Dec. 2009.

Viljoen, André et al. *Continuous Productive Urban Landscapes (CPUL): Designing Urban Agriculture for Sustainable Cities* Architectural Press, Elsevier, 2005.

Chapter 5: Agriculture as the New Golf:
Farming as a Development Amenity

"Cultivating the Capital, Food Growing and the Planning System in London," London Assembly, Housing and Planning Committee, Jan. 2010.

McMahon, Ed. Interview with the author.

Ranney, Vicky et al. *Building Community with Farms: Insights from Developers, Architects and Farmers on Integrating Agriculture and Development.* Liberty Prairie Foundation, Sept. 2010.

serenbecommunity.com

Chapter 6: In Praise of Technology

"Advantages of Vertical Farming," verticalfarms.com, accessed Sept. 2009.

Despommier, Dickson and Eric Ellingsen. "The Vertical Farm: The Sky-Scraper As Vehicle for a Sustainable Urban Agriculture," CTBUH 8th World Congress, 2008.

Dietz, Diane. "Culinary Connection — Foodhub Is an Online Resource Linking Area Food Buyers with the Region's Farmers and Food Processors," *The Register-Guard* Oct. 17, 2010.

Elton, Sarah. *Locavore: From Farmers' Fields to Rooftop Gardens — How Canadians are Changing the Way we Eat.* HarperCollins, 2010.

Fane, Stephen, Valcent CEO. Interview with the author, Oct. 2010.
"Growing Food Locally: Integrating Agriculture into the Built Environ-
ment," *Environmental Building News* Feb. 2008, buildinggreen.com,
accessed Jan. 2, 2011.
Roberts, Genvieve. "Fish Farms, with a Side of Vegetables," *International
Herald Tribune* Sept. 28, 2010.
Underwood, Nora. "The Future Has Begun, Vertical Farms Will Take Eating
Local to the Next Level — But Are They Safe?" *The Walrus* Jan./Feb. 2009.
University of Arizona Controlled Environment Agriculture Center,
ag.arizona.edu.
Valcent Products. "Vertical Growing Solutions," valcent.net, Sept. 2010.
Viljoen, André et al. *Continuous Productive Urban Landscapes (CPUL):
Designing Urban Agriculture for Sustainable Cities.* Architectural Press,
Elsevier, 2005.
Woody, Todd. "Selling Agriculture 2.0 to Silicon Valley, *New York Times*
April 22, 2010.

Chapter 7: Economic Sustainability: Making the Economics of Agricultural Urbanism Pay

Ableman, Michael, *Fields of Plenty: A Farmer's Journey in Search of Real
Food and the People Who Grow It.* Chronicle Books, 2005.
Ableman, Michael, organic farmer, Fairview Gardens. Interviews with the
author, May 2009 and Oct. 2010.
Allen, Will. Presentation at Growing Power, Inc., Milwaukee, Jan. 2010.
Brown, Stuart. "Is There Now an Opportunity for a Viable Small-Scale Sus-
tainable Agriculture to Emerge In Brisbane, Australia?" Charles Stuart
University, June 2008, spinfarming.com.
communityfoodenterprise.org
EPA. "How Does Your Garden Grow: Brownfield Development and Local
Agriculture," epa.gov.
growbiointensive.org
Holm, Wendy. Public presentation in Vancouver, Oct. 2009.
Integrity Systems Cooperative and Sustainability Ventures Group. "Adding
Values to Our Food System: An Economic Analysis of Sustainable Community Food Systems," USDA Sustainable Agriculture Research & Edu-
cation Program, Utah State University, Feb. 1997.
Jeavons, John. *How to Grow More Vegetables Than You Ever Thought Possible
on Less Land Than You Can Imagine.* Ten Speed Press, 2002.
Myers, Annie. "Vitalizing the Vacant: The Logistics and Benefits Of Middle-
to Large-Scale Agricultural Production on Urban Land," May 2008,
communityfoodenterprise.org.

Pawlick, Thomas F. *The End of Food: How the Food Industry Is Destroying Our Food Supply—and What You Can Do About It.* Greystone Books, 2006.

Scobie, Pauline, SPIN practitioner. Interview with the author, Nov. 2009.

Tunnicliffe, Robin. "Saanich Organics: A Model for Sustainable Agriculture through Cooperation," B.C. Institute for Cooperative Studies, 2008, cics.org.

Urban Partners. "Farming in Philadelphia: Feasibility Analysis and Next Steps," Institute for Innovations in Local Farming, Dec. 2007.

Chapter 8: Economic Development through Urban Agriculture: Chasing the Local Job Dream

American Planning Association. "Policy Guide on Community and Regional Food Planning," planning.org, 2007.

"A New Japan? Change in Asia's Megamarket," East Asia Analytical Unit Department of Foreign Affairs and Trade, Barton, Australia, 1997.

Cantrell, P. et al. "Eat Fresh and Grow Jobs," Michigan Land Use Institute and C.S. Mott Group, Michigan State University, 2006.

"Food for Thought: The Issues and Challenges of Food Security," Provincial Health Services Authority, Vancouver, B.C., phsa.ca. Aug. 2010.

"Food Justice: The Report of the Food and Fairness Inquiry," Food Ethics Council, foodethicscouncil.org, July 2010.

Harper, Alethea et al. "Food Policy Councils: Lessons Learned," Institute for Food and Development Policy, foodsecurity.org, 2009.

Hild, Chris. "The Economy of Local Food in Vancouver," prepared for the Vancouver Economic Development Commission, vancouvereconomic.com, Aug. 2009.

Ho, Mae-Wan et al. "Food Futures Now: Organic, Sustainable, Fossil Fuel Free," i-sis.org.uk, Aug. 2010.

Nasr, Joseph et al. "Scaling up Urban Agriculture in Toronto: Building the Infrastructure," Metcalf Foundation, June 2010.

Marqusee, Rob, Director, Rural Economic Development, Woodbury County Iowa, speaking online at a COABC conference, Kamloops, B.C., March 2010.

Shuman, Michael. "Frequently Asked Questions About Local First Campaigns," Business Alliance for Local Living Economies, livingeconomies.org.

Sonntag, V. (2008) "Why Local Linkages Matter: Findings from the Local Food Economy Study," published by Sustainable Seattle, quoted in Metro Vancouver Draft Regional Food Strategy, Oct. 2010.

Toronto Food Business Incubator, City of Toronto Food Sector, tfbi.com.

Walmart Local Food Sourcing: Good for Farmers and Local Economies?" locobc.com, Oct. 21, 2010.

Chapter 9: Rebuilding the Lost Food-Producing Infrastructure

Cantrell, Patty. Conversation with the author, May, 2010.

Campsie, Philippa. "Food Connects Us All: Sustainable Local Food in Southern Ontario," Metcalf Foundation, Feb. 2008.

Dillon, Casey. *Counties and Local Food Systems: Ensuring Healthy Foods, Nurturing Healthy Children.* NACo Center for Sustainable Communities, July 2007.

"Draft Regional Food System Strategy," Metro Vancouver, www/metrovan couver.org, Sept. 2010.

González, Novo, and C. Murphy. "Urban Agriculture in the City of Havana: A Popular Response to Crisis," in *Growing Cities, Growing Food : Urban Agriculture on the Policy Agenda.* Deutsche Stiftung für internationl Entwicklung, 2001.

Hild, Chris. "The Economy of Local Food in Vancouver," prepared for the Vancouver Economic Development Commission, vancouvereconomic .com, Aug. 2009.

Illinois Local and Organic Food and Farm Task Force. "Local Food, Farms & Jobs: Growing the Illinois Economy: A Report to the Illinois General Assembly," March 2009.

Moskow, Angela. "The Contribution of Urban Agriculture to Gardeners, Their Households, and Surrounding Communities: The Case of Havana, Cuba," in *For Hunger-Proof Cities: Sustainable Urban Food Systems.* International Development Research Centre, Ryerson Polytechnic University, Toronto, 1999.

Schnieders, Rich, retired Sysco CEO, in "Sysco's Journey from Supply Chain to Value Chain: Results and Lessons Learned from 2008," by Patty Cantrell, National Good Food Network, Wallace Center at Winrock International, Aug. 2009.

Viljoen, André et al. *Continuous Productive Urban Landscapes (CPUL): Designing Urban Agriculture for Sustainable Cities.* Architectural Press, Elsevier, 2005.

Chapter 10: Less "Waste," More Soil

American Planning Association, "Policy Guide on Community and Regional Food Planning," planning.org, 2007.

Baumgartner, Bettina and Hasan Belevi. "A Systematic Overview of Urban Agriculture in Developing Countries," EAWAG and SANDEC, eawag.ch, Sept. 2001.

Carrusca, Ken, Engineer, Metro Vancouver. Interview with the author, Dec. 2010.

Christiansen, Kendall. "Converting Banana Peels to Energy...under the Kitchen Sink: Gathering Food Waste for Production of Biogas," North American Clean Energy, nacleanenergy.com, 2010.

Clifford, Stephanie. "Walmart to Buy More Local Produce," *New York Times* Oct. 14, 2010.

Cordell, Dana. "The Story of Phosphorus: 8 Reasons Why We Need to Rethink the Management of Phosphorus Resources in the Global Food System," Global Phosphorus Research Initiative, phosphorusfutures.net /why-phosphorus, 2008.

Evans, Tim. "Environmental Impact Study of Food Waste Disposers," Worcestershire County Council, letswasteless.com, accessed Oct 2010.

"Food Waste into Biofuel: Sainsbury's Aims to Turn All Food Waste into Biofuel," seriousnature.com, Jan. 2009.

Gardner, Gary. "Recycling Organic Waste: USA Today," Society for the Advancement of Education, findarticles.com, Nov. 1997.

"Guidelines for the Safe Use of Wastewater, Excreta and Greywater, Volume 4: Excreta and Greywater Use in Agriculture, World Health Organisation, who.int, 2006.

Hild, Chris. "The Economy of Local Food in Vancouver," prepared for the Vancouver Economic Development Commission, vancouvereconomic .com, Aug. 2009.

Kantor, Linda Scott et al. "Estimating and Addressing America's Food Losses," Economic Research Service, US Department of Agriculture, ers.usda.gov, 1997.

Lawton, Graham. "Pee-cycling," *New Scientist* optimumnutrition.wordpress .com, Dec. 20, 2006.

Nasr, Joseph et al. "Scaling up Urban Agriculture in Toronto: Building the Infrastructure," Metcalf Foundation, June, 2010.

"Norway Turns to Human Waste-Powered Buses," *Agence France-Presse* March 23, 2009.

Shore, Randy. "High School Garden Project Grows into Full-Scale Urban Farm," *Vancouver Sun* Nov. 10, 2010.

Statistics Canada. "Human Activity and the Environment: Food in Canada, 2009," quoted in "Draft Regional Food System Strategy, Metro Vancouver," metrovancouver.org, Sept. 2010.

Sundström, Anders and Dagens Nyheter. "Separating Food Waste Is Profitable, Study Shows," Post Carbon Institute, energybulletin.net, May 20, 2008.

US EPA. "Food Waste Production," epa.gov.

Vancouver Food Policy Council. "Food Secure Vancouver: Baseline Report,"
    2007
van Hemert, James and Joe Holmes. "Healthy Food Systems," The Rocky
    Mountain Land Use Institute, Sustainable Community Development
    Code, law.du.edu, 2008.
Vermiculture Canada, vermica.com, March 2009.
"Waste and Resources Action Plan: Understanding Food Waste," in Carolyn
    Steel, *Hungry City: How Food Shapes Our Lives.* Vintage, 2009.

Chapter 11: Starting Young: Healthier Local Food
in Schools, Colleges and Universities

"2010–11 Take a Bite of B.C. Program," B.C. Agriculture in the Classroom
    Foundation, aitc.ca/bc.
Abdul-Kareem, Maryam et al. "Using Zoning to Create Healthy Food
    Environments in Baltimore City," Harrison Institute For Public Law-
    Georgetown University Law Center, prepared for Baltimore City Food
    Policy Task Force, Dec. 2009.
Bruske, Ed. "Cafeteria Confidential: Remaking School Meals in Boulder,"
    Grist, grist.org, Nov. 8, 2010.
Chase, Steven. "The Quest to Put Some Bite into Foreign Food Inspections,"
    Globe and Mail Nov. 20, 2010.
Davis, B. and C. Carpenter. "Proximity of Fast-Food Restaurants to Schools
    and Adolescent Obesity," *American Journal of Public Health* March 2009.
Davis, Doug, Burlington Schools Food Service. Presentation at Farm to Caf-
    eteria conference, Detroit, May 2010.
"Food for Thought: The Issues and Challenges of Food Security," Provincial
    Health Services Authority, Vancouver, B.C., phsa.ca. Aug. 2010.
Harris, Jennifer L. et al. "Fast Food Facts: Evaluating Fast Food Nutrition
    and Marketing to Youth," Center for Food Policy and Obesity, Nov. 2010.
Joshi, Anupama and Andrea Misako Azuma. "Bearing Fruit: Farm to School
    Program Evaluation Resources and Recommendations," Center for Food
    & Justice, Urban & Environmental Policy Institute, Occidental College,
    departments.oxy.edu, 2009.
National Policy and Legal Analysis Network to Prevent Childhood Obesity.
    "Creating a Healthy Food Zone Around Schools," nplanonline.org
Pollan, Michael. *The Omnivore's Dilemma: A Natural History of Four Meals.*
    Penguin, 2006; *In Defense of Food: An Eater's Manifesto.* Penguin, 2008;
    Food Rules: An Eater's Manual. Penguin, 2009.
Philpott,Tom. "Telling Whoppers: The Fast-Food Industry's $4.2 Billion
    Marketing Blitz," Grist, grist.org, Nov. 10, 2010.

Pothukuchi, Kameshwari. "Community and Regional Food Planning: Building Institutional Support in the United States," *International Planning Studies* Volume 14, Issue 4, Nov. 2009, 349–67.

Shore, Randy. "Windermere Student Farmers Reach Out with Mobile Composting Project, *Vancouver Sun* Nov. 15, 2010.

Chapter 12: Farmers Markets and CSAs: Making the Most of Direct Sales

"Are the Farmers Markets Really More Expensive?" Neighborhood Farmers Market Alliance, seattlefarmersmarkets.org.

Been, Vicki and Ioan Voicu. "The Effect of Community Gardens on Neighboring Property Values," New York University Law and Economics Working Papers. Paper 46, lsr.nellco.org, 2006.

"CSA Farms Come of Age," *Canadian Farm Manager Newsletter* Dec. 2010/Jan. 2011.

Clifford, Stephanie. "Walmart to Buy More Local Produce," *New York Times* Oct. 14, 2010.

Douglas, Ted. "Fresh Business Model," *Chicago Tribune* May 13, 2009.

Farmers Markets Canada. "National Farmers Market Impact Study 2009 Overview," farmersmarketscanada.ca.

Fisher, Andy and Nell Tessman. "State Implementation of the New WIC Produce Package: Opportunities and Barriers for WIC Clients to Use Their Benefits at Farmers Markets," California Department of Public Health, 2009, Community Food Security Coalition, Updated Sept. 2010.

Sands, Mike, Executive Director of the Liberty Prairie Foundation. Interview with the author, May 2010.

"The Greater Philadelphia Food Systems Study," Delaware Valley Regional Planning Commission, dvrpc.org and farmtocity.org, 2010.

USDA. WIC Farmers Market Nutrition Program, www.fns.usda.gov.

White, Monica, Dept. of Sociology at Wayne State University. Speaking at the Farm to Cafeteria conference, Detroit, May 2010.

Wiggins, Betti, Office of Food Service, Detroit Public Schools. Comments at public meeting, Farm to Cafeteria Conference, Detroit May 2010.

Wingfield, Nick and Ben Worthen. "USDA Data Cited in Copycat Farmers Markets Reap a Crop of Complaints," *Wall St. Journal* Sept. 24, 2010.

Worldwatch Institute. worldwatch.org.

Chapter 13: Growing Community with Community Gardens

"25th Anniversary of Collective Kitchens," Montreal, rccq.org, March 21, 2007.

American Community Gardening Association, livejournal.com.

"Food for Thought: Planting Seeds for Solutions: Building Communities with Food in Mind," B.C. Provincial Health Services Authority, phsa.ca, August 2010.

"Food for Thought: The Issues and Challenges of Food Security," Provincial Health Services Authority, Vancouver, B.C., phsa.ca. Aug. 2010.

Pothukuchi, Kameshwari. "Community and Regional Food Planning: Building Institutional Support in the United States," *International Planning Studies* Volume 14, Issue 4 Nov. 2009, 349–67.

Sanford, Jack. "Harvesting the City," *The McGill Daily* Oct. 24, 2005.

Scharf, Kathryn et al. "In Every Community a Place for Food: The Role of the Community Food Centre in Building a Local, Sustainable, and Just Food System," Metcalf Food Solutions, The Stop Community Food Centre, June 2010.

Chapter 14: Getting Food to Hungry People

"25th Anniversary of Collective Kitchens, Montreal," March 21, 2007, rccq .org.

Campsie, Philippa. "Food Connects Us All: Sustainable Local Food in Southern Ontario," Metcalf Foundation, Feb. 2008.

Centre for Cooperative and Community-Based Economy. "The Canadian Community Kitchen Movement," University of Victoria, socialeconomy network.ca.

Cooper, Karen. Personal interview conducted June 2010.

"Dietitians of Canada 2004,"in "Evidence Review: Food Security, Population Health and Wellness," B.C. Ministry of Health, June 2006.

Food and Nutrition Service, USDA, fns.usda.gov.

"Food for Thought: The Issues and Challenges of Food Security," B.C. Provincial Health Services Authority, phsa.ca, 2010.

Gailliot, Matthew T. and Roy F. Baumeister. "The Physiology of Willpower: Linking Blood Glucose to Self-Control," *Personality and Social Psychology Review* 11, 2007.

Gram, Claire, Regional Coordinator, Healthy Communities & Community Food Security, Vancouver Coastal Health. Personal interview conducted Nov 2009.

Kimmett, Colleen. "Secrets to Supporting Local Food," Dec. 17, 2010, TheTyee.ca.

Miewald, Christiana. "Food Security and Housing in Vancouver's Downtown Eastside," Centre for Sustainable Community Development, prepared for Vancouver Coastal Health, Population and Health Team, Aug. 2009.

Nord, M. et al. "Household Food Security in the United States, 2004," *Eco-*

nomic Research Report No. (ERR11) United States Department of Agriculture, ers.usda.gov, 2005.

Rocha, Cecilia. "Urban Food Security Policy: The Case of Belo Horizonte, Brazil," *Journal for the Study of Food and Society* Vol. 5, No. 1, Summer 2001.

Scharf, Kathryn et al. "In Every Community a Place for Food: The Role of the Community Food Centre in Building a Local, Sustainable, and Just Food System," Metcalf Food Solutions, The Stop Community Food Centre, June 2010.

Chapter 15: Ending Food Deserts

Bertand, Lise. Montreal Agency for Health and Social Services, Department of Public Health (DPH) World Town Planning Day Online Conference, PlanningTheWorld.net, Nov. 2009,

Bolen, Ed and Kenneth Hecht. "Neighborhood Groceries: New Access to Healthy Food in Low-Income Communities," California Food Policy Advocates, Jan. 2003.

Campsie, Philippa. "Food Connects Us All: Sustainable Local Food in Southern Ontario," Metcalf Foundation, Feb. 2008.

Durkin, Erin. "Vendors See Mixed Results After City's Green Cart Push to Sell Fruit, Veggies in 'Deserts,'" *New York Daily News* April 27, 2010.

Feldstein, Lisa, U.C. Berkeley Dept. of City & Regional Planning. Speaking at World Planning Day online conference, Nov. 2010.

Fisher, Andy and Nell Tessman. "State Implementation of the New WIC Produce Package: Opportunities and Barriers for WIC Clients to Use Their Benefits at Farmers Markets," Community Food Security Coalition, June 2009 (updated Sept. 2010).

"Food Access & Liquor Stores: Life and Death from Unnatural Causes," acphd.org, accessed Dec. 22, 2010.

"Food for Thought: The Issues and Challenges of Food Security," Provincial Health Services Authority, Vancouver, B.C., phsa.ca. Aug. 2010.

Gallagher, Mari. "Examining the Impact of Food Deserts on Public Health in Detroit," LaSalle Bank, 2007.

Pothukuchi, Kameshwari. "Attracting Supermarkets to Inner-City Neighborhoods: Economic Development Outside the Box," *Economic Development Quarterly* Vol. 19, No. 3, Aug. 2005 (available at peoplesgrocery .org).

Pothukuchi, Kameshwari. "Community and Regional Food Planning: Building Institutional Support in the United States," *International Planning Studies* Vol. 14, Issue 4, 2009.

Smith, Joel J. and Nathan Hurst. "Grocery Closings Hit Detroit Hard: City Shoppers' Choices Dwindle As Last Big Chain Leaves," *The Detroit News* July 5, 2007.

"S. LA Bans New Stand-Alone Fast Food Eateries," Dec. 8, 2010, KABC-TV, abclocal.go.com.

Spence, John C. et al. "Relation Between Local Food Environments and Obesity Among Adults," *BMC Public Health* Vol. 9, 2009.

Strategic Alliance Enact Local Policy Database, Arcata Formula Restaurant Ordinance, thrive.preventioninstitute.org.

sustainweb.org

thefoodtrust.org

"The Greater Philadelphia Food Systems Study," Delaware Valley Regional Planning Commission, dvrpc.org, 2010.

Wehunt, Jennifer. "The Food Desert: Major Swaths of Chicago Lack Access to Healthful Food," *Chicago Magazine* July, 2009.

Chapter 16: Is Local Food Safe?

Chase, Steven. "The Quest to Put Some Bite into Foreign Food Inspections," *Globe and Mail* Nov. 20, 2010.

Finster, Mary E. et al. "Lead Levels of Edibles Grown in Contaminated Residential Soils: A Field Survey," sciencedirect.com, accessed Dec. 2010.

Flynn, Dan. "Food Safety Leaders: Top Food Safety Stories of 2010." No. 1, Dec 31, 2010, foodsafetynews.com.

"Growing Food Locally: Integrating Agriculture into the Built Environment," *Environmental Building News* Feb. 2008, buildinggreen.com.

Morris, J. Glenn Jr., editorial in *Emerging Infectious Diseases*. Centers for Disease Control and Prevention, Jan. 2011, foodsafetynews.com.

Nasr, Joseph et al. "Scaling up Urban Agriculture in Toronto: Building the Infrastructure," Metcalf Foundation, June 2010.

"Raw Milk Dairy Responsible for *E. Coli* Outbreak," Dec. 23, 2010, food safetynews.com.

Starmer, Elanor. "Food Fight," Food & Water Watch, grist.org, accessed Nov. 2010.

Chapter 17: What We Can Do: Systemic Changes, Personal Choices

"Evidence Review: Food Security, Population Health and Wellness," B.C. Ministry of Health, June 2006.

euractiv.com

"'Food for Thought' Consultation with Canadians Shows Overwhelming Demand for Leadership," June 22, 2010, ndp.ca.

Gillispie, Mark. "New $1.1 Million Program to Create Urban Farms in Cleveland's Kinsman Neighborhood," *The Plain Dealer* Oct. 27, 2010.

Harper, Alethea et al. "Food Policy Councils, Lessons Learned," Food First and the Community Food Security Coalition, 2009.

Marqusee, Rob, Director, Rural Economic Development, Woodbury County Iowa, speaking online at a COABC conference, Kamloops, B.C., March 2010.

NewsCore. "US Soldiers Turn To Diet Pills, Liposuction To Meet Weight Standards," myfoxdc.com, Dec. 8, 2010.

"Policy Guide on Community and Regional Food Planning," American Planning Association, May 11, 2007.

Pothukuchi, Kameshwari. "Community and Regional Food Planning: Building Institutional Support in the United States," *International Planning Studies* Vol. 14, Issue 4, 2009.

Roberts, Wayne and Cecilia Rocha. "Belo Horizonte: The Beautiful Horizon of Community Food Sovereignty," *Alternatives International Journal* July 2008.

"Sweden Withdraws Proposal on Climate Effective Food Choices," euractiv .com, Jan. 12, 2010.

Notes

Preface

1. Frank Lloyd Wright in *Hungry City: How Food Shapes Our Lives*, by Carolyn Steel. Vintage, 2009, p. 304.
2. Matthew B. Crawford, *Shop Class As Soulcraft: An Inquiry into the Value of Work*. Penguin, 2009, p. 7–8.
3. Joel Salatin, speaking in Vancouver at a University of B.C. public lecture, Sept. 2010.
4. Les Bowser, Cedar Grove Organic Farm, Omemee, Ont.; Mark Trealout, Grassroot Organics and Kawartha Ecological Growers, Woodville, Ont., letter to *Globe and Mail* June 18, 2010.

Chapter 1: What's the Matter with Food?

1. Carolyn Steel, *Hungry City: How Food Shapes Our Lives*. Vintage, 2009, p. 94.
2. Dan Koeppel, *Banana: The Fate of the Fruit That Changed the World*. Plume, 2009, p. xvi.
3. Antony Froggatt and Glada Lahn, "Sustainable Energy Security: Strategic Risks and Opportunities for Business," Chatham House-Lloyd's 360° Risk Insight White Paper, June 2010, chathamhouse.org.uk.
4. "Lloyd's Adds Its Voice to Dire 'Peak Oil' Warnings," *The Guardian* July 11, 2010.
5. "Millennium Ecosystem Assessment," *Ecosystems and Human Well-Being: Synthesis*. Island Press, 2005.

Chapter 2: Past Forward to Local? Let's Be Real

1. James E. McWilliams, "Just Food: Where Locavores Get It Wrong and How We Can Truly Eat Responsibly," *Wall Street Journal* online.wsj.com, Aug. 22, 2009.
2. Natural Resources Defense Council, "Food Miles: How Far Your Food Travels Has Serious Consequences for Your Health and the Climate," nrdc.org/policy, Nov. 2007.
3. Stephen Budiansky, "Math Lessons for Locavores," *New York Times* Aug. 19, 2010.

4. Gary Nabham, "From the Field, to the Campfire and Kitchen: Stories of Where Our Food Comes From," garynabhan.com/press, accessed Sept. 2010.

5. Peter Tyedmers in "Debunking Our 'Fetish of the Fresh,'" by Jessica Leeder, *Globe and Mail* Nov. 24, 2009.

6. "Harvested Here: Delicious Thinking about Local Food," a Tyee special edition, 2010 Concurrent Media Ltd., TheTyee.ca, p 40.

7. Poll of public opinions toward agriculture, food and agri-food production in B.C. Ipsos Reid Public Affairs. Prepared for the Investment Agriculture Foundation of B.C., 2008.

8. "Buy-Local Push Prompts Ontario Grocers to Go Independent," cbc.ca, accessed Mar. 23, 2011.

Chapter 3: Preserving Rural Agriculture Land for Food Production

1. American Farmland Trust, Farmland Information Center, August 2010, farmlandinfo.org.

2. Tsur Somerville, UBC Sauder School of Business, public presentation to NAIOP, April, 2010.

Chapter 4: Converting Urban and Suburban Lands for Growing Food

1. "Swine Farm Neighbors Say Stink Bugs Them," by Linda Kane, May 28, 1998, amarillo.com.

2. Terry Bremner in *FarmFolkCityFolk's Newsletter* 58, Summer 2010, article by Michael Marrapese.

3. Jac Smit in *Continuous Productive Urban Landscapes (CPUL): Designing Urban Agriculture for Sustainable Cities.* by André Viljoen et al., Architectural Press, Elsevier, 2005, p. x.

4. Michael Cameron in "Chicago Restaurant Opens Organic Rooftop Farm" by Dave Hoekstra, *Chicago Sun-Times* Sept. 3, 2008.

5. "Using Zoning to Create Healthy Food Environments in Baltimore City," prepared for Baltimore City Food Policy Task Force by Seema Iyer and Anne Palmer, Harrison Institute For Public Law — Georgetown University Law Center, Dec. 2009.

Chapter 5: Agriculture as the New Golf: Farming as a Development Amenity

1. Vicky Ranney, Co-Developer of Prairie Crossing and Chairman of the Liberty Prairie Foundation, in *Building Community with Farms: Insights from Developers, Architects and Farmers on Integrating Agriculture and Development.* by Vicky Ranney, Keith Kirley and Michael Sands, Sept. 2010, Liberty Prairie Foundation.

2. Andrés Duany in "New Urbanism for the Apocalypse," by Greg Lindsay, fastcompany.com, May 24, 2010.

3. Galina Tachieva in "The Neighborhoods Issue," by Allison Arieff, good .is, April 18, 2010.

4. Steve Nygren in *Building Community with Farms: Insights from Developers, Architects and Farmers on Integrating Agriculture and Development.* by Vicky Ranney, Keith Kirley and Michael Sands, Sept. 2010, Liberty Prairie Foundation.

5. Unidentified speaker at a public meeting, Delta Community Centre, spring, 2010.

Chapter 6: In Praise of Technology

1. Bill Zylmans, CBC Almanac, Vancouver, podcast.cbc.ca, Oct. 8, 2010.

2. Joel Salatin, Polyface, Inc. speaking in Vancouver at a University of B.C. lecture, Sept. 2010.

3. Will Allen, "An Urban Farmer Is Rewarded for His Dream," *New York Times Magazine* Sept. 25, 2008.

4. Mark Vickars, "Urban Farming 2.0: No Soil, No Sun," by Jennifer Alsever, CNNmoney.com, Dec. 23, 2010.

5. Harley Smith, hydroponics specialist, in "Dwelling of Permanent Culture," by Katrina Sutcliffe, coursework in the Faculty of Environmental Design, The University of Calgary, Feb. 2010.

6. Paul Matteucci in "Selling Agriculture 2.0 to Silicon Valley," by Todd Woody, *New York Times* April 22, 2010.

7. Bruce Bugbee in "Urban Farming 2.0: No Soil, No Sun," by Jennifer Alsever, CNNmoney.com, Dec. 23, 2010.

8. "Dickson Despommier Speaks About the Vertical Farm," linked on Cityfarmer.info, accessed Oct. 15, 2010.

9. "The Rise of Company Gardens," by Kim Severson, *New York Times* May 11, 2010.

10. James Godsil in "Fish Farms, with a Side of Vegetables," by Genvieve Roberts, *International Herald Tribune* Sept. 28, 2010.

11. Paul Matteucci in "Urban Farming 2.0: No Soil, No Sun," by Jennifer Alsever, CNNmoney.com, Dec. 23, 2010.

12. James MacKinnon in "One Big Idea: Make Fresh Food Free for the Picking," by Ian Bailey, *Globe and Mail* Dec. 12, 2010.

13. Deborah Kane in "Foodhub Is Fast Becoming the Facebook of Local Food," by Leslie Cole, *Oregonian FoodDay* Aug. 31, 2010.

Chapter 7: Economic Sustainability: Making the Economics of Agricultural Urbanism Pay

1. Pauline Scobie, interview with the author, Nov. 2009.

2. Roxanne Christensen, interview with the author, Sept. 2009.

3. "Adding Values to Our Food System: An Economic Analysis of

Sustainable Community Food Systems," United States Department of Agriculture Sustainable Agriculture Research and Education Program, Utah State University, prepared by Integrity Systems Cooperative and Sustainability Ventures Group, Feb. 1997.

4. communityfoodenterprise.org, accessed Oct. 20, 2010.

5. "John Hantz Envisions Vacant Detroit Land As a Working Farm," by Laura Berman, *The Detroit News* July 23, 2009.

6. John Hantz, interview with the author, May 2010.

7. "Today's Fruits, Vegetables Lack Yesterday's Nutrition," by Andre Picard, *Globe and Mail* July 6, 2002.

8. Chris Bodnar, "The Cost of Local, Organic Food," by Glen Valley Farm cooperative, glenvalleyorganicfarm.blogspot.com.

Chapter 8: Economic Development through Urban Agriculture: Chasing the Local Job Dream

1. "Pricing Is a Black Art," by "nlo," TheTyee.ca, Oct 16, 2010.

2. Rob Marqusee, Director, Rural Economic Development, Woodbury County, Iowa, speaking online at a COABC conference, Kamloops, B.C., March 2010.

3. Patty Cantrell, Michigan Land Use Institute, interview with the author, May 2010.

4. Ken Meter, Crossroads Resource Center, speaking at Detroit Farm to Cafeteria conference, May 2010.

5. Peter Van Loan in "Deconstructing Dinner," Kootenay Co-op Radio CJLY in Nelson, B.C. deconstructingdinner.ca, July 2, 2009.

6. Dianne Dowling, vice-president of Local 316 of the National Farmers Union, in "Deconstructing Dinner," Kootenay Co-op Radio CJLY in Nelson, B.C. deconstructingdinner.ca, July 2, 2009.

7. Chris Parmer in a letter read at a public forum in Kingston, March 2009, in "Deconstructing Dinner," Kootenay Co-op Radio CJLY in Nelson, B.C. deconstructingdinner.ca, July 2, 2009.

8. Steven Shrybman in "B.C.'s Farming and Food Future, Local Government Toolkit for Sustainable Food Production Community Farms Program," prepared by Wanda Gorsuch for The Land Conservancy of B.C. and FarmFolk/City Folk, conservancy.bc.ca, Dec. 2009.

Chapter 9: Rebuilding the Lost Food-Producing Infrastructure

1. "Counties and Local Food Systems: Ensuring Healthy Foods, Nurturing Healthy Children," by Casey Dillon, NACo Center for Sustainable Communities, July 2007.

2. "Ten Ingredients for a Healthy Local Food Economy," by Colleen Kimmett, TheTyee.ca, Oct. 18, 2010.

3. "Walmart to Buy More Local Produce," by Stephanie Clifford, *New York Times* Oct. 14, 2010.

4. "Counties and Local Food Systems—Ensuring Healthy Foods, Nurturing Healthy Children," by Casey Dillon, NACo Center for Sustainable Communities, July 2007.

5. Joel Salatin, speaking in Vancouver, Sept. 2010.

6. David Van Seters, interview with the author, Feb. 2010.

7. "Local Food, Farms & Jobs: Growing the Illinois Economy: A Report to the Illinois General Assembly," by The Illinois Local and Organic Food and Farm Task Force, March 2009.

8. Jorge Peña Dílaz and Phil Harris, "Urban Agriculture in Havana: Opportunities for the Future," in *Continuous Productive Urban Landscapes (CPUL): Designing Urban Agriculture for Sustainable Cities*, by André Viljoen et al., Architectural Press, Elsevier, 2005, p. 139.

Chapter 11: Starting Young: Healthier Local Food in Schools, Colleges and Universities

1. "Food for Thought, The Issues and Challenges of Food Security," B.C. Provincial Health Services Authority, phsa.ca, 2010, p.56.

2. Theresa Ramirez, Office of Food Service, Detroit Public Schools, comments at public meeting, Farm to Cafeteria Conference, Detroit, May 2010.

3. Comments at public meeting, Farm to Cafeteria Conference, Detroit, May 2010.

4. "Culinary Connection: Foodhub Is an Online Resource Linking Area Food Buyers with the Region's Farmers and Food Processors," by Diane Dietz, *The [Eugene] Register-Guard* Oct. 17, 2010.

5. Christie Ralston, interview with the author, January 2010.

Chapter 12: Farmers Markets and CSAs: Making the Most of Direct Sales

1. "London's Food Markets Fight Clone Town Britain," lda.gov.uk, Nov. 7, 2005.

2. Woody Tasch, public presentation in Vancouver, July 13, 2010.

3. "CSA Farms Come of Age," Canadian Farm Manager Newsletter, Dec. 2010/Jan. 2011.

Chapter 13: Growing Community with Community Gardens

1. M. Brown et al., *The Ration Book Diet*. The History Press, 2005.

2. Domenic Vitiello, "Planning the Food Secure City: Philadelphia Agriculture Retrospect and Prospect," in "The Greater Philadelphia Food Systems Study," Delaware Valley Regional Planning Commission, dvrpc.org, 2010.

3. Barbara Finnin in "Oakland City Slickers Get a Permanent Home," by Twilight Greenaway, Nov. 17, 2010, civileats.com.

Chapter 14: Getting Food to Hungry People
1. Kathryn Scharf in "Better Than a Food Bank: The Stop in Toronto Has Evolved into a Dignified Model Connecting Local Producers with Low-Income Eaters," by Colleen Kimmett, TheTyee.ca, Nov. 5, 2010.
2. Christiana Miewald, PhD., "Food Security and Housing in Vancouver's Downtown Eastside," Centre for Sustainable Community Development, prepared for Vancouver Coastal Health, Aug. 2009.

Chapter 15: Ending Food Deserts
1. LaDonna Redmond in *Grub: Ideas for an Urban Organic Kitchen*, by Anna Lappé and Bryant Terry. Jeremy P. Tarcher/Penguin, 2006.
2. Kameshwari Pothukuchi, "Attracting Supermarkets to Inner-City Neighborhoods: Economic Development Outside the Box," *Economic Development Quarterly* Vol. 19 No. 3, Aug. 2005 (available at peoplesgrocery .org).
3. Kameshwari Pothukuchi, Director, SEED Wayne, speaking at World Planning Day online conference, Nov. 2010.

Chapter 17: What We Can Do: Systemic Changes, Personal Choices
1. Neil Currie in "The Growing Problem: Canada Slips from Agricultural Superpower Status," by Paul Waldie, *Globe and Mail* Nov. 23, 2010.
2. Kelly Brownell, Rudd Center for Food Policy and Obesity, Yale, interviewed on Sunday Edition, CBC radio, Sept. 19, 2010.
3. Darrin Nordahl, "Smart City Governments Grow Produce for the People," grist.org, Aug. 5, 2010.
4. Jerry Kaufman, Emeritus Professor of Urban and Regional Planning at the University of Wisconsin-Madison, speaking at World Planning Day online conference, Nov. 2010.
5. Robert Clark in *Locavore: From Farmers' Fields to Rooftop Gardens — How Canadians Are Changing the Way We Eat*. by Sarah Elton, Harper-Collins, 2010, p. 192.

Index

A

abandoned land. *See* urban land

abattoirs, 119–120, 235

Abbotsford, B.C., 40

Ableman, Michael, 85–86, 98

Aboriginal Front Door, 207

Adam's Sustainable Table, 77

aeroponics, 64

aggregators, 126–128

Agrarian Urbanism, 53

Agreement on Internal Trade (AIT), 114–115

agricultural land
  conflict with urban housing, 38–40, 56
  integration with residential, 42, 49–52, 53–59
  limiting sale of, 30–31
  loss of, 25–28
  preservation of, 28–30, 31–34, 71
  value to neighborhood, 40–41

Agricultural Land Reserve (ALR), 28–30, 32, 58

agricultural subdivisions, 49–52

agricultural urbanism, 53

agriculture
  effect of climate change, 7
  effect of water shortages, 4–5
  energy efficiency in, 16–18
  investment in sustainability, 68–70
  monocultures, 3–4

Agriculture Farm Bill, 244

agriculture-housing developments, 53–59

Agromere, 56

Alameda, California, 218

Aldergrove, B.C., 40

Alemany Farm, 84–85

algae, 3

Allen, Will, 44, 64, 74, 89–90, 109, 142–143, 194, 234

Allen Street Community Garden, 84

Almere, Netherlands, 56

American Community Gardening Association, 183

American Farmland Trust (AFT), 6, 26–27

American Planning Association, 251–252

anaerobic digestion plants, 135–136

antibiotics, 4

apetito, 135–136

Apple Lane Orchards, 167

apples, 17

aquaculture, 145

aquaponics, 72–75, 90

Aquaponics UK, 74

AquaRanch Industries, 74

Arcata, California, 225

Arizona, 17

Arkesteyn-Vogler, Andrew, 137, 139

Artscape Wychwood Barns, 122, 202

Arturo Toscanini School, 161

Asia, 4

Astyk, Sharon, 121

Atwater Market, 168

Australia, 6, 7, 74–75

B

Babineau, Lindsay, 155, 163, 165

Backyard Aquaponics, 74–75

balcony gardens, 93

Baltimore, 228

Banana (Koeppel), 3

bananas, 3

Bangladesh, 5

B.C. bud, 63

B.C. Federation of Agriculture, 29

B.C. Fruit Growers Association, 29

beef, water requirements of, 18–19

Beijing, 21

Bekkelaget sewage treatment plant, 148

Belo Horizone, Brazil, 212–214, 241, 248

best before dates, 136

Better Food Solutions greenhouses, 72

Big B Farms, 77

biodiversity, 3

biofuels, 6–7

biogas, 140, 141

Bodnar, Chris, 99, 172

Bohn, Katrin, 42

Boston, 218

boulevards, 45

Bradford, UK, 192

Brazil, 241, 257

Bremner, Terry, 41

British Columbia
  farmers' market program, 174
  farmland requirements, 26
  low income families, 200
  preservation of agricultural land, 28–30
  school vending machines, 154
  trust of farmers, 22

British Columbia Ministry of Agriculture, 26

Broadway Farmers' Market, 170

Brooklyn, 228

Brown, Les, 35

Brownell, Kelly, 246
Brusatore, Nick, 66
Budiansky, Stephen, 16
Bugbee, Bruce, 69
Burlington, Vermont, 85, 159
Burlington Electric, 94
Burns, Janie, 123
Buy Fresh Buy Local (BFBL)
    movement, 254
buying clubs, 178–179
Buywell Project, 226–227

C
calcium, 98
Calcutta, 145
Calgary, Alberta, 21, 33
California, 16, 33, 160
California Food Policy Advo-
    cates, 226
Campbell, Mark, 39
Canada
    beliefs about local food, 13
    farmer demographics, 8
    food banks, 199
    food costs, 9
    food safety, 155, 236
    health issues, 9
Canadian Agri-Food Policy
    Institute, 244
Canadian Diabetes Associa-
    tion, 9
Canadian Federation of Agri-
    culture, 244
CanAgro Greenhouses, 68
canning food, 20–21
Cantonal Library, 147
Cantrell, Patty, 105
CARE, 204
Cargill, 2
Carline, Cheryl, 137
Carmody, Dan, 120
cash value vouchers (CVVs),
    173
'Cavendish' banana, 3
CBC news, 23
Ceccarossi, Kristi, 194
Center for Nutrition Policy
    and Promotion, 153
Centers for Disease Control
    and Prevention, 9, 232
Centre for Food, 244

Certified Local Sustainable,
    113
Change4Life, 227
Chattahoochee Hills, Geor-
    gia, 32
cheese, 133–134, 231, 235
Chez Panisse Foundation, 160
Chicago, 47, 218
Chicago Park District, 47
Chicago Supermarket Ordi-
    nance, 224
chicken coops, 44–45
chickens, 91, 144, 249
Chill Room, 207
China, 6, 146
Chino, California, 224, 252
Choices Market, 66
Christensen, Roxanne, 90
cities
    conflicts with farms, 38–40
    edgeless, 42
    farm use zoning, 45–46
    farming-related business
        opportunities, 92, 94
    food security programs,
        248–250
    history of food produc-
        tion in, 37
    loss of farmland to, 25–28
    markets for produce, 86–
        87, 91
    urban food planning,
        251–253
    value of farm proximity,
        40–41
City Farm, 234
City Farm Boy, 45, 81
City Farmer, 76
City Slicker Farms, 190
Clark, Robert, 254
Cleveland, 45–46, 223, 249
Cleveland Urban Agricul-
    tural Incubator, 244–245
climate change, 3, 7
CO_2 emissions. See green-
    house gas emissions
cold storage, 122
Coleman, Eliot, 91
commercial kitchens, 124
commercial urban farms,
    81–83

Community Development
    Corporations (CDCs), 223
community food centers,
    122–123
Community Food Project
    Competitive Grants Pro-
    gram, 245
Community Food Security
    Coalition, 253, 255
community gardens
    contamination, 232–233
    contributions of, 184–186
    corporate, 193–195
    history of, 182–183
    in planned communities,
        52
    political power in, 186–187
    start up, 188–189
    tenure, 187, 190–192
    traits of, 181–182
    two-block gardens, 192–193
Community Gardens Act, 87
community groups, 255
Community Health Survey,
    199
community kitchens, 204–
    207
Community Supported Agri-
    culture. See CSAs
Community Supported
    Fishery (CSF), 78–80, 177
compost, 86, 139, 142–143
composting toilets, 147
Condon, Patrick, 58
Conference Board of Canada,
    244
conservation developments,
    53–57
conservation easements, 33
consumer demand, 253–256
contamination, 3–4
Continuous Productive Urban
    Landscapes (Viljoen, Bohn,
    Howe), 42
Contra Costa, California, 218
convenience stores, 217–220,
    225–227
CookShop education pro-
    gram, 205
Cooper, Ann, 155
Cooper, Karen, 209–211

Cooper, Steve, 179
corn, 2
Cornell University, 156
corner stores, 225–227
corporations, 2–3, 193–195
Courtauld Commitment, 135
Craigslist, 75
crime, 221–222
crop mobs, 75–78
CSAs (Community Supported Agriculture)
advantages of, 92, 94, 175–177
cost effectiveness of, 85
growth in, 13
in housing developments, 54
improvements in structure of, 178–180
Cuba, 131–132, 144
Currie, Neil, 243

D
D-Town, 187
dairies, 121
Dakar, 21
Dallas, 218
Dave's Supermarkets, 223
Davie Village Community Garden, 191
Davis, California, 22
Deist, Flanders, Belgium, 144
Denmark, 30–31, 147
Despommier, Dickson, 69–70
Detroit
commercial urban farms in, 95–97
fast food and schools, 151–152, 154
food stores, 217–218, 220, 221, 225–226
political power of gardens, 187
racism, 253
school programs, 157
slaughterhouses, 120
urban food production, 22
Detroit Black Community Food Security Network, 96, 187

Detroit News, 221–222
developments
integration with agriculture, 49–52, 53–59
loss of farmland, 6, 28
open space within, 49
taxes, 26–27, 191–192, 250–251
diabetes, 9
diet and health, 9–10, 209–211, 220
Dirt!: The Movie, 71
distribution, 122, 124–128
Dowling, Dianne, 110
Dr. Peter Centre, 203
Duany, Andrés, 53
Duke, Bob, 39
Duke, Michael T., 126
Dunn, Ken, 234
Dutch University, 56

E
E. coli, 4, 231–232
Eagle Heights Community Garden, 182, 183, 184
Earlscourt Park Community Garden, 187
EarthBoxes, 72, 162–163
East Calcutta Wetlands, 145
Eastern Central Market, 168, 217
Eco Spirit produce, 66
economic development
effect of local spending, 102–104
effect of organic farms, 107–109
employment opportunities, 109–111
foreign competition, 101–102
impact of local spending, 105–106
institutional procurement, 111–115
investments, 115–116
economic sustainability
cost of urban farmland, 81–85
in CSA structure, 92, 94
infrastructure, 86–87

niche markets, 85–86
profitability, 97–99
small-scale production systems, 87–92
urban opportunities, 94
using vacant land, 94–97
EcoTrust, 76, 159
Edey, Anna, 65
Edible Schoolyard (ESY), 160–161
Edmonton, Alberta, 171, 220
education, 130–131
Eglus, 44–45
Egypt, 5
electric fences, 63
electronic benefit transfer (EBT) cards, 173
The End of Food (Pawlick), 98
energy, 16–19, 68, 70–71
entrepreneurs, 81–85, 87–92, 94, 106–107
environment, benefits of local food movement, 19
Environmental Youth Alliance, 162
EPA (Environmental Protection Agency), 45, 134
Estrella Family Creamery, 235
Eto, Dave, 120
European Union, 140, 146, 242

F
Fairmont Waterfront Hotel, 43
Fairview Gardens, 94
Fairview urban farm, 85–86
Fallen Fruit, 138
FamilyFarmed EXPO, 128
FamilyFarmed.org, 128
Fane, Stephen, 65, 92
Farm Folk/City Folk, 80, 117
Farm Incubator Program, 94, 130–131
Farm Industry Review Board, 40
Farm to School programs, 157, 158, 255
Farmer Business Development Center, 51
farmers, income, 8–9

Farmers' Market Nutrition
Program (FMNP), 173–174,
201, 225, 247
farmers' markets
challenges for, 174–175
low income families and,
173–174
popularity of, 167–170
prices at, 170–173
transportation, 16–17
farmland. *See* agricultural
land
farms, small-scale, 87–92
FarmStart, 131
Farmview, Pennsylvania, 54
fast-food restaurants, 152,
224–225
Feast of Fields Day, 12, *14*,
117
Federation of Canadian Municipalities, 21
fertilizers, 69, 146
Finland, 241
Finnin, Barbara, 190
fish, 7–8, 72–75
flavor, 97–99
food
cost of, 9
diversity in, 3
future production, 5
safety of, 3–4, 22–23,
231–237
See also local food
Food, Conservation, and Energy Act, 244
Food and Agricultural Organization, 241
Food and Drug Administra-
tion (FDA), 235
food banks, 199, 200–201
food deserts
car dependency, 220–221
conversion of corner
stores, 225–227
effects of crime, 221–222
mobile programs, 227–228
programs for, 222–224
in urban centers, 217–220
Food Distribution Program
on Indian Reservations
(FDPIR), 201

Food Innovation Center, 106
food literacy, 159–162
food miles, 7, 15–17
Food Policy Council, 239–
240, 252–253
food production infrastructure. *See* infrastructure
Food Retail Expansion to
Support Health (FRESH)
program, 224
food riots, 5
Food Rules (Pollan), 153
Food Safety Modernization
Act, 236
food security
city programs, 212–214,
248–250
community kitchens,
204–207
corporate control, 6–8
effect of, 214–215
effect on health, 211–212
effect on taxpayers, 207,
209–211
encouraging local food,
104–105
oil dependency, 6–8
programs for low income
families, 201–203
state programs, 246–247
See also food banks
food system
corporate control of, 2–4
facets of plans, 239–241
oil dependency, 6–8
unsustainable agricul-
ture, 4–6
Food Trust, 218, 225
FoodHub, 76–78
FoodRoutes, 254
FoodShare, 122
Forbes 2020, 21
Forest Preserve District of
Cook County, 47
Forstbauer Family Natural
Food Farm, 167
Fort Vermilion, Alberta, 163
France, 30–31
Frankfurt, 30
Fraundorf, Josh, 74
Freishtat, Holly, 228

Fresh Food Access Initiative,
225–226
Fresh Food Financing Initia-
tive (FFFI), 223
Fresh off the Boat, 167
Fresia condominium, 81–82
Friendly Aquaponics, 74
Frontenac Farm, 43, 110–111
fruit, 98, 138
Fruitvale, Oakland, 226
funding, 87
Fusarium wilt, 3

G
garburators, 140–141
Garden Back to Eden, 167
General Agreement on Tar-
iffs and Trade, 241
genetically engineered corn, 2
genetically modified seeds, 63
Gennevilliers, France, 145
Germany, 30
Glenn, Doug, 236
Global Eco-Village Network,
255
Global Generation, 192
globalization of food system,
2–3
goat milk, 121
Goat's Pride Dairy, 167
Godsil, James, 74
Golden Town Apple Prod-
ucts, 123
golf course developments,
49, 57
Good Food Neighborhood,
254
Google, 72, 193
Goosen, Dan, 45
governments, 240–241,
244–246
grain, 2, 6
Gram, Claire, 212
Grand Central Bakery, 77
Grange Farm, 44
grants, 87
Granville Island Public Mar-
ket, 122, 168
Great Depression, 182, 201
Green Barn, 202
Green Carts, 228

Greenbelt Plan, 30
greenbeltfresh.ca, 76
greenhouse gas (GHG) emissions, 7, 15, 16, 17, 242
greenhouses
    advantages of, 67
    aquaponics, 72–75
    energy costs, 68, 70–71
    profitability of, 92
    rooftop, 43
    vertical growing, 64–68
    weather control, 62
Greening Food Deserts Act, 245
Greenmarket, 173
grocery stores
    car dependency, 220–221
    effects of crime, 221–222
    encouraging development, 222–224
    lack of, 217–219
    product diversity, 1–2
'Gros Michel' banana, 3
GROW BIOINTENSIVE Sustainable Mini-Farming, 90
Growing Home, 35
Growing Power, 44, 64, 74, 89–90, 122, 142–143, 178
guerilla gardeners, 47

H
Haiti, 5
Hamir, Arzeena, 193
Hanoi, 21
Hantz, John, 95–96
Hantz Financial Services, 95
Harmony, 113
Harston, Myles, 74
Hartmann, Michael, 231–232
Havana, Cuba, 132
Health Care Providers Against Poverty, 211
health issues, 9–10, 209–211, 220, 242
Healthy, Hunger-Free Kids Act, 242
Healthy Food Financing Initiative, 223
Hellman's, 194
Hobart, Tasmania, 148
Hodgins, Sean, 58–59

hog farms, 39
Holland, Mark, 59
home delivery services, 129–130
Homer-Dixon, Thomas, 14
Hometown Grocers Co-op, 22–23
Hong Kong, 21
Hooker, Oklahoma, 39
Hornbeam, London, 128
hospitals, 212
housing developments. *See* developments
Howe, Joe, 42
Howell, Julia, 39
Hui's Farm Specialty Mushrooms, 167
human waste, 144–148
Hummingbird Wholesale, 77
Hungry City (Steel), 102
hydroponics, 64–70

I
Illinois, 120, 130
Illinois Local Food, Farms, and Jobs Act, 112
imported food safety, 236
India, 6, 8–9, 146
Indian Springs Farmers Association, 128
industrial safety standards, 234–236
infrastructure, food production
    aggregators, 126–128
    cold storage, 122
    cost of, 123–124
    distribution, 122, 124–126
    home delivery, 129–130
    for small producers, 119–120, 121
    waste, 120
InSinkErator, 140–141
Insite, 207
Institute for Innovations in Local Farming (IILF), 88
institutions, local procurement, 111–115
interactive marketplaces, 76
International Composting Corporation, 139

international policies, 241
Internet, 75–80, 127, 130, 137–139
Intervale Agricultural Development Consulting Services, 94
Intervale Center, 51, 85, 94–95, 124, 130–131, 182
Intervale Compost Products, 94
Intervale Conservation Nursery, 94
Intervale Food Enterprise Center, 94
investments, 115–116
Ipsos Reid, 237
Ireland, 31
iron, 98

J
Japan, 24
JBS, 2
Jeavons, John, 90
jisan jisho, 24
job training, 36
John D. and Catherine T. MacArthur Foundation, 64
Jones, Stacy, 170
junk food, 152

K
Kamloops, B.C., 252
Kampala, 21
Kane, Deborah, 76, 77, 78, 159
Kansas City, Missouri, 125, 252
Katona, Peter, 123–124
Kaufman, Jerry, 252
Kellogg Foundation, 96
Kennedy School of Government, 223
Kentucky, 152
Keyakizaka, Tokyo, 44
King Portland Farmers' Market, 174
Kingdome Stadium, 148
Kingston, Ontario, 110–111
Kiss, Robert, 182
Kitchen Tables project, 207
kitchens, commercial, 124
kitchens, community, 204–207

Kitsilano Farmers' Market, 167–168
knowledge base, 130–131
Knoxville, Tennessee, 252
Koeppel, Dan, 3
Kohl's Department Stores, 193
Kootenay Alpine Cheese, 167
Kraft's Home Farming Initiative, 194
Kropf, Dale, 22–23
Kwantlen Polytechnic University, 131

L
Land Commission Act, 29
Land Conservancy, 114
land prices, 84–85
Landshare, 255
lawns, 45, 47
lead, 233
leases, 41, 46, 51, 131, 192
Left Coast Naturals, 124
Let's Move, 155, 158
Liberal Party, 244
Liberty Prairie, 50, 255
lighting, 63
Linsley, Benjamin, 71–72
Listeria, 3–4, 232, 235
Lloyds, 6–7
Loblaw, 9–10, 253–254
local food
　benefits of, 23–24
　cost of, 20
　diverse sources, 104–105
　environmental benefits, 7, 19
　origin of components of items, 17–18
　safety of, 22–23, 231–237
　storage of, 20
　transportation issues, 15–17
　urban food supply, 21
local food movement, 11–13, 14, 57
Local Food Plus (LFP), 113, 114, 254, 255
LocalHarvest.org, 176
locavores, 11–12
Lohr, Luanne, 107

London, 175, 226–227
London Food Commission, 170
Long Island Business Development Association, 44
Lorentz, Mike, 119
Los Angeles, 140, 224, 246
Love Food Hate Waste campaign, 136
low income families
　barriers to food security, 212
　effect of food security, 209–211
　food choices, 199–200
　programs for, 201–203

M
M&Ms, 151–153
MacKinnon, James, 11, 12, 20, 75
Making the Edible Landscape project, 186
Manhattan, 69
manure spreading, 40
Maple Leaf Foods, 232
marijuana, 63
Marin Agricultural Land Trust (MALT), 33
Marin County, 32–33
Marine Stewardship Council, 253
Marketplace IGA food store, 1
markets for produce, 86–87, 90–91
Marqusee, Rob, 105, 107–108
Martin Luther King, Jr. Middle School, 160–161
Mary, 217
Massachusetts, 158–159
Matteucci, Paul, 68, 75
Maxim Power Corp, 68
McConnell Foundation, 255
McDonald's, 153
McGill University, 144, 186
McMahon, Ed, 49, 56–57
McNeil Station, 94
McRae, Glenn, 94, 131
McVean New Farmers, 131
McWilliams, James, 15, 18

Meals on Wheels, 208
Meanwhile Projects, 192
meat
　control of market, 2
　effect on grain supply, 6
　energy use in production, 18
　greenhouse gas emissions and, 7
　processing plants, 119–120, 235
　water requirements of, 18–19
Melbourne, 30
mental institutions, 43
Merrigan, Kathleen, 9, 158, 245
Metcalf Foundation, 244, 255
Meter, Ken, 105, 106
methane, 68, 148
Metro Vancouver, 137
Metro Vancouver Regional Food Strategy, 120
Michigan, 125
Michigan Food Policy Council, 247
Michigan State University, 22, 96, 106, 125
micro farming systems, 87–92
Milwaukee, 46, 186
Minneapolis, 184
Minnesota, 231–232
Mississippi River, 3
Mobile Market Program, 227
Modesto, California, 139
monocultures, 2–4
Monsanto, 2
Montgomery County, 32
Montreal, 183, 232, 249
Mooney, Terry, 177
Mori Building, 44
Morocco, 146
Morse School farmers' market, 171
Mullinix, Kent, 58, 131

N
Nabham, Gary, 17–18
NAFTA (North American Free Trade Agreement), 114, 241

NASA, 69
National Farmers Union, 110
National Good Food Network, 125
National Resources Defense Council, 16
National School Lunch Program, 201, 232
national security, 242–244
Natural Resource Conservation Service, 33
Nature's Path, 19, 193
Needy Family Program, 201
Neighborhood Progress, 223
NeighborSpace, 47
Nelson and Pade, Inc., 74
Netherlands, 54, 147
New Farm Project, 110
New Jersey Department of Corrections, 43
New Oxford American Dictionary, 11
New Seasons Market, 107, 128
New Town, Missouri, 54
New Urbanism, 53
New York City, 158, 185, 218, 224, 225, 252
New York City Food Bank, 199, 202, 205, 212
New York Daily News, 228
New York Department of Agriculture and Markets, 247
New York State Council on Food Policy, 246–247
New York Times, 126
New Zealand, 17, 171
NewSeed Advisors, 69
niacin, 98
niche markets, 85–86
nitrogen, 3, 69, 146, 148
noise, 40
NoMix toilets, 147
non-profit farms, 94–95
Nordahl, Darrin, 248
Norman, Diane, 204
Norway, 18, 30–31, 241
Novo, Gonzàlez, 131–132
nutrient film technique (NFT) hydroponics, 67
nutrition, 97–99
Nygren, Steve, 57

O
Oakland, California, 190
Obama, Michelle, 155, 245
obesity, 6, 9
Ogallala Aquifer, 5
Ohio State University, 249
Ohm, Laura, 77
oil, use in food system, 6–8
Oklahoma Food Cooperative, 127–128
Oliver, Jamie, 160
100-Mile Diet, 11, 19, 20
online communication networks, 75–80, 127, 137–139
Ontario, 30, 199, 254
Ontario Food Terminal, 168
Oppenheimer Park, 207
Oregon, 112
Oregon Department of Agriculture, 106
Oregon State University, 106
organic farms, 107–109
organic food, local food versus, 19, 22
Organically Grown Company (OGC), 128
O'Rourke, P.J., 63
Oslo, Norway, 148
Ostara Nutrient Recovery Technologies Inc., 147
Ouellette, Jacynthe, 204
Outstanding Young Farmers program, 179
Overwaitea Food Stores, 154

P
packaging, 135–136
Paignton Zoo, Devon, UK, 65–66
Pakistan, 7
Panama disease, 3
Pappy's Restaurant, 35
parks, 84
Parmer, Chris, 111
Pawlick, Thomas, 98
peak oil, 6–7
Pennsylvania, 223, 254
People's Food Policy Project, 244
Pepsico, 193
Perry, Jan, 224

Peru, 204
pests, in monoculture, 3
Petrini, Carlo, 170
petrochemicals, 233–234
Philadelphia, 46, 84, 174, 175, 179, 187, 218, 224, 225
Philadelphia Water Department, 88
phosphate, 146–147
phosphorus, 146, 148
Pig Clubs, 183
pigs, 144
Pingree, Hazen, 182
Plan Against Hunger, 241, 257
planned communities, 52
Planning for Agriculture and Food Network (PAFN), 130
Policy Guide on Community and Regional Food Planning (APA), 251–252
Pollan, Michael, 153
population, 5
Porter, Edward, 58
Portland, Oregon, 103
Portland Green Parenting, 77
Portland Hotel Society, 211
Postmedia News, 237
potassium, 146, 148
potatoes, 98
Pothukuchi, Kameshwari, 222, 226, 244
Prairie Crossing, 49–52, 57, 124, 131, 177
Prairie Crossing Homeowners' Association, 52
prairies, 4
preservation of food, 16, 20–21
prices, 97–99, 170–173
prisons, 43, 109–111
Procter and Gamble, 142
Public Health Agency of Canada, 206
Public Produce (Nordahl), 248

Q
Qroe Farm Preservation Development, 54
Quebec, 30

Quebec Collective Kitchens Association, 204
Quest Outreach Society, 137, 203

R
Raap, Will, 51, 94, 177
rainwater, 86
Ralston, Christie, 162, 184
Ramirez, Theresa, 157
Ranney, George, 50
Ranney, Vicky, 50, 57
Raoul, Mr., 148
The Ration Book Diet, 183
Red Deer County, Alberta, 27
reliability of food sources, 22–23
residential developments. *See* developments
resiliency, 14
restaurants, 12, 43–44, 57, 254
Retail Chicago, 223
riboflavin, 98
Richard the Pesto Man, 167
Richmond, B.C., 19, 161
Ridsdill-Smith, Mark, 93
Robbins, Mark, 34
Rochester Economic Development Corporation, 224
Rock, Joyce, 205–207
Rodas, Cuba, 21
rooftop gardens, 43–44, 67
Royal Institute of International Affairs, 6
Rubin, Jeff, 15
Russia, 5, 7

S
safety of food, 3–4, 22–23, 231–237
Sainsbury's, 140
salad mixes, 4, 83
Salatin, Joel, 63, 127, 175, 176, 235–236, 237
salmon farms, 18
Samel, Linda, 127
San Francisco, 248
San Francisco farmers' market, 170
San Francisco Food Systems, 212

San Francisco Public Utilities Commission, 41
Sandhill Organics, 51
Sands, Mike, 83
Santa Clara, California, 218, 246
Santoni's Supermarket, 228
Santropol Roulant, 208
Sao Paulo, 30
Saputo, 154
Saskatchewan, 19
Satzewich, Wally, 87–88, 91
Saudi Arabia, 4
Schantz, Gwen, 44
Scharf, Kathryn, 200
Scheuer, David, 57
Schmidt, Ellie, 203–204, 212
School Community Connections, 155
School Fruit and Vegetable Nutritional Program, 154
school programs
    container gardening, 162–164
    food literacy, 159–162
    local procurement, 103, 157–159
    marketing healthy foods, 156
    promoting change, 255
    snack foods, 151–155
Scobie, Pauline, 88
Scotland, 18
Seaboard Farms Inc., 39
seafood, 253
Seattle, 103, 249
Seattle University, 170
Serenbe, Georgia, 32, 54, 57
sewage treatment, 144–146
Shanghai, 21
Shared Harvest, 137
Sheaffer, Matt and Peg, 51
Shiva, Vandana, 71
Singapore, 21
skip gardens, 192
Sky, Florida, 54
Slow Food, 116–117
Slow Money model, 115–116
Slow Money (Tasch), 176
Smith, Alisa, 11, *12*, 20
Smithfield, 2

SNAP (Supplemental Nutrition Assistance Program), 173, 201
Sobeys, 22–23
Sociètè d'Aménagement Foncier et d'Etablissement Rural (SAFER), 31
soil, 4, 71
soil contamination, 232–234
Sole Food Farm, 251
Solviva Solar Greenhouse, 65
Somerton Tank Farms, 88–89
Somerville, Massachusetts, 84
soup kitchens, 197–199
South Village, Vermont, 54, 57, 177
Southlands, 58–59
Souza, Herbert de, 213
Sowing Seeds, 131
soybeans, 2
Spareground, 255
Spetifore, George, 58
SPIN (Small Plot Intensive Farming), 87–89, 90
Spitzer, Eliot, 246
SPUD (Sustainable Produce Urban Delivery), 129–130, 136, 179
Spuds in Tubs, 163–164
Stahlbrand, Lori, 20, 114–115
Standard Motor Products building, 44
Statistics Canada, 9
Steel, Carolyn, 2, 102
Steiner, Rudolf, 176
Stephens, Arran, 19
Stockholm, 141
The Stop, 122–123, 187, 202
storage of food, 16, 20–21
Stray Cat Flower Farm and Market, 94
Strobel, Otto, 78, 177
Strobel, Shaun, 80
Strobel, Sonia, 79–80
Stump, Jeff, 33
subsidies, 100
suburbs, 42
Success on Farms, 131
Sudan, 243
Sugarsnap Café, 94
Sunol Agriculture Park, 41

Sunset Magazine, 193
supermarkets. *See* grocery
 stores
Surrey, B.C., 29, 40
Sustain, 128
Sustainable Agricultural
 Education (SAGE), 41
sustainable agriculture,
 investment in, 68–70
Sustainlane, 183–184
Sutherland, Kate, 193
Sutherland, Kim, 38
Svanholm Gods, 147
Sweden, 31, 147, 242
Sweet Water Organics, 74
Sysco, 124–125, 126, 254

T
T. and J. Bison and Grains, 167
Tachieva, Galina, 54
Take a Bite of B.C. program,
 157
Tasch, Woody, 115–116, 176
taxes, 26–27, 191–192, 246,
 250–251
Taylor Made Farms, 77
technology
 aquaponics, 72–75
 increasing production,
 71–72
 online communication
 networks, 75–80, 127,
 137–139
 weather control, 61–63
Terra Nova Farm, 161, 193
TerraSphere Systems, 66
Teulon, Ward, 45, 81–82, 84,
 85, 86
Texas, 160
thiamine, 98
Tiberius Caesar, 62
toilets, 147
Toledo, Ohio, 227
tomatoes, 83
Tops Markets, 224
topsoil, 4
Toronto, 21, 23, 246
Toronto and Region Conservation (TRCA), 131
Toronto Food Business Incubator, 106

Toronto Public Health, 234
toxic metals, 233
Toyota, 193
Trade, Investment, and La-
 bor Mobility Agreement
 (TILMA), 114
Transfer of Development
 Rights (TDR), 31–32
Transition Towns, 255
transportation, 15–17, 220–221
Triscuits, 194
Troy Gardens, Wisconsin, 54,
 161, 162, 184
Tsawwassen, B.C., 53, 58–59
The Two-Block Diet, 193
Tyedmers, Peter, 18
TheTyee.ca, 124
Tyson, 2

U
UK. *See* United Kingdom
UK Department of Health,
 227
UK Food 2030, 241, 243
UN Food and Agriculture
 Organization, 5
UN Millennium Develop-
 ment Goal, 213
UN Millennium Ecosystem
 Assessment, 7
Uncommon Ground, 43–44
Union Gospel Mission,
 197–199
United Kingdom
 chickens, 44–45
 consumer trips, 17
 food miles, 15
 food policy, 243
 food provisions during
 war, 182–183
 food safety, 233
 GHG emissions, 242
 oil dependence, 6–7
 public land leases, 192
 urban farms, 41
 urban food production,
 21–22
 waste, 134–136, 141
United States
 Army weight standards,
 243

farmer demographics, 8
food banks, 199
food imports, 6
food product availability,
 1–2
gardeners, 24
health issues, 9
imported food safety, 236
phosphorus, 146
preservation of agricul-
 tural land, 31–32
urban food production,
 21, 22
Victory Gardens, 182
universities, 112–114
University of British Columbia, 31, 131
University of Oregon, 149
University of Pennsylvania,
 187
University of Toronto, 112, 114
Urban Edge Agricultural
 Parks, 41
urban farms
 commercial operations,
 81–83
 infrastructure, 86–87
 markets for produce,
 85–86
 micro-scale, 83–84
 production rates, 21–22
 related business opportunities, 94
 small-scale, 87–92
urban land
 agricultural development,
 95–97
 benefits of gardens, 84
 secure tenure, 46–47
 zoning changes, 45–46
Urban Land Trust, 190
Urevit, 147
urine, 146–148
USDA (US Department of
 Agriculture)
 CSAs, 176
 definition of farm, 34
 farmers' markets, 175
 food policy, 244
 food programs, 153, 201
 grants, 245

loss for farmland, 25
school programs, 157, 161

V
vacant land. *See* urban land
Valcent Products Inc., 65,
68, 92
Van Loan, Peter, 109–110
Van Seters, David, 129–130,
136
Vancouver, B.C.
community gardens, 184–
185, 191, 192–193, 194, 239
edible landscaping re-
quirements, 45
food and poverty, 206
food policy, 248
land costs, 123
loss of farmland, 28
mentally ill residents, 210
tax breaks, 250–251
Vancouver Area Network of
Drug Users, 207
Vancouver Coastal Health
Authority, 206
Vancouver Community
Kitchen Project, 204–205
Vancouver Convention and
Exhibition Centre, 254
Vancouver Downtown East-
side Neighborhood House,
205–207
Vancouver Food Bank, 137
Vancouver Food Policy
Council, 134
Vandersteen, Gail, 91
vegans, 18
vegetables, 98
Vercammen, Jim, 26
vermicomposting, 148–149
Vermont Housing and Con-
servation Board, 131
vertical growing, 64–68
Vickars, Mark, 66
Victoria, B.C., 181–182, 250
Victory Gardens, 21–22, 182
Viljoen, André, 42

Village Homes, 22
Vilsack, Tom, 161
vitamin A, 98
vitamin C, 98
Vitiello, Domenic, 187
Vlad's Apiary, 167

W
Waldrop, Robert, 106
Walker, Ian, 124
Walmart, 125–126, 135, 254
War Gardens, 182
Ward, Richard, 7
Washington, D.C., 127
Washington Grown Fresh
Fruit and Vegetable Grant
Program, 159
Washington State, 159, 246
waste
alternatives to sewage
treatment, 144–146
biogas, 140
composting, 139, 142–143
energy required, 133–134
perishable foods, 1, 136–139
prevention of, 135–136
from processing plants,
120
under-sink food waste disposer, 140–141
urine, 146–148
worm composting, 148–
149
Waste and Resources Ac-
tion Programme (WRAP),
135–136
water, 4–5, 18–19, 86
Waterloo, Ontario, 123
watermelons, 172
Waterville Elementary
School, 164
weather, effect on agriculture, 61–62
Weins, Linda, 49, 50
West Germany, 30–31
West Oakland, California,
221

Western Sahara, 146
Weston, Galen, 9–10, 253
wheat, 4, 5
Whisenant, Blake, 72
White, Monica, 187
Whole Foods, 155
*Why Your World Is About to
Get a Whole Lot Smaller*
(Rubin), 15
WIC (Special Supplemental
Nutrition Program for
Women, Infants, and Chil-
dren), 173, 200, 201, 252
Wiggins, Betti, 157, 159
Williams, Melissa, 77
Windermere High School,
144, 162
Windowfarms Project, 72
Wisconsin, 231
Women's Land Army, 183
Wood Street Urban Farm,
35–37, 41–42
Woodbury County, Iowa, 107,
124, 251
Worcestershire County, 141
World Bank, 241
World Environment Day, 12
World Health Organization,
146
World Trade Organization,
241, 242
World War I, 182
World War II, 182
worm composting, 148–149

Y
Yahoo, 193
Yakini, Malik, 96, 187
Yarrow Eco Village Farm, 167
Year of Urban Agriculture,
249
Yohay, Mike, 75

Z
Zabar, Eli, 43–44, 68, 233
Zylmans, Bill, 61–62

About the Author

PETER LADNER is a lifelong food gardener and student of urban planning who became especially interested in urban agriculture while serving as a Vancouver City Councillor in 2002-2008. He worked with the Vancouver Food Policy Council in initiating the city's program to add 2010 food-producing community garden plots by 2010 as an Olympic legacy.

Peter has been publisher, president and part owner of the Business in Vancouver Media Group, which he co-founded by establishing the award-winning *Business in Vancouver* weekly newspaper in 1989. He has more than 35 years of journalistic experience in print, radio and television and is a frequent speaker on business, community and sustainability issues.

He brings an invaluable mix of communication skills, food- growing experience and business savvy to the urgent need to bring more local, fresh affordable food back into urban living.

From 2009-2011 he was a Fellow at the Simon Fraser University Centre for Dialogue, researching, teaching and organizing public events around the theme Planning Cities as if Food Matters. He is on the board of The Natural Step Canada.

He lives in Vancouver with his wife Erica on a lawn-free city lot dedicated to food production. They have four grown children.

If you have enjoyed *The Urban Food Revolution,*
you might also enjoy other

BOOKS TO BUILD A NEW SOCIETY

Our books provide positive solutions for people who want to
make a difference. We specialize in:

Sustainable Living • Green Building • Peak Oil
Renewable Energy • Environment & Economy
Natural Building & Appropriate Technology
Progressive Leadership • Resistance and Community
Educational & Parenting Resources

New Society Publishers

ENVIRONMENTAL BENEFITS STATEMENT

New Society Publishers has chosen to produce this book on recycled paper made
with **100% post consumer waste,** processed chlorine free, and old growth free.
For every 5,000 books printed, New Society saves the following resources:[1]

31	Trees
2,838	Pounds of Solid Waste
3,123	Gallons of Water
4,073	Kilowatt Hours of Electricity
5,159	Pounds of Greenhouse Gases
22	Pounds of HAPs, VOCs, and AOX Combined
8	Cubic Yards of Landfill Space

---

[1]Environmental benefits are calculated based on research done by the Environmental Defense
Fund and other members of the Paper Task Force who study the environmental impacts of the
paper industry.

For a full list of NSP's titles, please call 1-800-567-6772 *or check out our website* at:

www.newsociety.com

NEW SOCIETY PUBLISHERS